Inn-Sanity:
Diary of an Innkeeper Virgin

"Entertaining and well worth reading! Each motel should have copies for reading during guest stays, like the Gideon Bibles!"

-- Pat & Connie S., Frequent Travellers

"I really liked your book! While fun to read by anyone, it would be super for first-time owners of inns, motels, hotels, or resorts."

-- Dianne H., Innkeeper

"Good stuff! I enjoyed reading it! I may even use some of the incidents as case studies in the lodging courses I teach at university."

-- Dr. Gabor F., Professor of Hospitality & Tourism Management

"A real page-turner!"

-- Librarian stating the obvious

Praise for

Humour on Wry, with Mustard

"We have proof that your funny book is being read in our cottages. We place it on the coffee table in the living areas and, after our guests check-out, we find it in the bathroom next to the toilet! Don't worry, no pages are missing."
—— Pam & Peter F., Innkeepers

"I am on my second reading of this wonderful book during my train trips across Ontario."
—— Connie P., Salesperson

"Most entertaining and well written! When I want a chuckle, I will reach for your book."
—— Vena J., Retired Innkeeper

"Arriving home, I dropped my groceries on the kitchen counter and opened my just-acquired copy of your book, intending to sample one or two of your 88 short stories before I put the groceries away. One or two led to one or two more, then one or two more ... while ice cream and frozen peas slowly melted. I need to shop again tomorrow, but it was worth it!"
—— Hazel G., Retired Innkeeper

INN-SANITY:
DIARY OF AN INNKEEPER VIRGIN

AN EPIC JOURNEY OF DISCOVERY
(WITH MANY POTHOLES ALONG THE ROAD)

To Paul &
Dana & Maren
Keep Smiling!

Bruce Gravel

Bruce Gravel.

Wigglesworth & Quinn
Peterborough

INN-SANITY: DIARY OF AN INNKEEPER VIRGIN

For information, contact: bruce@brucegravel.ca.

Published by: Wigglesworth & Quinn, Peterborough, Ontario, Canada
Ordering Information: bruce@brucegravel.ca
Printed in the United States of America

First Edition: July 2009

Library and Archives Canada Cataloguing in Publication

Gravel, Bruce M. (Bruce Magnus), 1952 -
    Inn-sanity, diary of an innkeeper virgin: an epic journey of discovery (with many potholes along the road) / Bruce Gravel.

ISBN 978-1-4486-0057-1

    I. Title.

PS8613.R369I55 2009   C813'.6   C2009-903859-5

Dedication

To Frances and Scott

For their steadfast love and encouragement,
their wonderful inspiration and honest feedback.

And for their patience, as I wrestled this out
of my head and into the computer.

And for their threats of bodily harm
if I didn't get this polished and published.

Acknowledgements

The cover illustration was done by Bob Sherwood, a
professional caricaturist living in Ontario.
Contact Bob at: 905-659-5498.
Email: cartoonbob@cogeco.ca.

Many thanks to Frances Gravel for her great work in the
formatting and lay-out of the entire book, getting it all
print-ready, including the back cover.

Many thanks to Scott Gravel,
for designing the front cover and electronically
enabling the printing of this book.

Author's Note

My inspiration for writing this book was to record some of the true stories I've heard from innkeepers of small to medium-sized properties during the 24 years I've spent managing their non-profit association, which celebrates its 60th Anniversary in 2009.

So while this story is fictional, **most of the incidents are based on actual experiences that happened to innkeepers**, all members of the Ontario Accommodation Association, formerly Motels Ontario, formerly the Accommodation Motel Ontario Association, formerly the Ontario Motel Association, and originally, in 1949, the Ontario Tourist Courts Association. (Talk about an identity crisis!)

These heroic innkeepers are warmly thanked for sharing their tales with me. All names have been changed to protect the embarrassed.

This novel went through three drafts: 2001 (first draft), 2007 (second draft) and 2009 (third draft). Many thanks to those friends, relatives and innkeepers who read the first draft and provided constructive feedback, especially Pat and Connie Slinn, Dave Warren, Ed Gadzala, Dianne Hounsome, Jim and Vena Johnstone, Dr. Marion Joppe, Dr. Gabor Forgacs, and Frances and Scott Gravel.

Bruce Gravel
Peterborough, Ontario
May, 2009

Windsong Inn

Guest Register

Prologue

Of Motels And Murder

Smothered amidst miles of rolling farmland, deep in Eastern Ontario, lies the small city of Wackimac, population: 74,001. It's biggest problem is that it's a town that thinks it's a city. But don't tell its politicians that.

How the sleepy burg received its unusual name is a matter of bored conjecture. One theory is that it originated from the indigenous First Nations people, when they first encountered European explorers centuries ago. When the explorers asked what this area was called, the natives misunderstood. They thought the Europeans were asking what the natives thought of them. So the aboriginals said "wackimac" which, loosely translated, means "dresses funny and smells bad." (Makes you wonder what 'kanata", from which Canada distilled its name, *really* means.)

Another theory is that Wackimac is derived from an old Gaelic word used by the area's early Scots settlers, meaning "grrrreat place for a still."

Some say it came from the name of the settlers' leader, who was prone to irrational behaviour (usually involving equal parts whiskey and swordplay): one Angus "Wacky" MacDonald.

Anyway, because of that still and its fertile soil, Wackimac took root and stumbled through history, slowly but stubbornly growing despite the best efforts of its ruling elite to keep it "small and manageable".

As happened with cities and towns throughout North America, clusters of motels sprang up on the outskirts of Wackimac in the l950s and 60s. In the boom of post-war prosperity, families embraced lengthy road trips in their shiny new automobiles, and motels answered the need for affordable accommodation and a life-saving break from squabbling backseat kids.

One of those new motels on the edge of town was christened the Pleasant Holiday Inn. It first opened for business on May 7, l953.

Camped on the banks of the Woebegone River (a minor waterway that meanders in almost-unmapable serpentine confusion through Eastern Ontario), the motel is on a 4.2 acre lot. The size of the lot gives the place good privacy from neighbouring inns; a special setting not typical of the usual pattern of motels bunched together in tiresome sameness.

The building is L-shaped, surrounded by pleasing lawns on which the first owner planted a variety of saplings.

When it first opened, its 23 rooms were outfitted with the latest features, many of which had yet to be found in most people's homes, such as television. Back then, motels were trend-setters.

The motel went through several owners over the succeeding decades. Each new owner treated the property well enough, until its last one: a disreputable brute named Hal Owens. Much to my disgust, and despite anything I could do, he ran the place into the ground during his eight-year ownership.

When he had wrung every last penny out of the place, Owens sold it. To a pair of naive big-city folk.

The new owners are a married couple: Pete and Ellen Tomlinson. He's a gent of 52, with a small beer belly and a seriously-balding head. What hair remains is grey. Tall, with a permanent pinched expression to his mouth, he looks pompous and professorial. Comes off like a professor when he speaks, too: a dry monotone. His moon-face has muddy blue eyes and a high forehead that's prone to wrinkling. He walks in a hurried, jerky fashion, like he's always late for something.

I wonder about him.

Ellen is a lady of 47, with reddish-brown hair and a ready laugh. Her smiling face has a pert nose beneath sparkling green eyes, anchored by a prominent chin. Her hair style is indeterminate, as if her only concern is keeping it out of her eyes. Her voice reminds me of a cascading brook, bubbling merrily. She has a nice figure, though you'd hardly know it because she loves drowning it in loose-fitting clothing.

All of five feet one inch in height, she's a little dynamo of energy and enthusiasm. She sometimes talks to things, giving them encouragement or admonishment. On her first day at the motel, she told it that she hoped it liked its new owners, and that they'd do their best to restore it to its former glory.

I liked her immediately.

They moved here from a sterile highrise condo in Toronto. They wanted a complete lifestyle change from the bustle of urban living and their previous demanding jobs. They have no experience with country life: the weather, the people, the small-town politics and cliques, and that wonderful "country air" that wafts in from the surrounding farms twice a year when the fields get manured.

They also know nothing about innkeeping. Their first mistake was paying far too much for this dump.

Me, I've been at this motel since the third month after it opened in 1953. While motels usually cater to transient guests, you might say I'm a long-term tenant here. Though not by choice.

Seventy-four days after the Pleasant Holiday Inn welcomed its first guest, I checked-in with my boyfriend for a night of wild, scandalous sex. When he left, I stayed.

Since the violent death of a local farmer while fixing his threshing machine was eventually ruled accidental (a verdict his widow celebrated by marrying their farmhand two days later), that meant I was Wackimac's first, and only, murder victim of 1953.

That nice new owner, Ellen, keeps a Diary. You'll read more about me there.

Boo.

Our First Week

In Which We Buy A Motel Under Great Misconceptions

Dear Diary:

Well, Pete and I finally did it! We bought our own business: a 23-room motel nestled in lovely countryside just outside the small city of Wackimac. It's charming – or at least it will be once we renovate it. The real estate agent said the place "needed a little work." As soon as he saw it, Pete said "no kidding" and briefly considered suing the agent for misrepresentation.

But we can see – especially if we squint hard – that the inn has potential.

The motel is surrounded by wide lawns, which would normally look quite nice. Unfortunately, the grass hasn't seen the underside of a mower in weeks. Many mature trees dot the grounds; a mix of deciduous and evergreen. The building itself looks extremely tired; it hasn't known the touch of a paintbrush in years.

Behind the motel sits a putrid rectangular mess that, in better days, was a swimming pool. Built over 20 years ago, we were told the pool hadn't been used in at least four years.

Our two grown children think we're nuts. Why we would sink our life savings into a dilapidated motel, and move away from The Centre Of Canada's Universe (Toronto), is quite beyond them. Dawn, our daughter who lives in Calgary with her oh-so-important career and her husband (in that order), actually e-mailed her brother wondering if we weren't succumbing to early-onset Alzheimer's.

From his 43-foot sailboat somewhere in the Caribbean, our son, Clint, replied that we had the right to do whatever-the-hell we wanted, even if it was completely stupid.

Thanks, kid.

Pete figures what really upsets them is that we've just spent their inheritance.

I've set myself the personal goal of keeping a diary of our new life as innkeepers. At the end of each week, no matter what, I intend to record the highlights of the previous seven days. I've never kept a diary before, so this will be another new experience for me. At the very least, it will document this bold venture of ours, so our absentee children can read about it.

We're both eager to start our new lives. This will be the perfect semi-retirement project for us; Pete used to be a high school teacher and I was secretary to a team of high-pressure, hard-drinking, chain-smoking salespeople. Pete took early retirement and I quit my job (throwing the sales team into an almost-suicidal tizzy) so we could fulfill our dream of running our own business while we're still young enough .

We figure running the motel will only take half of our time, and we'll spend the remaining hours enjoying the quiet pleasures of country living. We immediately subscribed to several magazines and two monthly book clubs – we love to read, but never had much time before with our full-time jobs. We also plan to indulge in our other hobbies, and even take up golf.

Our Toronto friends are *so* envious.

The fact that neither of us has any prior experience operating a motel doesn't bother us. "Heck, how hard can it be?" scoffed Pete. "You just make beds and clean bathrooms!"

Those words – and *something* else – would come back to haunt us.

Monday:
The sale closed today, June 15. A red-letter day!

In the afternoon, we met the vendor, who reassured us about our new venture.

"Mr. and Miz. Tomlinson, most motel owners had no experience before they bought," said Hal Owens, a grizzled red-faced man with an enormous stomach. "I was a used car salesman before I bought here, eight years ago, and I succeeded! Anyway, don't worry, I'll be around to guide you over the rough spots for the first few months."

What a nice man!

Tuesday:

We took possession of the motel today. Five minutes after Hal Owens drove away, promising to return that afternoon to give us our first lesson on running a motel, we had our first guest! He wanted a room with two double beds.

"Yep, no problem, Sir," said Pete smoothly from behind the front desk. He looked at me: "Ellen?" I stared back blankly; we had no idea which rooms had which beds!

With that unspoken instant communication that comes from 21 years of marriage, Pete turned back to the guest, fumbled behind the desk, and by sheer luck, located a registration card, which he asked the man to fill out (as soon as he located a pen).

Meanwhile, as casually as possible, I palmed the master key and eased out the side door of the office. I then ran madly down the motel, opening doors to check each room. Luckily, all the rooms were clean – and I soon located one with two doubles.

I raced back to the front office, smiled at the guest, and whispered "Number 12" into Pete's ear.

Then I went back outside and collapsed, gasping until I caught my breath.

Mr. Owens did not return that afternoon.

Wednesday:

Today, Pete threw a bum off the property and we almost lost our housekeeper.

As part of our arrangement when we took possession, we had

agreed to keep on the housekeeper.

"You won't find a better maid anywhere; she makes those tired old rooms sparkle," Hal Owens had promised. "Angie Huycke is her name. Now, she has Mondays and Tuesdays off, so you two'll have to do the rooms yourselves those days."

We were anxious to meet Angie today. Though we hadn't had many guests yet, doing the housekeeping chores cut into precious time that we needed, as new owners, to familiarize ourselves with things. But the day wore on with no sign of Angie.

"Actually, the only person that came to the door today was some grubby bag lady," said Pete as we took a mid-day break from the chores. "I asked what she wanted here, and she just glared at me and mumbled something. She tried to push past me into the office, so I lost my temper and told her to get out. She swore at me under her breath, but left. I hope that's the last we see of her!"

Finally, around 2:00 pm, I called the number Hal had scrawled on a dirty scrap of paper. A boy answered, and I asked to speak to Angie Huycke.

"Oh, you mean my Mom," he replied. "Well, she's so mad, she can't come to the phone. Seems her new employers wouldn't let her work at the motel today!"

It hit me like a rifle shot. The "bag lady" was Angie.

It took much apologizing and cajoling, after I finally connected with Angie, to convince her it had all been a horrible mistake. She agreed to return tomorrow, but she expected an apology directly from "that pompous idiot" (as she referred to Pete), before she'd consider the matter closed.

Still no sign of Owens.

Thursday:

I was pleased to meet Angie today. She looked to be in her late fifties, with scraggly grey-blonde hair that insisted on escaping from whatever hat or kerchief she put over it. Tall and "big-boned", she would not look out of place on a football team. She had the same shape no matter which direction you looked at her: a mountain on two legs. A small mouth gave birth to a deep gravel rasp. I think she sounded that way because her voice-box was rusty from underuse; she rarely spoke. No matter how cheerfully you talked to her, she answered in grunts and her face remained dour as she went about her work.

"Definitely not someone we want greeting the public from behind our front desk," commented The Pompous Idiot, displaying the keen insight that made him a legend in his own mind.

Following Pete's (grudging) apology, Angie went to work. Though she did indeed look like a bag lady, she worked wonders on the rooms. She had an unusual cleaning technique: She seemed to absorb the dust and dirt onto herself, like a human dust mop. As the room got cleaner, Angie got dirtier.

I soon discovered that Angie took great pride in cleaning rooms. It was a matter of honour with her. She regarded housekeeping as a noble profession, and woe be anyone who thought otherwise.

Mr. Owens finally did return to give us our first lesson – two days late. The lesson lasted a whole 20 minutes. Then he told us he'd just signed up for a five month vacation, and abruptly left. Through the cloud of dust raised by his car as it sped out of our unpaved lot, we heard:

"Good luck, suckers! You'll need it!" followed by a braying laugh.

What a nasty man!

Friday:

Pete and I make a good team. We each like doing things that the other dislikes. (Except for cleaning toilets; we both hate that.) I'm a morning person, while Pete is a nighthawk. You don't want to be around Pete first thing in the morning. He's like a bear freshly awakened from a winter's hibernation: growling, grumpy, and ravenously hungry.

The guest that roused Pete out of bed very early today should have known that. One look at Pete as he stumbled into the front office should have set off alarm bells.

It's too bad I was away that morning; I had to leave before sunup to drive to Toronto to buy new linens and towels at a doorcrasher sale. (What was in the rooms desperately needed replacing. The textiles were so threadbare that even the Goodwill didn't want them.)

If I had been at the motel, we might have saved a customer. After all, the poor man simply wanted to check-out. But disturbing Ol' Baloo from his hibernation sealed the guest's fate. The stress of our first week as innkeepers certainly didn't help Pete's mood either, and he had not had his all-important first cup of coffee.

Our motelier neighbours down the road later told me they could hear Pete bellowing from there.

We never saw that guest again.

Note to self: Never let Pete do the desk in the mornings.

Saturday:

It was really hot again today; it hadn't rained for weeks. We had sprinklers out everywhere, trying to keep our grass green in the withering heat.

Our motel was originally on its own well and septic system. However, in the 1980s, the city extended its water and sewage systems out to the "motel strip". When the motel switched to municipal water and sewage, the owners kept the well operating to supply water to the outside faucets. This saved a lot of money watering the large front and back lawns and filling the pool (during the years the pool was in operation), since commercial businesses using city water were on meters.

The guest rooms had ancient individual air-conditioning units, which cooled the rooms, but with a horrible racket. However, the unit in our front office refused to work, no matter what we did to it. Judging by the cobwebs inside the grill, it had not worked in years. We were sweltering at our front desk.

When we first toured the motel building on Monday, we noticed a few unusual things, like two or three pails stacked in each guest room closet, in the office, and in the closets of our small apartment behind the office. There was also a large fan in the laundry room, blowing on the well pump that served our outside faucets.

"That fan doesn't make any sense there," Pete muttered, as we suffered through our sauna today, so he took the fan away to cool our office.

One hour later, we lost water in all the sprinklers. Cries of complaint filled the air from the children who'd been playing under the spray. (Something we encouraged, to mollify upset families when they discovered our advertised swimming pool was, in fact, a stagnant pond.)

Entering the laundry room, an acrid burning smell hit our nostrils. We soon discovered the source: the well pump had seized. Now it was our turn to fill the air with cries of complaint.

We found out from the time-and-a-half plumber who (finally) arrived, that the pump was only two years old and was woefully underpowered for the job. That cheapskate Owens had kept the fan on it 24 hours a day during the spring and summer, to keep it from overheating while it was in use!

We dipped into our modest renovation fund, and purchased a new stronger pump – and a new air-conditioning unit for our front office.

Sunday:

Our first week as innkeepers was drawing to a close. Somehow we had made it through, learning some basics of motel operation by trial and error (mostly error), as we bumbled along. Some part-time semi-retirement job! We were on the go from sunrise to way past sunset. Pete and I both agreed that we had never worked harder before in our lives.

"Anyway, it's bound to be easier next week," opined Pete wearily. "You'll see; we'll have more time to relax. Things can't get any worse."

We soon discovered that Pete's ability to predict the future was on par with that of the weather-forecasters at Environment Canada.

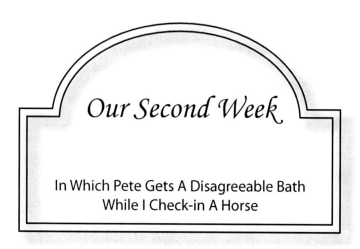

Our Second Week

In Which Pete Gets A Disagreeable Bath While I Check-in A Horse

Dear Diary:

Monday:

This week started bad and went downhill from there.

The morning mail contained a thick envelope from a law firm with more names than the starting line-up of the Toronto Blue Jays. Opening it, I started reading the letter. Two paragraphs in, I was hollering for Pete.

"We're being sued!" I exclaimed as he bounded into the office, out of breath.

Our place was called the Pleasant Holiday Inn. Charming name. Unfortunately, the worldwide Holiday Inn chain thought so too – and they had it trade-marked. Reading the multi-page letter, with frequent use of our dictionary to translate legalese into English, we pieced together the story.

Seems the previous owner, Hal Owens, had been receiving letters about this for over a year – first from Holiday Inn, then from their lawyers. Though the motel had been using that name since it opened in 1953, it had only recently come to Holiday Inn's attention. Owens had been warned to change the name, but he had ignored each increasingly-nasty letter. Now they were suing.

"Well, the solution's obvious," I said. "We can't fight Holiday Inn. We'll write and say we're the new owners and that we'll find a new name." Pete agreed and we sent off a letter.

And thus touched off The Great Name Debate.

Tuesday:

For a couple that usually agreed on everything, we could not agree on a new name for our motel. We didn't want something obvious, like naming the place after the small city on whose outskirts we perched. The Wackimac Motel didn't float our boat. (Especially since we'd likely soon become known as the Wacky Motel.)

Nor was the Sparkling River Inn suitable, since the Woebegone River that flowed past our backyard only sparkled in spring. By early summer, it was stagnant. By late summer, it had expired into a mud flat. (Hence its name.)

In his ever-increasing dour moods, Pete suggested names like Dead End Motel or the Money Pit Inn. (In just one week, all by himself, he had managed to become wracked with doubts about our new career as innkeepers.)

I wanted something cozy and cheerful, like Mallard's Rest, in honour of the ducks that made their home along the river bank.

"But the ducks leave when the river dries up," the Pompous Idiot objected. "Hey, how about the Phantom River Inn, or the Departed Duck Depot?"

I threw a shoe at him.

We realized today that changing our name meant changing our road sign, our brochure and letterhead, and everything else with the old name on it. We had wanted a fresh look to our advertising materials, of course, but had planned to phase it in gradually. Now we had to do it all at once.

"Well, there's more money gone from our renovation fund," I said woefully.

That fund would take a major hit the next day. So would Pete.

Wednesday:

We were doing chores, still arguing about names, when Angie, our housekeeper (otherwise known as the Human Dust

Mop), approached us. Her expression was more gloomy than usual.

"Toilets won't flush," she muttered.

I looked at Pete, the *de facto* maintenance maestro of our little enterprise.

"Well, we gotta plunge 'em, I guess," he proclaimed.

He found a plunger, marched into a room, and attacked the toilet bowl with great zeal. It was the first toilet Pete had plunged in his life – at our Toronto condo, the custodian had handled all the maintenance.

Sploog! Sploog! Sploog! went the plunger. Great showers of water erupted from the bowl, landing in equal measure on the floor and Pete. (Luckily it *was* just water.) But it still wouldn't flush when he tried it.

Dripping wet, Plumber Pete aggressively plunged the toilets in three other rooms, duplicating the mess in each. Same results: They still wouldn't flush.

Frustrated, he took a break while Angie and I swabbed up the water. After some thought, he said:

"Y'know, with the outside water line, when the well pump seized last week and after the new pump was installed, the plumber had to bleed the line to remove air bubbles, to get it to flow properly. Maybe it's the same principle with the sewer line. There's probably a big air bubble in it."

Pete used to teach high school. Not tech courses, but history. His expertise with hands-on repairs consisted of using his hands to search the Yellow Pages for help. Still, he seemed confident and his logic made sense in a Pete-sorta-way. I tagged along, in case he needed help. Or someone to call 911.

We went into the basement, where he found the plug at the end of our main sewer pipe. He took a big wrench to it with gusto. ("Gusto", to a male, means lots of sweating, straining and swearing – in equal proportions.)

The plug came off very suddenly and very fast, shooting past Pete like a cannon ball, barely missing him. I caught a quick glimpse of my man, eyes bulging in surprise, as a solid stream of foul brown waste water hit him and bowled him over.

Angie had silently materialized beside me.

"Huh," she said, watching as the rest of the pipe's reeking contents emptied onto my husband. "Shoulda kept his mouth shut."

Draped in that awful mess, coughing and spitting, Pete no longer looked Pompous, but he sure had the Idiot part covered.

I could swear Angie was almost smiling.

The hastily-called plumber banished Pete from the basement while he fixed our system. The plumber said that we should have shut off something called a sewage injector before taking that cap off. Since our property slopes down away from the road, a sewage injector is needed to push the waste out to the main sewer line by the highway. This means our main sewer pipe is under a lot of pressure.

As Pete had found out the hard way.

My hubby had to take several disinfectant showers, then get a shot at the hospital for what had landed in his mouth.

His motel name suggestions for the next few days were extremely colourful and have no place in this Diary.

Thursday:

The day after the Sewer Incident, Pete's father suddenly graced us with a visit. Bowed with age, Bill moved slowly with the aid of a cane. But his mind was still sharp, as was his mouth. With large black-rimmed glasses dominating a thin severe face, he looked like a hawk moonlighting as a librarian.

He still had his driver's licence and loved to take rambling car trips all over North America. It was his one remaining passion since his wife, after 46 years of marriage, had left the miserable old coot six months after he retired. She simply could not put up with his grumpiness 24/7. (No mortal woman could, unless she had severe masochistic tendencies.) The divorce had deepened Bill's negative outlook of women in general and wives in particular.

He didn't much like me; despite my best efforts, we had never hit it off, even though I'd been married to his son for over two decades. However, he was a major investor in our business: We had needed his money after the banks refused to loan us enough to buy the place on our own.

Thanks to someone's genius inspiration, Bill had been nick-named Sarge because of his stint as a Master Sargent in the U. S. Army during World War Two. That background was still very evident as he toured the motel, passing out acerbic comments on what needed changing.

When Sarge found out that we had to rename the place and couldn't agree on a new name, he thought a minute, then suggested: "Why not call it Ellen's Fubar Motel?"

"Fubar? What's that mean?" I asked. "And what about Pete's name?"

Sarge fixed me with a shrewd look. "Fubar? Why, it doesn't mean anything, Ellen. Just like Xerox or Kodak, it's an invented name that will come to represent a unique product – in this case, your motel. And it should be just under your name, since a feminine name conjures a sense of home and comfort. Besides, I reckon buying this place was mostly your idea."

Pete sided with his dad (typical!). He liked the logic. My objections were overruled. So we called a local printer and started the ball rolling on new brochures. She wasn't busy that time of year, so we had graphic designs ready for our approval early the next morning.

Sarge left for home. He seemed amused by something. I mentioned it to Pete, but he shrugged it off.

Friday:

I got a phone call this morning from the local tourism bureau.

"Since you're not a member, we normally don't refer enquiries to you," the lady said tartly. "But there's a big horse show in town this weekend and every other place is full. Do you have any rooms available?"

I replied that I did. She hung up before I could thank her, or say that, as new owners, we were interested in joining the bureau.

One hour later, an expensive pickup truck pulling a gleaming white horse trailer arrived. "Crawford's Purebred Arabians" was painted on the side of the trailer. Crawford himself was the driver. He rented our largest room, after first asking if it had air conditioning and if it worked. We were still in the middle of a major heat wave.

As I try to do with every guest, I chatted him up during the registration process and discovered he spoke about his horses the way most men talk about their wives or girlfriends. Then Crawford drove off, to spend the rest of the day and evening at the horse show.

Late that afternoon, Pete and I approved the artwork for our new brochures and told the printer to print 20,000 copies. I was a bit nervous with the large quantity, but Pete said: "We must distribute our brochure everywhere, over a wide area, El. Even though we're small, we have to think big! That's how we'll succeed."

I found myself getting used to our new name: Ellen's Fubar Motel. Had a nice ring to it. Maybe Sarge was finally declaring a cease-fire in our decades-long strained relationship.

Saturday:

Early this morning, some very upset guests checked out of the rooms on either side of Number 17. They said there had been very weird noises all night in that room, which disturbed their sleep.

After they left, I realized that Number 17 was rented to the owner of that show horse, who had returned late last night. I went over to have a word. After some pounding on the door, it finally opened.

The smell hit me first.

"What have you been DOING in here?" I demanded of Crawford, who was standing bleary-eyed in the doorway wearing nothing but his boxers, blinking in the morning sunlight. "It smells like a BARN!"

The second thing to hit me was a big wet set of nostrils. Horse nostrils. Poking out past Crawford, from INSIDE the bedroom!

"My God! You brought your HORSE in with you!" I exclaimed, as I shoved the horse's head away from me. "Are you NUTS?"

"Not usually," he replied defensively. "It was far too hot and muggy to leave him outside in his trailer all night. And I was worried someone might steal him. This is, after all, a prize-winning Arabian! Don't worry, I brought in straw to cover the floor where he was, so there should be no damage to your carpet. I'll clean out the straw and his poop before I leave."

"Straw? POOP!" I was sputtering with rage. "I don't care if this nag won the Triple Crown! This is a MOTEL room, not a STABLE! Have you no sense? You wouldn't try this at the Royal York Hotel in downtown Toronto, so why the blazes did you do it here?"

"Well," he replied archly, "this is not the fancy Royal York, is it? It's just a small country motel."

"Even here in the country, we know that bedrooms are for humans and barns are for animals!" I shot back. "Do you have ANY idea of how hard it's going to be to clean and disinfect this room? We take great pride in our rooms, Sir! They are NOT for the use of horses!"

Crawford fixed me with a crafty look: "Oh, really? Y'know lady, the Innkeeper's Act of Ontario states you must board the horses of your guests. That Act may be over 100 years old, but it's still valid."

The British have a unique expression for when something totally takes you by surprise, causing your jaw to drop and your eyes to look like saucers: gobsmacked. It perfectly describes how I looked and felt at that moment.

"Wh-what?" I said. "I've never heard of the Innkeeper's Act."

"Ignorance of the law is no excuse. Look it up: It says you gotta give me a room and you gotta board my horse, too."

"Well, it might very well say that, mister, but I'm damn sure it doesn't say we must let your horse stay in your room!"

"Since you don't have a barn, where the hell else could I put it? Say, you wouldn't know where I can buy more horse feed, do you? Used the last bag last night."

I just glared at him and pushed past him into the room. Which seemed much smaller with a full-grown horse in it. I quickly noticed that the bathroom door had been removed. Peering inside, I saw that the sink was now a container for oats. The bathtub was full of hay.

Normally I'm a cheerful person. But this morning I lost it.

When Pete found me, I had finished making venomous comments about Crawford's ancestors, and was working on the ancestors of his horse. The air was blue. Pete surveyed the scene and promptly took over the shouting. I left to see if we still had that shotgun among those unpacked boxes from our move here. If I found it, my next task was to call a dog food factory to find out the going rate for fresh purebred Arabian horse meat.

The horse and Crawford were gone before I returned. Lucky for them; I'd found the gun. Pete had charged the jerk a hefty amount to cover the cleaning bill.

Pete suggested we change our motel name again, to Inn Tolerable, or maybe Inn Frustration.

I wasn't very good company for the rest of that day.

Sunday:

I had recovered most of my composure, following the trauma of the Horse Incident. After a mere two weeks as owners, Pete and I realized that for every bad-news customer, there were nine decent ones. (Which is what makes this business enjoyable, especially if you like people. It's also what keeps most innkeepers from committing suicide.)

I was checking out one of those nice people this morning: a charming elderly gentleman, touring Ontario with his wife. He noticed the artwork for our new brochure on the table behind our front desk, and laughed.

"What's so funny?" I asked as I gave him his credit card

receipt.

"Why, that name on the brochure over there. I haven't heard that phrase since World War Two. It's a gag, isn't it?"

"Gag?" I said, as a small knot started in my stomach. "What do you mean? That's going to be the new name for this motel."

"It is? My dear, don't you realize what Fubar means?" When he saw that I did not, he went on: "Well I can't very well tell you because ... ah, it's language unsuitable for a lady's ears."

I was really concerned now. "Oh, don't worry about my ears. You should have been here yesterday – and Wednesday too, for that matter. So, what's Fubar mean?"

The old gentleman was silent for a long moment. Then he said:

"It came out of the Second World War. The Americans coined it, I believe, just like they did SNAFU. It's an acronym; FUBAR is short for F**ked Up Beyond All Recognition."

"Oh. Really. I. See." I said, and forced a smile.

I thanked the man for his information, and stood in the doorway waving until they had driven away. Then I tracked down my husband, while working myself into another monster rage.

"THAT'S what it means?" Pete was incredulous. Then he saw I was seething with fury.

"That miserable old father of yours set us up! He's an American war vet! He knew bloody well what Fubar meant! What a dirty trick to play on us! Especially on me: it's ELLEN'S Fubar Motel!"

I was yelling now. Pete stepped back before my verbal assault. Then his mouth fell open.

"Omigod!" he blurted "We've just ordered 20,000 brochures with that name!"

That shocked me into silence. Of course, being Sunday, we could not reach the printer to cancel the order.

"I'm sure she hasn't started printing it yet," I said, and almost believed it. "I'll call her first thing tomorrow."

"Unless something else happens," said Pete, thinking positively again.

Our Third Week

In Which Angie Discovers The Bare Necessities
And
We Get A Native Experience

Dear Diary:

Monday:

Something else happened: At about 7:00 am, the power went out across the city. We endured complaints from guests who had to take cold showers and we had to handwrite all receipts on check-out. The power finally came back on around 9:30 am, just as the last disgruntled guest drove off.

What a great start to the week!

One of the things that worried Pete and I when we decided to open our own business together, was whether there'd be too much together. Before we bought the motel, we both had separate jobs. No matter how much we loved each other, how would we be if we were together 24/7, at work and at home? How could we take breaks from each other?

To help keep our relationship harmonious, one of our strategies was to give each other some Personal Time by ourselves to do stuff. I took some Personal Time this morning.

We still needed a new name. So I drove through the countryside to air my brains and hopefully get inspired.

That's when I discovered the Giggling Squirrel.

It was a gift shop and restaurant tucked away in a quiet glen between the highway and the Woebegone River. It was full of neat and unique things, including wind chimes. Lots of them, some made of metal and some of wood. I was captivated – and the light bulb went on.

I bought a dozen of the largest chimes. I planned to hang them from the limbs of the stately shade trees on our property. These softly tinkling creations would give us our new name:

Windsong Inn.

Pete was less than enthusiastic.

"That's kind of an airy-fairy name, isn't it?" he groused after I returned and told him of my brainstorm.

"It's much more suitable than anything you – or your *father* – have come up with!" I snapped back. (Hmmm, perhaps I needed more Personal Time?) "And I think we should call it an inn instead of a motel, because I noticed during my drive that many of our motel neighbours call their properties inns. I stopped in and talked with one, and he said it's because 'motel' had a negative connotation among today's travellers, reminding them of a seedy joint that rents rooms by the hour."

Pete wondered if hosting prostitutes might be a steady source of revenue, then he saw my face and shut up.

He eventually agreed to the new name and helped me hang the chimes with thick cord. The air was soon filled with their cheerful music, as the light breeze stirred them. Even Pete, who at first doubted he'd enjoy hearing "those clinking things" all the time, grudgingly admitted that the sounds were restful.

The motel – sorry, *inn* – kept us both too busy to listen to much radio or watch TV. So we never heard the weather forecast for later that week.

Tuesday:

This was the most unusual day we'd had since we bought the place. Nothing happened.

No disasters, no incidents, no jerk guests. We couldn't believe it. But we should have known.

The fates were merely regrouping.

Wednesday:

First thing today, our printer drove up and unloaded several large, heavy boxes on our doorstep. "Your new brochures!" she announced proudly. "Hot off the press!"

"Ohmigod! I completely forgot to call you to cancel the order!" I said, horrified.

"Cancel it? You're kidding, right?"

"No, unfortunately. Y'see, we just found out what FUBAR really means last Sunday. I meant to call you first thing Monday, but stuff happened and it completely slipped my mind."

"Well, it's too late now. Oh, here's your bill."

The woman left and I stared at the stack of boxes holding 20,000 copies of glossy, colourful Ellen's Fubar Motel brochures. I glanced at the invoice in my hand: A nice bill – and we had nothing to show for it, except an expensive pile of recycling!

Pete made some snarky comments about my screw-up (yeah, like Mr. Perfect never screws up!), then loaded the boxes into our battered old station wagon, whose springs creaked in protest at the weight. Grumbling to himself, he drove off to dump them at the city's recycling depot.

Angie, the Human Dust Mop, did a wonderful job cleaning the bedrooms. She was also the type of person who wouldn't get excited if Elvis suddenly walked up to her, admitted he really had been in hiding all these years, and shook her hand.

That's why I knew instantly that something was very wrong when Angie came up to me today, looking flustered.

"Miz. Ellen, I done a terrible mistake when I went ta clean Number Seven," she said. "In 10 years of doin' rooms, this ain't never happened. You're gonna be hearing about it, sure."

My phone rang just then. I scooped it up and listened to an explosion at the other end. One very angry guest. Who'd been in Number Seven with his wife when Angie had entered. Both quite naked. In bed. On top of the sheets. Doing the horizontal mambo. Very enthusiastically. In a position that would never receive missionary approval.

Angie had done what she always did before entering a room: knock, announce "housekeeping", then upon getting no response, use her passkey to enter. This entire procedure took less than two seconds, the standard at hotels and motels worldwide. The guests had not used the deadbolt or the chain. Angie had barged right in – and got quite an eyeful.

I stammered apologies to the irate guest and chided him for not securing the door with deadbolt or chain. He retorted angrily that the rented room was his private domain and my housekeeper had no right entering unbidden. (I found out weeks later that wasn't true; we had the right to enter for housekeeping.) They had not heard Angie's knock (not surprising, considering their athletic activity at the time). He screamed that their privacy had been violated and that his wife was so traumatized, she'd locked her naked self in the bathroom and wouldn't come out.

Then he announced that he was a lawyer. And he was going to sue us. (Naturally.)

I hung up the phone, smiled at Angie, and said I'd straighten everything out. She went off, still flustered, to continue her duties. Pete had returned by then and I braced myself when I told him about it, but he surprised me. He questioned me on every little detail. When I'd finished, not only did he stay calm, but he insisted on handling it himself.

He went over to the room, apologized profusely, said that our poor housekeeper was equally traumatized, that it had been an honest error, of course their stay would be complimentary, and offered them another complimentary stay on their next trip here. Mollified, the lawyer agreed and they shook hands. Then the man spent an hour talking his wife out of the bathroom.

Pete wore a huge goofy grin the rest of the day. And mentioned several times how he maybe should do some housekeeping chores, to relieve Angie's burden.

Men!

Thursday:

Shortly after Angie started work today, there was a terrific banging sound. Pete and I dashed outside. Angie was pounding lustily on a bedroom door with a rubber mallet.

"What the heck are you doing?" we yelled in unison (another

ability gained from 21 years of marriage).

Angie replied that this was her new method of announcing herself, before she entered a room to clean. "Mr. and Miz. Tomlinson, no one'll miss me knockin' on them doors now," she said with satisfaction.

While her enthusiasm was admirable, we commanded her to cease and desist immediately. Besides the long-term damage to our doors if she continued, we imagined the shock to our guests when they suddenly heard the thunderous blows.

"Probably give some old geezer a heart attack!" proclaimed Pete, considerate as ever. Muttering, Angie retired the mallet.

After lunch, I visited our printer and ordered another 20,000 brochures, this time with our Windsong Inn name.

"Now, you're sure about this name, right?" she asked.

"Yessss," I gritted, forcing a smile.

The wind picked up after supper. The sweet music from our 12 wind chimes increased in volume. By 10:00 pm, the wind was approaching gale-force, and the chimes were now very loud and no longer musical.

The wind had blown in cooler air, breaking the crushing heat wave. Our guests, and ourselves, had the bedroom windows open to take advantage of the refreshing air. But we couldn't get a good night's sleep thanks to the Windsong Inn Symphony Orchestra.

Just before midnight, Pete abruptly left our bed. I heard him rummaging around in our storage room, then heard the outside door slam. I suddenly realized what he intended. Throwing on some clothes, I dashed out into the night.

Lit by our parking lot lights, a wild sight greeted my eyes. The wind was howling and the chimes were making an awful racket as they danced like demented marionettes. There was Pete, with at least six guests, the gale tearing at their clothes and hair while they madly attacked the sturdy cords from which my beloved chimes hung. Pete was the most effective; he had our big machete.

The wind chimes were soon retired to the ground. The guests cheered. Pete fixed me with a look, then stomped off back to bed.

Friday:

When Ol' Baloo finally awoke, we had a "discussion". Pete convinced me that we really didn't need 12 big wind chimes to justify our new name. We negotiated, and settled on three, which we re-hung. The rest went back to the Giggling Squirrel.

"Besides, just the sound of the wind through all our trees justifies our name," he said.

It was then that we heard the nerve-jangling squawks of what sounded like a BIG duck. Very close. Very loud.

We quickly came upon Angie outside a bedroom door, removing a large duck caller from her mouth.

"So that WAS you sounding like Donald Duck in heat!" Pete exclaimed.

"Yup," she replied. "Since you don' want me poundin' on them doors, I figgered this here caller would be better. Will certainly git the attention of anyone in there."

"Especially in duck hunting season, when it will become a threat to your personal safety." I said. "We're not going to disturb our guests with that awful sound."

We confiscated her caller. And hoped that was the end of that.

That afternoon, I was working in our small rear apartment when the front desk bell rang. When I entered, a hat was barely showing above our counter top. I peered over. That hat was perched on the head of the smallest man I'd ever seen. And the thinnest; you could see the outline of his cheekbones clearly.

He introduced himself as Jean-Michel Laurence Simpson McTavish-Jones. (His name was longer than he was tall!). He said he was from the government and was here to help. (Uh-oh.)

He was the local tourism officer from the Ontario Ministry of Economic Development, Trade, Technology, Information, Culture, Recreation, Communication, Bagpipe Licensing and Tourism. When I remarked that tourism looked like it had been tacked onto his Ministry as an afterthought, he smiled a pained little smile.

"Yes, well at least our tourism industry is represented by a senior Minister in Cabinet," he said stiffly.

As we were new owners, he had personally troubled himself to come out and meet us. He outlined a number of helpful government programs developed specifically for tourism businesses which we'd be eligible for – if only we were larger.

There wasn't much help available for a small 23-unit inn. And the government had cancelled the sole financing program that could have been used to expand our operation.

"You'll find the banks won't be of much help either, if you want to expand or renovate, Mrs. Tomlinson," he explained. "These days, they have little desire to lend money to tourism operations. On their scale of acceptable lending risks, I believe tourist accommodation is near the bottom, just below hog farming."

He gave me a thick file of complaints that his Ministry had received from guests at the motel, when it had been run by Hal Owens. The file covered just the past year. On a quick flip-through, I saw many complaints that were hair-raising.

"You see the negative reputation you've got to overcome," he noted mournfully. "However, you've made a good start by changing your name. Well, best of luck and DO call me whenever you feel that I MAY be able to help you."

"Oh, you've certainly been a big help so far," I said.

He winced at my sarcasm and walked away with quick, precise little steps. He drove off in an energy-efficient eco-friendly tiny car that looked like a child's toy. The only thing missing was a wind-up key sticking out of the roof.

Saturday:

AOOOGAH! AOOOGAH!

The morning quiet was shattered by the blare of what sounded like a submarine's diving klaxon. In fact, it WAS a submarine diving klaxon, as we discovered when we raced up to Angie and yanked the battery-powered horn out of her hands.

"Enough is enough!" I exclaimed. While Pete calmed down startled guests, I took Angie aside for a talk. I finally realized just how disturbed she had been by Wednesday's incident. These loud alerts were her over-compensating (to put it mildly!) to prevent it happening again.

I reminded her that it had been the only such incident in her 10 years of housekeeping. It was a fluke. All she had to do in future was knock just a little louder, and wait just a little longer before opening the door

I finally convinced her and she promised no more mallets, duck calls, or klaxons.

In late morning, I checked-in a large group of First Nations people, who'd come to our area for a native festival. It was a fund-raiser for a community program. One of the organizers asked if we would promote the festival to our other guests and I readily agreed. I put up one of their posters in our lobby and placed some flyers at the front desk.

In early evening, Pete was doing the lawn when he noticed smoke wafting out of Number 20's open window. He yelled for me to call 911, while he grabbed a fire extinguisher and kicked open the door to the room. He was hollering to the occupants to get out; his first concern was for their safety. But what he saw as he charged inside stopped him colder than a pair of skinnydippers at the annual January Polar Bear Plunge into the Woebegone River.

The room had been cleared of furniture; the beds were propped up against the walls, and the chairs and tables had been piled in a corner. In the centre of the room, two men, two women and a pair of teenage boys were sitting cross-legged and chanting – around a small blazing campfire!

(We later discovered that they had liberated one of our garbage can lids and built the fire on top, out of consideration for our carpet. How nice. They had also removed the batteries from the room's smoke alarm.)

Pete ran up to the fire and gave it a hearty dose from the fire extinguisher. That put out the fire, but it also scattered glowing embers all over the carpet and created billowing clouds of smoke, which quickly filled the room. Coughing and swearing, everyone staggered outside except Pete who, eyes streaming, stomped out the embers. Then he too stumbled outside, where he had the first word:

"What the bloody HELL were you doing? Are you trying to burn down our place?"

The oldest adult, a fiftysomething man with long flowing hair who had been leading the chant, regarded Pete solemnly, then replied that they had been conducting a native cleansing ceremony using sweetgrass. He was quite indignant that it had been interrupted.

"YOU'RE indignant? How do you think WE feel? Just look at what the smoke has done to our walls and curtains! And those embers have ruined our carpet!" Pete bellowed.

"Well Sir, it seems to me that most of the smoke and all of the ember damage were caused when you blasted the fire with your extinguisher," the man said. For a long moment, Pete seriously considered blasting him with the extinguisher as well.

"Why the hell were you even doing this native ceremony anyway? Pardon my noticing, but all of you are so white that your skin probably glows in the dark! That couple next to you have red hair!"

The man snorted. "So? We attended the First Nations festival this afternoon and totally got into the whole native thing, man. It's so *earthy.*"

"Yeah," chimed in one of the women. The man continued:

"So we bought some sweetgrass and brought it back here to have our own purifying ceremony, ya know?"

I ran up to the group about then, clutching our first aid kit and some blankets. Pete was waving his arms and yelling:

"What possessed you to do your sweetgrass ceremony inside our room? Campfires are meant for the outdoors!"

"Because open fires have been banned throughout this county, due to the high fire hazard risk. It's been a very dry season. The wind is very strong today and we did not wish to endanger the environment."

Before Pete could express his opinion of this logic, the police and firemen arrived, sirens wailing. Another wailing soon joined the cacophony: me. When I looked into the bedroom and saw the damage.

That's when Pete discovered I could yell louder than he could.

The police eventually calmed everyone down. Charges were laid against the adults for violating the Fire Code and for room damages. We asked them to leave our property immediately, which they did, although with an air of greatly-injured dignity.

It was our second heavily-damaged room in two weeks.

Tonight, I cried myself to sleep.

Sunday:

This morning, one of the guests checking-out said, with a huge grin: "Love that sign you folks have on the back of the room door! Little touches like that are why we stay at small independent motels like yours."

I smiled graciously and thanked him. I had no idea what he was talking about.

As soon as he left, I went to his room. Tacked to the back of the door was a photocopy of a small hand-printed sign. It read:

IMPOTENT NOTICE

Before you has any sexual relatives,
inshore your primacy by fasting
the deadbeat, also use the chain.

Tank you.
Mangerment

I did a quick check of those rooms that were vacant. The signs were in all of them.

Angie. She'd had the last word after all.

In early afternoon, Pete and I were discussing a potential guest who had just telephoned, asking that we accept his pet, a small poodle. Because of last week's Horse Incident, we had decided upon a strict No Pets Policy. When informed of this, the caller had become abusive, insisting that we were obligated to accept Fluffy.

"No, you're not," came a deep voice from outside, through our screen door. The door opened, and in walked a man and a woman, both in their early sixties. "You have the complete right to set your own pets policy, whether to accept them or not," continued the man.

"In fact," added the woman, "The only pets you must accept, by law, are service animals, trained to assist people with disabilities such as blindness or epilepsy."

They introduced themselves as Bert and Madeline Monahan. Tall and dignified, with a completely-bald head, Bert had piercing grey eyes and a stern mouth – which could erupt into a glorious smile without warning. Madeline was small and vivacious, with coiffed black hair streaked with grey, and blue eyes that were always flicking from subject to subject like a hummingbird after nectar.

They owned and operated a 102-room property on the other side of Wackimac: the Best Western Countryside Inn. They'd been in this business for over 25 years, and had expanded their place from a small tired 1950s-style motel into a large full-service modern inn, affiliated with the international Best Western chain. Bert and Madeline were now semi-retired (HAH! Like Pete and I were supposed to be!), and their daughter handled most of the day-to-day operation of the inn.

Hearing of us new owners, they'd come over to make our acquaintance and see if they could offer any advice.

Pete and I couldn't believe our ears. We immediately asked if we could adopt them as our new parents. If not, then at least as our legal guardians.

Maybe this would be the turning point in our fledgling enterprise? Maybe our problems were over?

Diary, I'm dreaming, aren't I?

Our Fourth Week

In Which We Discover A Different Use For A Toilet Bowl And A Regular Guest Drops In

Dear Diary:

Monday:

We really enjoyed meeting Bert and Madeline Monahan yesterday. They were now our official Guardian Angels. It was wonderful of them to come over and meet the "newbies". We had a nice long chat. One of their first recommendations was that we must quickly improve our "curb appeal".

"You've got to make your inn more appealing from the highway," Bert advised. "If it looks tired from the outside, people will think your rooms are tired on the inside. The type of clientele you're after will just pass you by."

"But our rooms ARE tired on the inside!" I protested. "We were going to tackle them first."

"No," admonished Madeline. "Your rooms are priority two. Priority one is your curb appeal. You must make it attractive, so folks will stop in. What you want is a nice flower garden out front, or a charming gazebo; something attention-getting. Also a fresh coat of paint on all your exterior walls, with pleasing colours that complement each other."

"And pave your parking lot, too," added Bert. "It's dusty when it's dry and a quagmire when it rains."

This morning, Pete and I discussed it. We decided to pave the parking lot and create a front garden first, and leave the painting until fall. But I was still convinced that our tired rooms needed attention now, as much as the outside did.

"Tell you what, dear," offered Pete. "You work on redecorating the rooms and leave the exterior stuff to me. I'll arrange the paving and garden."

Made sense to me, so I agreed. (In hindsight, I recall that no mental alarm bells went off at all.)

Wasting no time, Pete charged off to a garden centre. Hours later, when he returned, he said that our gardening materials would be delivered Wednesday. He seemed inordinately pleased with himself.

Tuesday:

Our new brochures with our new name – Windsong Inn – were delivered today. They looked great! Pete and I made plans to drive to each tourist information booth in a wide radius around our inn, and drop off a bunch. The Monahans suggested other places for distribution, too. We also ordered a new roadside sign – whose cost made me lose my appetite for lunch – and it would be installed soon.

The Windsong Inn was being born!

Late this afternoon, I was working the front desk when a very agitated man burst in.

"Come quickly!" he yelled. "It's my daughter! She's stuck in the bathroom!"

Now this, I knew how to handle. I'd grown up with three younger siblings, who had sometimes locked themselves inside the bathroom. Grabbing a wire coat hanger and a pair of pliers, I ran to Number Four, the scene of the crisis.

The girl's parents were frantic. "Our Katie is crying in there and says she can't come to the door to unlock it!" said the mother. "Something's very wrong!"

Using the pliers, I cut a straight length of wire from the coat hanger, inserted it in the bathroom door knob and tripped the lock. We flung the door open. And stared.

On the edge of the bathtub, sat one hugely embarrassed girl

in shorts and tank top, who looked to be about 8 years old, with her right foot planted in the toilet bowl!

Tears streaked her face. "I'm really sorry! It's stuck! Can you please hurry and get it out? It really hurts," she whimpered.

Accompanied by sobs, Katie's story gushed out: "We'd just returned from sightseeing and I was VERY hot. So I ran in here, locked the door, pulled off my shoes and socks, sat on the edge of this tub, and put my feet into the toilet bowl to cool them off quickly. I guess I went too far in with one foot and now it's stuck at the bottom! And it REALLY hurts."

"Why on earth didn't you just use the bathtub?" I said. "You could have put your feet under the faucet!"

The girl stared at me as if I'd just made a shocking revelation, such as one day she'd actually like boys.

"I ... I didn't think," she stammered. (Duh.)

Her whole foot was inside the drain, past her heel. It was probably swollen by now, too. I called for Pete, who soon arrived. After he recovered from the same shock that had hit me, he tried to work her foot free. I tried to work her foot free. Then we both tried. Her parents tried. The girl yelped with pain every time.

No luck.

"Well, we'll just have to break the bowl, I guess," Pete muttered grimly. He left and soon returned lugging a toolbox. "Let's see what we've got in here."

Pete rummaged around in the huge toolbox that, along with the Human Dust Mop, had come with the inn. Now, Pete with a toolbox is like a politician with a smile: both are just for show. So I don't know what I expected him to pull out, but it certainly wasn't THAT: a big crowbar.

"Pete! Are you sure about using that thing?"

"Yep," said the person to whom "handyman" was someone listed in the Yellow Pages. "It's the only way! We gotta break the bowl around the drain, and we gotta be careful so we don't hurt Katie here."

Katie was regarding the crowbar like it was a giant needle with her name on it.

"Wait!" I yelped, and reached behind the bowl to shut off the valve on the water pipe feeding the toilet. I then used the ice bucket to quickly empty the tank and bowl of water. Pete sheepishly muttered thanks. He then squared his shoulders and, with chivalrous determination, set about rescuing the fair damsel.

"Oh, DO be careful!" gasped her mother.

Pete was careful. At first. But as he struggled to break the porcelain without hurting Katie, he got more and more frustrated. Which made him angry. You wouldn't like Pete when he's angry.

He had removed the bolts fastening the bowl to the floor, since he figured he could break the drain from underneath. The bowl was now rocking violently back and forth as Pete furiously tried to break off a porcelain piece large enough to free the girl. Katie's father was holding her steady so she wouldn't be rocked off the tub edge.

Finally, Pete gave a mighty heave on the crowbar. Many things happened at once. A large chunk of porcelain broke off the drain area, freeing Katie's foot – Pete lurched sideways and fell, hitting his head on the sink – and the entire bowl crashed on its side, ripping the water pipe from the wall. The pipe broke, ahead of its shut-off valve. Water gushed from the broken pipe right into Pete's face. Which helped revive him from the knock on his head.

"Master valve!" Pete sputtered through the water. "El, go shut off the master valve!"

Good advice. Very logical. Except I had no idea where the master valve was. As Pete sat up holding his bleeding head, moving out of the stream of water, he revealed a horrible secret: He had no idea where it was either!

And the water flowed in merrily. It had already covered the bathroom floor, and was spreading out into the bedroom. Katie and her parents had fled.

While Pete did what he always does in a crisis (swear and panic), I used the bedroom phone to call the Monahans across town. Madeline answered and in response to my screamed "WHERE DO I FIND THE MASTER SHUT-OFF VALVE FOR

THE WATER?", quickly gave me directions to several likely places. I hit pay dirt at the second location and shut off the water. But by then, much of the bedroom was flooded. We relocated the family to another room. Then I drove Pete to the hospital; he needed stiches for his head.

Another note to self: One of us HAS to take a course on general repairs.

Wednesday:

On check-out, Katie's parents refused to pay for damages to Number Four. They insisted it was Pete who had caused the disaster. While not admitting that they had a point, I said it had been their foolish daughter who had stuck her foot in the toilet bowl in the first place and we had damaged the room when freeing her. The parents refused to change their minds, berated me for "trying to con them", and left in a huff.

In late morning, Angie found me in Number Four, still mopping up. "Delivery guy here with a load of what he sez is garden stuff ordered by the Pompous Idiot," she mumbled. "Wants ta know wheres ya want it."

"Oh, just tell him to dump it on the front lawn near the highway," I replied. I didn't want to disturb Pete; he was staying in bed today nursing a terrific headache. Angie gave me a funny look, then shrugged and walked off.

About five minutes later, an earthquake hit. There was a huge crash and the ground shook. I ran out of the room and saw a large dust cloud obscuring our front lawn. Then the dust cleared.

I was looking at a mountain of giant boulders!

I found out from the delivery man that this was exactly what Pete had ordered. When Pete told me on Monday that he'd ordered supplies for our new front garden, I'd assumed it was a load of earth and flowers and shrubs. But the garden shop had talked Pete into putting in a rock garden, which was very trendy. Pete, convinced we needed a dramatic attention-getter to stop travellers on the highway, had (as usual!) gone overboard and ordered huge BOULDERS. Lots of them. The smallest one could crush a compact car.

"Well, you can't just leave them HERE," I said to the delivery man.

"Sorry ma'am, but I was told to put 'em here. Once they roll off my dumper, there's no way I can move 'em around," he replied. "You'll need a large backhoe for that. Sign here, please."

I couldn't wait until Pete felt better. So I could give him another headache.

Thursday:

The first of the magazines to which we had subscribed four weeks ago arrived today. With some ceremony, I cleared a space on our small coffee table for it. I was sure we'd get to it soon.

Pete's Rock Pile was already proving to be quite an attention-getter, but it was the wrong kind of attention. An official car with Ministry of Transportation on its doors pulled into our lot today. Two uniformed functionaries emerged, and walked around our rocks. One took notes while the other took pictures. When I went up to them, they said:

"Ma'am, you can't leave these rocks here. (No argument from me on that score!) They're obscuring the line-of-sight for oncoming traffic on the highway, especially for people exiting your parking lot."

They gave us 48 hours to move the rocks, after which we'd get a substantial fine. Hurt head or no, Pete had to do something fast. This incident made me realize that Pete and I should work together on major projects. One benefit would be that the Significant Other would be spared unwelcome surprises. I'd also discovered that the bedrooms needed a lot more than simple redecorating. So I put them on hold, while we worked together to fix up our exterior.

Friday:

As if we didn't have enough headaches, today was the day my French-Canadian Aunt Genevieve arrived for an extended stay. Aunt Ginny recently had major surgery and wanted a change of scenery to recuperate. I'd offered to take her in (soft-hearted me). I put her in Number One, next to our apartment behind the inn's office.

In her early sixties, my Aunt was small with a well-padded pear-shape, topped by a cherubic face and obviously-dyed blonde hair. She looked the perfect cliche of a grandmother, right out of a Hallmark card. Appearances were deceiving.

Aunt Ginny was notorious within my family. Extremely bigoted, she felt any non-white in Canada should be packed off "back where they came from". This included our First Nations people; the fact that they were here first didn't derail her logic.

She held strong opinions on just about everything, and refused to let those opinions be affected by facts. When she read the newspapers, she only read the headlines of each article, then insisted on speaking authoritatively about the story. She was a widow (her husband had died years ago in a mysterious hunting accident), with three grown children: two sons and a daughter. She doted on the daughter while completely ignoring her sons; she hated males.

Pete was up and about today, though his head still ached. He spoke darkly about having to put up with "one of my crazy relatives". I looked at him and just said two words: "Sarge. Fubar." Shut him right up.

Aunt Ginny had many obsessions, but her biggest one was squirrels. She loathed those "vermin" because they wrecked one's garden, chowing down on what you were trying to grow. She soon discovered the big vegetable garden behind the inn planted by the former owner, which contained several rows of corn. She made it her personal mission to keep our corn safe from squirrels.

I was amused, but didn't give it much thought. At least it kept her occupied.

After several phone calls, I'd located a backhoe operator to come out tomorrow and move our boulder mountain. Pete had wanted to get a backhoe from the Rent-All place and operate it himself to save money. I firmly put a stop to that idea. Pete had the same prior experience with backhoes as with plumbing repair: none. He sulked for the rest of the day.

One of the few things Hal Owens had bothered to tell us before he fled was that we had a contract with the Ontario Ministry of Natural Resources for two bedrooms on the last Friday of May through September. It was for four people, doing fish planting and forest surveying in our area. The contract stipulated that they must have our two end units: Numbers 23 and 24 (though we had only 23 rooms, there was no number 13). These rooms were next to our treeless side lawn (which had originally covered the septic tanks and field before the motel switched to city sewage treatment). It was guaranteed business, and Owens had said the MNR crew usually dropped in around 5:00 pm.

He wasn't kidding about them dropping in.

At 5:10 pm, I heard a low throbbing noise, which slowly grew louder. Coming out of the office, I realized the sound was coming from the sky. The noise was quite loud now; the air itself seemed to vibrate. Several guests had come out of their rooms to investigate; as did Pete, interrupting his attempts to revive a comatose TV in Number 15.

Suddenly, coming up on us from behind, a large yellow and black helicopter thundered over the roof of the inn, very low. After slowly circling overhead, it hovered over our side field and started coming down. They were landing!

It was a big machine. I saw an Ontario Provincial Air Service symbol on its door as its skids touched down. The sound of its engines changed in pitch and the four large rotor blades started slowing.

"My gosh," I said to Pete, who had joined me, "These must be our MNR guests! Owens never said they came in a helicopter!"

Pete was in seventh heaven. He'd been a huge chopper fan ever since he was a kid, and to have one parked at his doorstep was quite a treat. He soon struck up a conversation with the Air Service pilot, Scott Andrew, and the two of them discussed the aircraft's specifications in the secret language of chopper geeks: a BK-117 by Messerschmitt-Bolkow-Blohm and Kawasaki Heavy Industries, two Lycoming LTS 101-650-B1 turbine engines with 500 shp each, four-bladed rigid rotor, 240 km/h cruise speed, 13 m overall length, 455 lb/h fuel consumption, 3200 kg maximum gross weight, standard passenger capacity of seven plus pilot.

Boys and their toys.

Anyway, the Windsong Inn could now boast of a heli-pad! Not only was the chopper a great hit with our guests, but people staying at neighbouring motels noticed it and also came over to gawk. I felt a swell of pride – how's THAT for one-upping your competitors!

But having such a crowd-pleasing attraction had a price.

Saturday:

The sun rose today at 6:04 am. So did we all.

A high-pitched whine woke some of us first. The whine changed to a deep throaty roar, which woke the rest of us. Then the sounds repeated, so the noise was now in stereo, which drove even the die-hard stay-a-beds to their windows. (Yes, even Pete.) A swishing sound added its voice to the chorus.

The helicopter had just fired up its twin jet turbine engines. At 6:04 am! We had to endure the racket for what seemed like forever. Then a man came out of Number Nine, a bedsheet wrapped around his middle, and walked towards the aircraft, shaking his fist. With the engines finally warmed up, the pilot chose that moment to lift off. The powerful turbine sound intensified, the angle of the rotors changed as they circled much faster, and the big chopper slowly lumbered into the air.

The guest shaking his fist didn't know much about helicopters. As the strong downdraft from the big rotors hit him, his bedsheet was whipped away. The guy went back into his room much faster than he had come out. (Nice show!)

As the chopper flew away and the *thup-thupping* sound of its rotors faded, Pete (never a morning person) groggily remembered that last night the pilot had mentioned something about an early start.

We heard about that early-morning wake-up call from all of our guests today. We had to do something about future MNR visits, though we didn't want to lose their business. The crew liked the convenience of not having to rent a car to get from the small airport on the other side of Wackimac to our inn. "Perhaps have them land at the airport and we'll shuttle them back and forth in our car?" I suggested.

"I guess so," said Pete gloomily. He had so enjoyed having a helicopter here.

"Or maybe we can talk them into leaving later, like around 7:30 am," I added hopefully.

The backhoe operator showed up at 8:00 am to move our rocks. He said he wanted an early start. Pete and I looked at each other and laughed.

By 2:00 pm, all the boulders were artfully repositioned in the centre of our front lawn, well back from the highway. (The job would have been finished much sooner, but SOMEONE couldn't make up his mind as to their final positions.) Those rocks too heavy for the backhoe to lift, had to be dragged. Our lawn now had deep skid marks. It looked awful. Besides the earth we'd ordered so we could plant flowers around the rocks, we'd need an extra load to repair those scars.

We decided that motel improvement works the same way as home improvement: It causes a domino effect, where one action causes many unplanned others.

Sunday:

Well, today marked the end of our first month as innkeepers! Here's what we've learned so far from the School of Hard Knocks:

Nine out of 10 customers are fine, decent people.
But, oh, that 10th person!
Never underestimate the public's ability to surprise you.
Some people do really stupid things.
This is no semi-retirement project.
Pete is no handyman.

Diary, I wonder what our second month will bring?

Our Fifth Week

In Which A-Haunting And A-Hunting We Will Go

Dear Diary:

Monday:

"BINOCULARS!" announced Pete triumphantly, as he strode into our front office waving a package.

I looked up from trying to fit three advance reservations into two rooms, and said: "What?"

Pete gave me his patented "Oh, get a clue, lady!" look and repeated: "Binoculars! You know, to check on our competition! Remember, the Monahans recommended we get a pair for our front desk? So we can spy on our neighbour motels' parking lots every evening, to see if they have more cars than ours? That lets us know their occupancy, so we can see how we're doing compared to them. The Monahans said EVERY innkeeper does it!"

I laughed: "Oh Pete, I think they were pulling your leg! Really! Spying on our competition! It's so...so...CHILDISH!"

"Not at all, my dear," replied Secret Agent Pete, in his best Sean Connery James Bond imitation. "It is modern industrial espionage." He unpacked the binoculars, put them to his eyes and fiddled with the focus. "There! I'm looking at our closest neighbour now – and he has more cars than WE do already!"

"Sure, Peter. And so he should – he's twice our size!" I left my *Secret Agent Man* to his research and returned to my reservations book.

About ten minutes later, I heard a power saw, followed by hammering. By this time, Pete was at the edge of our front lawn hiding behind a tree, playing *I Spy* on our farthest neighbour down the highway at the end of the "motel strip". (Oh, I wish he'd *Get Smart*.) It was up to me to investigate.

I tracked the commotion to our backyard, where I found a workman building something – a BIG something – around the corn plants in our vegetable garden. Aunt Ginny was hovering nearby, a big smile on her face.

"What is going on?" I asked her.

"Well, Ellen dear, I told you last week that I was making it my personal mission to keep your corn safe from squirrel vermin. I shooed them away all weekend, but there's simply too many around here! And I know from when I had a garden back home, that trapping and releasing them far away doesn't work, because other squirrels just move in to take over the territory.

"So I looked in the Yellow Pages and hired Tony here to build us a big cage around the plants! A sturdy wood frame covered by chicken wire. That should keep the little devils away from your corn!" Aunt Ginny stopped to catch her breath. Her eyes were shining with a fanatic's zeal.

"I ... see," was what my mouth said, but my brain was saying "you're nuts, lady."

Tony methodically went about his work, mumbling that in 18 years of construction, this was the first time he'd built a cage for corn. Aunt Ginny had even directed him to sink chicken wire 12 inches below the ground, to keep the squirrels from digging under the cage walls.

Shaking my head, I left them to it. That little rotund woman sure was obsessed about squirrels.

Tuesday:

It was another glorious sunny day today. Of course, I was too busy around the inn to enjoy it, but some of our guests certainly took advantage. Especially one lady.

It was early afternoon and I was just finishing another load of laundry. Pete, who usually helped me with this tedious chore, had been AWOL for over an hour. Coming out of the laundry room, I caught sight of him over by our side lawn.

"What are you doing?" I yelled.

"Just some yard work!" he hollered back. I glared at him, muttered something about poor timing, and went to place fresh towels in the rooms.

About 30 minutes later, a flustered mother came up to me, with two young children in tow. She demanded that I immediately put a stop to "such disgraceful behaviour." Seeing my blank look, she enlightened me:

"There's a topless woman sunbathing on your side lawn, which I find highly inappropriate for a family motel!"

I raced over and saw that it was true. A well-proportioned brunette in her late 20s was lying on her back on a towel, with just her micro-bikini bottom on. Her exposed skin glistened with sun screen.

I also saw Pete, some distance away, busily engaged in his "yard work", which conveniently gave him an unobstructed view of the almost-naked sunbather. *Pig!*

I went up to the woman, introduced myself as one of the owners, and asked her to please replace her top.

"Absolutely not!" she replied. "I have every right to go topless! There was that court case a few years ago, remember? It ruled that women have the right to go topless in Ontario! So leave me be!"

Keeping my temper in check (a difficult task, knowing that Pete The Pervert had been ogling her for over an hour), I said that some of our other guests were disturbed by what she was doing.

"Well, that's their problem, not mine!" she retorted. "They should just go somewhere else where they can't see me!"

Fuming, I left. Then I had a brainstorm. I yelled for Pete to come fix the sink in Number Five, as it kept backing up. (Not true, but since it really wasn't broken, then Pete had a good chance of fixing it.)

Pete reluctantly complied, but took one last look at the

Dynamic Duo as he walked away and banged into the corner of the inn, cutting his lip. Served him right!

Meanwhile, our statuesque sun-worshipper had resumed lying on her back, with her hat over her eyes. So she never saw me as I quietly positioned our lawn sprinkler so that its spray would drench our almost-naked beauty.

Now, our inn's outdoor taps draw water from a well that's 93 feet deep. What comes out of that well is clean and cold. Very cold. Especially when I run the hose for several minutes to get rid of the sun-warmed water in it, before connecting it to the lawn sprinkler. As the topless woman found out with a loud shriek when I switched on the sprinkler.

In a manoeuver worthy of an Olympic Gold in gymnastics, she catapulted straight up from her prone position to land on her feet. She screamed at me, but I smiled and said it was our regular time to water the lawn. She made a rude gesture, gathered her things and moved to another location, well away from the sprinkler.

I let her get settled, waited about 10 minutes, then moved the sprinkler and repeated the process.

This time, what came out of her mouth was most unladylike.

She relocated again. So did the sprinkler. By the fourth time, she finally got the message and flounced back to her room, slamming the door behind her. When he returned from fixing a sink that had nothing wrong with it, Pete was very disappointed she had gone. And wondered why the lawn was wet.

Wednesday:

First thing today, I spoke with Bert Monahan about the Topless Incident. He chuckled and complimented me on how I had handled it. He said that our inn was private property, which gave us the right to set our own reasonable rules about guest behaviour.

"For example, you already have rules about no noise after 11:00 pm. and no pets," he explained. "This is the same thing. Simply put up a sign in your lobby that states your establishment caters to families and that appropriate attire is required while on your premises."

Pete made half-hearted objections when I put up the sign, but gave up when I said curtly that we were trying to build a reputation as a NICE place.

A curious thing happened in early afternoon. A young couple arrived and asked if this used to be Ellen's Fubar Motel.

"Wha ... What? Where'd you hear that name?" I said, stunned.

The man yanked a glossy brochure out of his jeans pocket, saying: "This. Reading it, this seems like a nice place, though the name is kooky. Your address is the same as the brochure, so we figured you just changed your name. Right?"

I looked at the brochure. It was one of the 20,000 that were supposed to have been junked!

"Where did you get this brochure?" I said.

"Dunno. Somewhere. We've collected a whole pile of brochures an' guides an' stuff since we arrived in this area. Anyway, do you have a vacancy?"

I did. After they'd checked-in, I gained custody of the offending brochure and showed Pete. He had no idea where it might have come from.

(Arrgh! I'd have to think about this mystery later.)

Aunt Ginny's anti-squirrel corn cage had been finished since late Monday. I asked her how it was working. She replied that it seemed to work fine so far, though the vermin were trying their darnedest to get in. She was going to place paper bags over the ears of corn, figuring that if the squirrels couldn't see them, then they wouldn't try so hard to break into the cage.

With a vague sense of uneasiness, I told Aunt Ginny not to spend so much time on this. She needed to relax more. After all, she was supposed to be recuperating from a serious operation. Then I put it out of my head; I had an inn to run.

When the Human Dust Mop arrived today, I spoke to her about Number 11. I was very particular about our rooms. I knew they were tired and that they badly needed a major renovation. But until then, I insisted that they be spotlessly clean (Angie was great at that), and that the "little touches" I'd placed in them be arranged just so. For example, the amenities in each bathroom had to be placed a certain way in their basket next to the sink, the vase of dried flowers had to be centred on the dresser, and the clothes hangers must all be hung neatly on the left of the closet rod. Angie was great at those arrangements too – except for unit 11. For weeks now, every time I checked it after she'd finished, the items were never where they were supposed to be. The bathroom amenities were placed haphazardly in their basket which was on top of the TV in the bedroom, the vase was to the far right of the dresser, and the clothes hangers were scattered on the closet floor.

Today I finally had the chance to ask her why. She replied:

"Oh, I tried fer days after yous took over here to arrange tings jest as you sez, as I does in all them other rooms. But Number 11 is HER room, an' she has to have some tings HER way, Miz. Tomlinson. It's jest her way a tellin' us she's still around."

"HER room?" I asked, confused. "Who do you mean, Angie?"

Angie fixed me with a look that she usually reserved for the Pompous Idiot and said: "Why, the ghost. Brenda Ames. Didn't ya know, Miz. Ellen? Ev'body round here knows 'bout poor Brenda."

I certainly didn't, but Angie wouldn't say any more (she was the poster lady for taciturn), except for a parting comment that Brenda wasn't harmful and most guests never even knew she was there.

My head was spinning. GHOST? We had a GHOST? As if we didn't have enough problems!

I made myself a cup of tea and thought about it. While I believed that certain inanimate objects sometimes had personalities all their own (like men watching TV, or when our aged station wagon refused to start on cold winter mornings), I certainly didn't believe in ghosts. I decided that Angie was kidding me.

I marched into Number 11, re-arranged the items that were out of place and left. Twenty minutes later, I re-entered the room with fresh linens. The items had all been moved.

Convinced that Angie was playing an elaborate joke, I returned the items to their proper places. I left the room, walked ten steps, then turned and quickly went back in. The items had all been moved again!

"Okay, okay, that's it!" I said. I checked the room carefully, looking for a hidden prankster. I now suspected Pete was the culprit. Didn't that man have enough to do?

There was no-one in the room. I re-arranged the items yet again. Then I sat down in a chair and waited, watchful. Nothing. Thirty minutes crawled by. Nothing. I got up and announced loudly: "Ghost, eh? HAH!"

Suddenly, the air grew cold. Extremely cold. I could see my breath. The hairs on the back of my neck rose. I felt the presence of someone standing behind me and I was filled with an overwhelming sense of sadness. I whirled around. Empty air.

In the closet, the hangers crashed to the floor. I ran over and flung open the closet door. No-one was inside.

There was a thump in the bedroom. I looked back and saw the amenities basket from the bathroom was now on the TV. Then, right before my eyes, the vase slowly moved to the right of the dresser.

Waves of melancholy washed over me, so powerful that I suddenly felt like crying.

I fled.

Thursday:

Not surprisingly, I didn't sleep well last night. I didn't say a word about the ghost to Pete. Instead, mid-morning found me at the Best Western Countryside Inn, having a cuppa with Madeline. Feeling embarrassed, I told her what had happened in Number 11 yesterday.

"Oh yes, my dear," she said when I'd finished, "That was Brenda Ames all right. Why, everyone around here knows her story – oh! I forgot; you and Pete aren't from around here! Living in Toronto, you wouldn't have heard about our local tragedy."

So Madeline told me about Brenda Ames. Back in 1953,

she'd been quite the popular girl at the local high school. She had no shortage of young men interested in her. Two lads in particular made her short list and she played one off against the other throughout the senior year. Finally, Prom Night loomed, and she had to choose one over the other. The loser flew into a rage and wasn't seen around the school for the entire week before the prom.

On Prom Night, Brenda and her beau drank a lot of alcohol in the parking lot outside the dance. They left and managed to rent a room at the newly-opened Pleasant Holiday Inn, under assumed names. The room was Number 11. They had been inside for about an hour when the door crashed open. The rejected boyfriend barged in, quite drunk himself, holding his father's shotgun. He'd found them by cruising around until he saw her beau's car in the motel lot, parked in front of Number 11.

There was much screaming and swearing. Suddenly, the intruder pointed the shotgun directly at the boyfriend in the bed. With a wicked curse, he pulled the trigger. At the same moment, Brenda flung herself in front of her lover. Both barrels erupted, hitting her in the chest, killing her instantly.

"That poor girl, cut down in the prime of her young life," finished Madeline. "Well, her ghost has haunted that room ever since. I've never heard of her harming any one; mostly she just moves a few things around. And she never goes outside that room. If you treat her with respect, she's fine. You should be proud; you own Wackimac's only haunted motel!"

I just stared at her. Pride was not what I was feeling right now.

"You know, Ellen, you could even use this in your marketing. You'd be surprised how many people want to stay at haunted places. There's an Ontario country inn near London and an historic tavern inn at Niagara-on-the-Lake, each with a ghost, and it's quite the tourist draw for them!"

When I returned to our inn, I cracked open two beers for Pete and me, and told him everything. When I was done, he reacted like I hoped he wouldn't: scornful disbelief.

"It's your over-active imagination, El! And Madeline and Angie are just playing to it! Well, we'll just see about this so-called ghost!" he proclaimed. He finished his beer, grabbed another and marched into Number 11.

He lasted five minutes. Later, from his gurney in the hospital Emergency Room, he told me what happened:

He strode in loudly denying that there were such things as ghosts. He said the whole story was a fabrication to fool the gullible and to give the place some notoriety. In fact, if Brenda had ever existed, she had probably been the town slut. Then he placed the items that had been moved back to their proper places and DARED them to change positions while he watched.

That's when the amenities basket came flying out of the bathroom to smash Ghostbuster Pete in the face. He hardly felt it, though, because his beer bottle was wrenched out of his hand and sent crashing upside his head. Pete fell next to the dresser and rolled on his back just in time to see the vase tilt over the edge and plummet downwards at him. His next memory was waking up in the ambulance.

So much for my "over-active imagination".

I later found out from Madeline that, besides his insults, Pete's drinking had infuriated Brenda.

"Drinking was what led to her death, so she's very intolerant about it," she explained. "Mind, I never heard of Brenda ever being violent like that."

I replied that Pete could bring that out in people; it was a gift.

I didn't return to Number 11 for days. Until then, I refused to rent it.

Friday:

Angie came up to me today and showed me two bath towels from Number 14. Each one had a five-inch strip torn off across the entire width of one end.

"Same ting happened yesterday," she said. "I replaced them towels, but in all yesterday's excitement, I fergot ta tell yuz abouts it."

I swore. Not at Angie, but at the jerk who had mutilated my NEW towels. I had just bought them in Toronto a month ago!

I marched up to Number 14 and pounded on the door. It was answered by the father of the brood that was occupying the room. They had checked-in on Wednesday.

"WHY in heaven's name did you cut these strips off my new towels?" I demanded.

The guy scratched himself behind his back and said: "Well, we needed extra face cloths."

It never occurred to the Moron Family to simply call our front desk and request more face cloths.

Fighting the urge to strangle him, I told him that an extra amount would be on his bill to cover the ruined towels. Then I stormed off, muttering nasty comments about shallow ends of gene pools.

When they checked-out, they left behind a Guest Comment Card that noted the "Manager Lady" as being very rude and unreasonable.

Saturday:

I was hauling the laundry cart past Number Eight this morning, when I suddenly heard a muffled *poom*. It seemed to come from the vicinity of our office. I knew Pete was asleep courtesy of prescription painkillers, so it wasn't him.

The muffled *poom* repeated.

As I walked toward the area, Aunt Ginny came out of Number One, her room, closing the door behind her. She looked flushed and excited.

"Oh hello, Ellen dear," she gushed. "I'll be right back. I've just got to put something in the garbage!" She disappeared around back of the inn.

I walked along the front of Numbers Two to Four, but didn't hear anything unusual. Angie came by and I asked if she'd heard that *poom* sound. She hadn't; she'd been vacuuming with the ancient shrieking machine we'd nick-named the Howler. Then she sniffed the air.

"Y'know, Miz. Tomlinson, if I din' knows better, I'd swear that's the smell of gunpowder," she announced. "Smells jest like my Fred's clothes when he comes back from his fall deer hunt."

"Gunpowder?" I said. "You mean someone's just fired a GUN here?"

Angie looked at me and our eyes grew wide together. We forced ourselves to calmly walk to the office, where I called the police.

They quickly arrived and used my passkey to check rooms Two through Six. They found nothing, except a few guests upset at being disturbed.

"You sure about what you heard and smelled?" asked the senior officer when they'd finished their search. I nodded. She regarded me suspiciously.

Suddenly, the *poom* sound came again.

An officer came running around the side of the motel, gun drawn and yelling: "Someone's shooting from inside a room! I was just checking out the backyard when I saw a squirrel get hit! The thing was blasted apart! Shot came from that room!"

I gasped. The cop was pointing at Number One. Aunt Ginny!

The police flung open her door, and entered crouching with their guns at the ready. (Just like on TV!) They found a cherubic little grandmother standing by the rear window – holding a smoking hunting rifle.

She'd been shooting squirrels through the open window!

Aunt Ginny was quite vexed at having her squirrel hunt interrupted.

"You don't understand!" she protested as the cops led her away. "Those damn vermin had dug under the cage, past the buried wire, and were eating the corn! I had no choice! I got the ones in the cage and this last one on its way to the cage! I was saving your corn!"

Pete would never let me hear the end of this.

I suddenly wondered if my Aunt had somehow been involved

in that "mysterious hunting accident" that had killed her husband years ago. She'd just demonstrated that she was a crack shot.

I felt profoundly ashamed that she was related to me.

Sunday:

A saying from Goethe, that I've remembered since I learned it in college Psychology class, seems appropriate here: "Superstition is rooted in a much deeper layer of the psyche than skepticism."

Goethe got that right, because:

After church today, fortified with religion, I went back into Number 11. Alone. To have a chat with a ghost. (I can't *believe* I did that!)

"Look, Brenda, we have to talk. Pete and I believe in you now, okay? He's sorry about what he said and so am I. What happened to you was very tragic and unfair. I understand why you're so sad and why you got angry. But what you did to Pete was also unfair. You can't do things like that again. I wouldn't feel safe renting this room to guests and if I kept this room closed, I suspect you'd get very lonely, right?"

I paused. Nothing. I felt a little foolish. (Okay, a *lot* foolish.)

"So look, Brenda. You can arrange those few things in here to suit yourself, like you were doing, okay? And I promise that Pete won't say anything nasty about you again. But in return, you have to promise not to terrify or hurt any guests that stay in this room, or anyone else, like us or our housekeeper, Angie. Okay? Do we have a deal?"

In the closed room, a soft cool breeze ruffled my hair. I took that as a yes.

Our Sixth Week

In Which No Means No And Sleeping Beauty Almost Drowns

Dear Diary:

Monday:

We hadn't had a lick of rain since we moved here six weeks ago. Well, last night the drought abruptly ended just before midnight. With a vengeance. Rain sheeted down in torrents and we soon discovered another secret that our inn (and its former owner) had hidden from us:

The roof leaked like a sieve.

We first noticed it in our bedroom, where not one, not two, but three leaks started – right over our bed! We couldn't move our bed anywhere else in the cramped room, so Pete surprised both of us by coming up with an ingenious temporary solution.

We cut and stretched three layers of big plastic garbage bags over our bed, tacking the ends to the walls, to catch the drops. Then we settled back under our cozy sheets, to resume our interrupted sleep.

That's when the phone started ringing.

It was our guests calling, one after the other, squawking about roof leaks in their rooms. Pete and I looked at each other, as the revelation hit us simultaneously: During Week One, we noticed each room had two or three pails stashed in the closet. Now we knew why.

We apologized and told our guests to place a pail under each leak and go back to bed. As did we.

Early this morning, I was awakened by Pete whispering in my ear. Normally, Pete whispering in my ear in bed means one thing. Not today.

"Don't sit up, El. Stay flat and slide out of the bed. Now would be a good time."

I was on my back and opened my eyes. There was enough light in the room for me to see swollen green plastic – two inches from my face!

With perfect self-control, I said: "GAH!"

I stifled further outbursts and did as Pete had instructed, sliding out and landing with a thump on the floor. Then I scuttled away from the bed and stood up against the wall.

Our garbage bag canopy had slowly filled with raindrops all night and was now bulging downward, straining to contain a small lake just inches from where our faces had been. If it had ruptured, we would have drowned! Or at least received one helluva wake-up call.

Luckily, Pete, never a morning person, had been awakened by a call of nature and saw that we were in imminent danger of an unexpected deluge of Biblical proportions.

I looked at him, standing against the other wall, and gasped: "Wow. Close call."

"Yeah."

We spent most of the morning using a wet-vac to drain the hanging lake in our bedroom and emptying pails from the guest rooms. We gave our slightly waterlogged guests a discount on their stay, to compensate for their interior rainshowers.

After such a horrible start to the day, we received a wonderful surprise when we later opened our mail: a thank-you letter from a recent guest praising us for our hospitality. Wow! It was one of our goals to change our inn's reputation, from a tacky place previously run by a miserable man, into a friendly, family haven. This letter showed that we were starting to make a difference!

We knew from the visit three weeks ago of the short multi-named tourism official, that the only letters Hal Owens had ever received were ones of complaint and lawsuit.

That nice letter really made our day! I was determined to hold onto this warm fuzzy feeling as long as I could, before another nasty reared its ugly head.

Today's mail also contained more magazines to which we had subscribed, back in the euphoria of Week One. I added them to the reading pile on our coffee table. The pile was growing. Today also saw the arrival of the first books from the two monthly book clubs that we'd joined. I placed them next to the magazines.

Soon. We'd have the time to get to them soon.

Tuesday:

BAM! BAM! BAM!

It was very early in the morning. Like 2:00 am early.

BAM! BAM! BAM!

Sounded like someone was using a hammer. On our front door!

"Can't that idiot find our doorbell? It's even lit up!" groused Pete as he fumbled out of bed and found his way to the door. He opened the solid inner door and through the screen door, addressed the man standing impatiently outside: "Yessss?"

"Well, it's about TIME you answered! I've been pounding on your door for EVER!" said the candidate for this year's Medal of Diplomacy. "I need a room; I've been travelling since dawn!"

"Sir," replied Pete with great self-control, considering he had only gone to bed at midnight, after another 15 hour day, "It's 2:00 in the morning and our No Vacancy sign is on!"

"Yeah, I saw it. But, c'mon, you have to have something available, buddy! You can't tell me you're completely full! That's the same bull the other motels fed me!"

"Read my lips: WE'RE COMPLETELY FULL! That's what No Vacancy means, you twit! So get out of here and let us go back to sleep, or I'll sic the dog on you!"

The man let loose with a string of unprintable oaths, which Pete cut off when he slammed the inner door shut. Airing a few choice oaths himself, Pete returned to bed. We were just slipping back to sleep when we heard what sounded like a rifle shot. We were too tired to investigate; sleep overpowered us.

Come morning, I was the first one up and about, as usual. I was shocked to see a neat round hole in the centre of our office window facing the parking lot. It looked like a bullet hole!

Pete concurred, when he awoke later. We called the police, who came to investigate. They couldn't find a bullet, but we lodged a complaint anyway. We were sure it had been caused by our early morning visitor and Pete provided a description of his car. The officer departed, muttering that the alleged perpetrator was likely miles away by now.

Pete was really upset: "Too bad we don't really have a dog! I'd have loved to turn a snarling Rottweiler loose on that nut job!"

"Yes, dear," I said. "But you know how I feel about pets and we also have a No Pets policy here at the inn. How would it look if we had a dog ourselves?"

Pete conceded the point. He promised he'd figure something out, so we wouldn't be taken advantage of next time.

Wednesday:

Today was a momentous day: Our new roadside sign was installed! Now everyone driving along the highway could see WINDSONG INN in flowing script, with a graphic of stately trees, all in restful colours. Gone was the last vestige of the Pleasant Holiday Inn!

Pete and I also finished planting the last flowers around our Boulder Garden today. It made a lovely display, complementing our new sign. And the pavers were due to arrive soon, to do our lot. Our Curb Appeal was improving!

I was very concerned about one of our guests: Mrs. Litresits in Number 16. A dignified elderly lady, she was staying with us for the week, while she visited her husband at the Regional Health Centre. He was in for a serious heart operation and his chances were only 50-50. Their children, like ours, were living their busy lives scattered all over the world; she was alone here with her husband. She spent most of the day and evening with him at the hospital. Every night when she returned to our inn, she looked increasingly pale and worried.

I decided she needed a pick-me-up

This afternoon, during my Personal Time, I returned to the Giggling Squirrel, the unusual gift shop/restaurant where I'd discovered the wind chimes that had inspired our name. There, I purchased a very soft and hugable 18-inch-tall stuffed bear, with light brown fur, limpid brown eyes, and the cutest button nose. Later that evening, I presented it to Mrs. Litresits.

"Something to keep you company and to hug when you need to," I said. "Pete and I hope all goes well with your husband."

The old woman regarded first the bear, then me, in surprise: "You do this, for me? Oh, how very, very kind of you! This bear, it is so sweet!" With tears in her eyes, she thanked me profusely. Embarrassed, I shushed her. Her husband had just had his operation today and the next few days were crucial. I repeated our best wishes.

Thursday:

Pete used his Personal Time today to visit an electronics store. He returned with a CD player and two outdoor speakers. He spent two hours installing the speakers beneath the roof overhang outside our front door, then another hour re-installing them when they didn't work the first time and he finally conceded to read the Owner's Manual. He didn't tell me anything about this project and what happened next put it out of my mind:

Aunt Ginny checked-out. Following her arrest last Saturday, she had hired Wackimac's best female lawyer. The charges against her had been settled and she paid a hefty fine.

She was furious with me, "a fellow woman", for having called the cops on her. I protested that I hadn't known it was her doing the shooting when I'd called the police and besides, she had gone overboard shooting squirrels with a rifle from inside her room. My words fell on deaf ears.

"Some gratitude! I did it to save your CORN," Aunt Ginny

shouted. She was so mad, her double chins were quivering. "You'll see! Without my efforts, those squirrels will eat it ALL! Well, you can rest assured that I'll not darken YOUR doorstep again! In fact, just like I did with my two sons, I'm writing YOU out of my Will! You'll not get a penny from ME, Ellen Tomlinson! My boys won't know I've disowned them until I'm dead, but I'm telling YOU right now so you can stew over it for years! My dear daughter Carol-Ann will inherit everything!"

With that, and a curt nod to Pete who had just finished loading her 600-pound suitcases into her car (I guess males have their uses), she squeezed her pear-shaped frame behind the wheel and started the engine.

"Safe home, Mrs. Fudd!" called Pete, as she sped out of our lot, tires spraying stones. She didn't slow down when she reached the highway; she roared onto it without checking for oncoming traffic. Horns blared and tires screeched as cars braked or swerved to avoid her.

In a perfect imitation of Bugs Bunny, Pete repeated one of the rabbit's classic sayings: "She's a NICE lady. Eeeeugh!"

I didn't care if the stupid squirrels ate the stupid corn and it certainly didn't bother me whether I was in her damn Will or not. However, as far as I could tell, Aunt Ginny's sons were devoted to her; visiting regularly, treating her kindly and never forgetting special occasions. I suddenly realized that she had secretly disowned them for the sole reason that they were male. I knew she hated males – but her own sons?

I promised myself to send a note to both guys, cousin to cousin. They deserved to know now, while their strange mother was still alive, so they could discuss it with her. That would spare them the trauma of discovering how she really felt about them only after she died, when it would be too late to talk to her about it. Something like that would prey on their minds forever.

Friday:
Our first bank statements from VISA and MasterCard arrived in today's mail. They summarized the credit card use of

our guests from last month, who'd used the cards to pay for their accommodation. Examining the statements, I was startled to see the high service charge both banks took off the totals: 4.5%.

Pete whistled when I showed him my discovery. He grabbed a calculator. "Geez, that merchant fee means we lose $2.93 off every $65 room we rent! With 23 rooms, if each was rented every night, that would add up to $2,022 over 30 days! That's potentially $24,597 a year! Ouch!"

I called Madeline Monahan and asked her about it.

"Oh, my dear!" she exclaimed. "Bert and I forgot to tell you about a very important thing: Join our industry association! Their member benefits include a low merchant rate of only 1.7% for those credit cards. It'll save you thousands of dollars a year in bank service charges! In fact, you'll recoup your association membership dues in just one or two months and the rest is pure savings!"

I promptly phoned the toll-free number Madeline gave me. "Lodging Ontario," answered a chirpy female voice.

"Oh, I'm sorry, I was told this was the number for the Ontario Motels, Inns, Resorts, Campgrounds, Lodges and Yurts Association," I said.

"It is, it is," replied the chirpy voice. "We've just changed our name to Lodging Ontario. It's SO much shorter! We've had a number of names over the years, you know. We change names as the industry changes. For instance, we were originally called Tourist Courts of Ontario, because that's what most motels were called back in the 1940s and 50s."

Chatting with the happy bird, I found out the non-profit association was now 60 years old. They had gone through EIGHT names in that time! It seemed that every five years or so, they got the itch to re-name themselves. They were famous for it.

But their benefits were genuine. So I joined up then and there. They promised that our lower merchant rates on the credit cards would take effect soon. They would also send us a big Welcome package, outlining all their 45 benefits and services. (Great. More stuff for our reading pile.)

With some nervousness, I had decided to re-open Number 11, our infamous Haunted Room. I rented it today to two burly men, part of a construction crew repairing a bridge in our area. I figured two big guys like that wouldn't notice any tell-tale signs of Brenda Ames, the room's permanent spook, and if they did, it wouldn't faze them.

I found out that you really can't judge a book by its cover.

Saturday:

Despite what they say, it's a proven fact that sometimes lightning DOES strike twice. For the second time this week, we were rudely awakened by a furious pounding on our front door. This time, it was 12:45 am.

Pete roused himself with more energy than I would have expected. He grabbed my arm and urged me out of bed with him.

"C'mon, El, you'll enjoy this," he said.

We had been running with a full house all week and our No Vacancy sign was lit. That didn't stop this jerk from creating a ruckus in the middle of the night.

As Pete opened the front door, the guy immediately demanded:

"I need a room! And don't tell ME you're full; I know how you small motels work! When you want to call it a night, you just flip on your No Vacancy sign. So I KNOW you have a room!"

"We don't play games like that here, Sir," Pete replied with Pompous Idiot dignity. "We really are full up. You should pull off the road earlier, at a decent hour – you'd have a much better chance of getting a room."

"DON'T give ME any CRAP, Mister! I'm in NO mood for CRAP! You rent me a room right NOW, or you'll really regret it!"

Pete looked at me and I was astonished to see a big smile erupt on his face. Then the smile vanished and he turned back to the belligerent moron standing outside our screen door: "Look fella, you get back in your car and drive outta here, or I'll sic our Dobermans on you!"

"BULL! You ain't got no Dobermans!"

"Well, I warned you!" Pete drew back out of the man's sight. Suddenly, there came the distant throaty cry of a pack of large dogs, that quickly grew closer. Pete was yelling: "Here boys! Here! GET HIM BOYS!" Their ferocious barking and snarling increased in volume, until it sounded like they were almost upon us!

Our late-night (early morning?) visitor fled back to the safety of his car. The roar of his engine starting was almost drowned out by the deafening sound of howling dogs out for blood. He raced out of our lot.

Abruptly, the canine cacophony ended. Pete motioned to the CD player on the small table just inside our front door and said:

"A special CD of sound effects! Played through those outdoor speakers! Did you SEE that guy run?" He collapsed with whoops of laughter. I must admit, **Diary**, that I joined him. Pete really outdid himself on this one!

When we'd finished laughing, Pete said: "I've also got other neat sounds on the same CD, like machine gun fire, bombs, alien ray blasts and a nasty cat fight! Ellen, I can really have fun with this! I almost hope we get more idiots like him!"

I hoped we didn't. Can you imagine loud machine gun fire in the middle of the night?

We figured this was enough excitement for one day and that the rest of today would be much calmer.

Wrong.

Oh, the day passed sanely enough – at least for this business. By early evening, we'd been lulled into a false sense of security. Then our front desk phone rang. It was the guest in Number 12, shouting that water was pouring into her room through the right-hand wall shared with the unit next door.

Number 11.

Pete and I dashed outside and ran towards the unit. Just as we neared it, its door crashed open and the two beefy construction workers charged outside.

"GYAAAAH!" one screamed. He was wearing only his

boxers.

"Ay! Ay! Ay! MOMMA!" yelled the other. All he was wearing were water droplets.

Just another typical evening at the Windsong Inn.

I ran inside Number 11, grabbed the top sheets off the beds, and threw them to Pete. He chased after the two men, who were still running away. Meanwhile, I went through the room and quickly discovered that the bathtub was overflowing. This bathroom's floor was tilted slightly, so that the water flowed toward the adjoining wall instead of into the bedroom. Sloshing through the lake on the floor, I turned off the taps and opened the drain.

"Oh, Brenda!" I said sternly. "I'm so disappointed with you! I thought we had a deal!"

Sometime later, Pete returned to our office with the two men in tow. They looked quite shaken. We took them into our kitchen, where Pete poured them both a stiff shot of whisky. They quickly drained their glasses. Mid-way through their second glass, their story tumbled out.

They'd been working really hard since dawn today, so they were quite tired by the time they returned to their room. Carl, the guy in the boxer shorts, had flaked out on the bed, watching the ball game on TV. Since it was the Toronto Blue Jays, he had quickly fallen asleep.

Meanwhile, his buddy, Rob, had decided to treat his aching muscles to a nice hot soak in the tub.

Carl was rudely awakened by a vigorous shaking. When he looked around, there was no one there. Figuring it was his imagination, he settled back down to sleep. He was roughly shaken into wakefulness again. Thinking that Rob was playing a joke on him, he yelled out something crude towards the bathroom. Receiving no response, Carl heaved his bulk out of bed and padded over to the closed bathroom door.

Again, he called out. No response.

Concerned, he yanked open the door. Peering into the hot steamy room, he saw Rob lying on his back in the bath, with the taps on and the water overflowing the tub. He was snoring lustily.

Carl knew that explained why Rob hadn't responded; the guy could sleep through a nuclear explosion.

Then Carl suddenly realized that Rob's head was not resting on the edge of the tub. It was forward of the edge, surrounded by water, yet it was being held upright somehow. Carl could clearly see what looked like the impressions of invisible hands pressing against Rob's thick mane of hair!

Carl jumped forward and grabbed Rob under the armpit, trying to haul him out of the tub. Something grabbed Rob's other armpit, and the sleeping giant was lifted out. When Carl realized that an unseen something was helping him lift Rob, he released his grip and stepped back. So did the unseen something. Rob crashed to the floor. That woke him up.

White-faced, Carl blurted out what had just happened. Rob had obviously fallen asleep as the tub was filling and the overflow drain at the top must have been clogged. He would have slipped beneath the water and drowned except that something had held his head up.

Rob shook his head in disbelief:

"Whaddya mean, Carl? I wuz saved by a ghost? That's pure bull, buddy, an' you know it! Ain't NO such thing as spooks!"

To that, Carl replied: "Eep". He pointed past Rob.

A towel lifted itself from the rack and slowly floated towards the wet naked man on the floor. It halted over Rob, then dropped onto his crotch. Rob instantly became a believer. Then the hot humid air abruptly became very cold.

Both men totally lost it at that point and raced to be the first one out of the motel room. Which is where we came in.

If it hadn't been for Brenda Ames, Sleeping Beauty would have drowned. I owed her an apology.

We told the guys about Brenda's ghost. For two big construction workers, they were real wusses about the supernatural. (Listen to me! Just last week, I ran from the ghost myself!) Anyway, Carl and Rob refused to return to their room. Pete got them settled in the spare room in our apartment, while I returned to Number 11 to gather up their things.

Upon entering the room, I said: "I'm very sorry I doubted you, Brenda. Thank you for saving that man's life."

The room lights dimmed, then brightened again. She had accepted my apology. Either that, or the hydro was going to quit again.

Sunday:

This afternoon, Mrs. Litresits came to the office with terrific news. Her husband was out of danger and mending fast. In fact, he was being discharged tomorrow and they'd be returning home.

"That's wonderful! We're so happy for you!" I exclaimed.

Without warning, the old woman stepped forward and embraced me. "Thank you so much for your caring, Mrs. Ellen! Your nice words and especially that lovely bear! That was so special! You are so caring! And that is what I am going to tell everyone – this is the caring inn!"

I stammered that she shouldn't make such a big deal out of it, but she waved me into silence. "IS big deal!" she stated firmly. "You and Mr. Peter, you are good people."

Mrs. Litresits reached into a bag and produced the bear. "Here, you take and give to next customer who needs something to hug during sad times. And you tell customer that it works."

Pete came into the office about then and was ambushed by a big hug from Mrs. Litresits. Then she left to return to the hospital.

I told Pete what had just happened. Then I waited for one of his smart remarks, but he surprised me. With an admiring look, he put his arm around my shoulder and squeezed, saying:

"You did something that a large impersonal hotel chain would never have thought of, much less have done, for a guest. You done good, El. You done real good."

Flummoxed, I sat down hard. I wondered: Was Pete possessed by Brenda? Should I book an exorcism? (Why? He was nicer this way.)

Our Seventh Week

In Which An Automobile Gets A Hole-In-One
And Guess Who's Coming To Breakfast?

Dear Diary:

Monday:

As the early riser in our two-person enterprise, mornings are my special time. I like to take a walk around all 4.2 acres of our property, while the dew still sparkles on the ground and the air has that refreshing early-morning sweetness. Birdsong surrounds me; I call it the "Dawn Chorus." I usually have the place to myself; few guests are outside at 6:15 am.

But today, I was not alone. I came around a corner and saw a man and a woman in our backyard, by the banks of the mud flat that, in Spring, had been the aptly-named Woebegone River. With quiet, graceful movements, they were doing Tai Chi. I didn't disturb them; I knew it was a discipline requiring great concentration.

However, as I passed, the lady said: "Good morning. You have a lovely, peaceful place here. We'll be back!" I thanked her and walked on. What a nice way to start the week.

By late afternoon, we again had a full house. (No complaints from us!) It was the last day of a big convention (the Canadian Society of Left-Handed Sheep Shearers) in Wackimac and all available accommodation was booked solid.

At about 8:30 pm., Pete and I were working our front desk when a taxi arrived. It disgorged one very large, very drunk passenger. A gentleman we'd checked-in earlier today. He stumbled into our office.

"Heylo, folks!" he announced. Waving back and forth, he marshalled his thoughts with great effort and said: "Just gots throwed out ... er ... I mean, back froms th' cornvenshun. I know I gots a room here, but I forgets whisht one."

"Number Three," I said. "It's on your room key."

"Key? I have a key?" The man labouriously searched through his pockets. "No key," he concluded mournfully. He looked like he was about to cry.

"It's okay, Sir, here's a spare," said Pete and gave it to him. "Your original key will probably turn up tomorrow. Now your room is just three doors down from the office here. Okay?"

Pete had to repeat the room number twice, before the besotted conventioneer finally got it. He thanked us and wobbled outside. On our front step, he stopped and went a deathly shade of pale. Then he said:

"BWAAACK!" as he threw up all over our front step. He wiped his mouth, looked back at us and smiled like a little boy who'd been caught stealing from his mother's purse. He staggered off towards his room. Halfway there, he vomited again. Reaching his door, he took a long time trying to fit his key into the lock. Finally succeeding, he turned the knob and disappeared inside.

Pete saw my disgusted look and said: "Well, look at it this way, El. At least now he won't puke in the room!" He went outside to hose the mess away.

Yeah, what a way to start the week!

Tuesday:

Late this morning, our over-indulgent conventioneer appeared at our front desk. He was very hung-over.

"I want to thank you for your courtesy last night," he said contritely. "I apologize for getting sick outside there. You folks are a helluva lot nicer than some other motels. Last convention, the place where I stayed, I ralfed in their lobby. The owner herself fetched a bucket and mop, and made me clean up my own puke then and there!"

After he left, I said to Pete: "Maybe we should do the same, next time!"

In preparation for our parking lot being paved, I'd called the city to have them replace the crumpled culvert at the head of our driveway with a new one. We also wanted it sunk deeper, so there would not be a bump when our new pavement covered it.

The road crew arrived in early afternoon. Their backhoe operator must have been new, because he enthusiastically dug a huge deep trench across half of our driveway, large enough to bury an elephant! The plan was for them to lay the new pipe in that half, re-fill the hole, then dig up the other half. This way, guests could still access our inn throughout the procedure.

Everything went well with the first half of the driveway. But after they'd dug up the second half, they realized they needed more crushed stone fill because of the larger-than-expected trench. So the crew took a break under one of our shade trees, while the dump truck went to fetch the stones.

That nice couple in Number 17, who had checked-in an hour ago, chose that moment to leave in a great hurry. They jumped in their compact car and sped toward our entrance.

I don't know if it was the late-afternoon sun in their eyes, or they just weren't paying attention, but they headed right for the half of the driveway that was still an open pit! At the last minute, the driver noticed the hole and slammed on his brakes. The car slewed sideways, but its momentum carried it over the edge. With an awful *CLUNK*, the small car fell completely into the hole. Air bags deployed, then retracted.

The car was really wedged in the deep hole. So tightly that the doors wouldn't open. The man, who'd been driving, started screaming at the workmen, who'd run over to help. He shrieked insults and commands to get them out of there NOW. The woman just sat there with a horrified look on her face.

Around then, the Pompous Idiot arrived on the scene. Completely ignoring the people in the car, Pete accosted the foreman of the road crew, yelling:

"What the HELL were you thinking? Look at the accident you've caused! You should have put a barrier around the hole! You bloody fools! These poor people could have been badly hurt!"

The guy in the car was still screaming profanities. Pete turned on him and bellowed: "QUIET, BUDDY! I'm doing the shouting here, okay!"

"Well, excuse ME, 'buddy'! WE'RE the ones stuck in here!" the guy shot back, chasing those words with a string of colourful adjectives.

Then the foreman gave vent to his injured feelings, also using colourful vocabulary. Some of it was quite inventive, too. Soon all three men were screaming red-faced at each other. The road crew gathered around, enjoying the show. No one was helping extricate the trapped couple. Pete and the car's driver discovered that insults were not the right way to deal with unionized city workers. After several minutes, the foreman made a rude gesture, then he and his crew turned their backs on the scene and returned to their shady resting spot.

I'd seen more than enough testosterone in action. I called for a tow truck. Meanwhile, by some awful coincidence (or a vindictive workman with a cell phone), a photographer with our local newspaper, the *Wackimac Expositor & Farmers' Chronicle*, discovered the accident and snapped several photos.

Wednesday:

Pete and I were horrified when we received today's morning paper. The front page had a close-up photo of the stuck couple under a big banner headline: SCANDAL AT LOCAL MOTEL?

Seems the driver of the car was a prominent councilor at City Hall. Unfortunately, the lady next to him was not Mrs. Councilor! Being new here, we didn't know them from Adam. They'd rented the room for the night, so we never suspected they only wanted it for an afternoon "quickie".

And here we were trying to re-build our inn's reputation!

In late morning, a man showed up asking if we knew where Ellen's Fubar Motel was. He waved a glossy brochure in the air and said he'd been driving up and down the strip trying to find it, because it seemed like a nice place according to the brochure.

I explained, with forced calm, that he had found the place, but it was now called the Windsong Inn.

"Oh, okay," he said. "Well, I don't wonder that you changed the name. Ya know what FUBAR means, eh?"

"I assure you, I do," I replied. "Um, where did you get that brochure?"

He looked blank. "Huh. Ya know, I completely forget. Somewhere around here."

(Where the *hell* were these damn brochures coming from? They should have all been turned into toilet paper by now!)

That afternoon, Pete returned from a quick trip to the hardware store and went immediately to our side lawn. He was there for some time, so I went over to see what he was up to.

He was spray-painting a huge H on the grass, in white paint!

"What ARE you doing?" I exclaimed, afraid that the stress of innkeeping had snapped his fragile mind after only seven weeks.

"Painting a huge H on our lawn," he replied serenely. I resisted the urge to whack him; you must be kind to your loved ones, especially when they are mentally ill.

"Yes. I. See. That. WHY?"

"It marks our official helicopter landing pad, El! It helps the pilot target us and alerts guests that choppers land here. We're the only motel in Wackimac with a heli-pad!"

"No, we're the only motel in Wackimac with a huge H spray-painted on our lawn. Besides, it's not the last Friday of the month yet," I said, referring to our standing arrangement with the Ministry of Natural Resources. Pete then explained that MNR had called earlier today and booked rooms for a crew that was fighting a large forest fire north of Wackimac. They'd be arriving in the same helicopter that had landed here three weeks ago.

"But Pete!" I protested. "The business is nice and the chopper is a wonderful attraction for the guests, but we can't have them taking off at six in the morning again! Remember the awful racket those jet engines made? Our guests will kill us!"

"Don't worry, honey. I've solved that problem. They'll only leave later, at around 7:30 when most everybody is awake."

I had to rush back to answer our front desk phone and so didn't have time to ask him to explain further.

The big chopper thundered in after supper, landing precisely on Pete's H. It was the same pilot as before: Scott Andrew. While he and Pete renewed acquaintances, the grimy, exhausted fire-fighters trudged to their rooms. Once again, the bright yellow and black helicopter was a great attention-getter for our guests.

Thursday:

Pete is a late evening person. This means I'm up at least two hours before Ol' Baloo usually rises. So I should have realized something was amiss when I emerged from the shower, to find Pete gone. With a towel around my hair, and another around my body (barely covering what needed to be covered), I walked into the kitchen to put the tea kettle on for my wake-up cuppa, my head full of plans for the day.

The kitchen was filled with nine husky men, all of whom stopped what they were doing to gawk at me. Pete was at the stove. He gawked too.

I, of course, handled the situation with perfect aplomb.

"AAACK!" I shrieked and beat a speedy retreat.

Later, fully dressed, I mustered my dignity and made my grand re-entrance. After enduring some good-natured ribbing, I got the story: Pete had discovered that the chopper crew lifted off at the crack of dawn to get to the airport diner for breakfast as soon as it opened. This gave them an early start to the day. So Pete had made them a deal: He'd cook them breakfast, in return for them leaving later.

Except that Pete had forgotten to tell ME about it! Talk about being shocked wide awake! Speaking of shocks ...

In our mail today was a letter from the company that insured the inn. They were notifying us that they would not be renewing our insurance! Something about a poor claims record. They'd given us a whole three day's advance warning. Fighting panic, I called the company. After an eternity in voice-mail hell, I finally connected with a live body.

I found out it was the poor claims record of the former owner, Hal Owens. There had been numerous claims over the past two years, most highly suspect. Owens had been treating the insurance policy like a renovation fund. When part of the roof had been wind-damaged, he'd insisted that the whole roof be replaced. When three old doors were damaged, he'd argued for a complete set of 23 new doors, "so that they all matched". When water damage was caused by faulty plumbing, he'd tried to get all new plumbing and a complete room renovation paid for by the policy.

He had not won all his battles, but when he did, he kept the money from the claim, instead of spending it to fix what was damaged. The insurance company had had enough of these shenanigans and refused to renew the policy. No matter how much I pleaded, explaining that we were new owners and Owens was gone, the "customer service" rep stuck by the company's decision. Finally, he hung up on me!

Several calls to local insurance brokers revealed that some didn't write commercial policies, while those that did wouldn't touch us because of our claims record. I was in despair. We couldn't operate the inn without insurance! (Especially with Handyman Pete's "expertise"!)

When I told Pete about it, he was all for driving to the company's Toronto office and throttling the inconsiderate suit until he changed his mind. I thought it would be more productive to call Madeline Monahan, which I did. She immediately told me to contact Lodging Ontario, the association we'd joined last week. Seems they had a group property/casualty insurance program, with a great policy and competitive rates.

When I called the association, the same cheerful bird I'd talked to last week told me that the Welcome Kit she'd sent us had full details on the insurance program. Had I received the Kit yet?

I had. It was in our reading pile, being slowly devoured by the magazines arriving almost daily.

The nice lady at Lodging Ontario helped me connect with Dave Matthews, President of their insurance broker, Warren & Associates. He was an absolute joy to deal with. Once he verified that we really were new owners, he signed us up on the association's program. We received a pleasant surprise: The premium was much less than the old policy.

Whew! One more crisis resolved!

Friday:

Another major improvement to our exterior appearance: The paving crew arrived today to do our parking lot. The sub-surface foundation had been prepared last week. We directed our guests to park on our lawn during the work. Mindful of the Car Pit Incident earlier this week, I waited with great nervousness for another disaster to occur.

Surprise! Everything went well. When the pavers were done, our place looked wonderful with fresh black asphalt covering what had been earth and gravel.

Around mid-afternoon today, we experienced our first belligerent rate haggler. We'd had some people haggling about rates since we bought the place, but it was very minor compared to what happened today.

A late-model silver Lincoln Town Car drove up and a well-dressed older gentleman emerged and came into our office.

"Good afternoon. I'd like a room, please," he said. We had vacancy and I so informed him.

"Excellent," he replied. With a flourish, he placed a card on the desk. "I'm a senior citizen and here is my Canadian Alliance of Relaxed Pensioners card. I expect your seniors' discount, of course."

"I'm sorry, but we have a fixed-rate policy here," I said. "We don't discount our rates; it's the same rates for everyone."

"For everyone ELSE, certainly, but not for seniors. You must give me my seniors' discount. Ten percent is customary. It's my right and it's your obligation."

"Sorry, Sir, but I believe it's up to each business to set their own prices and that includes whether to offer seniors' discounts. We have fixed room rates here, which we believe represents fair value for the accommodation we offer. We do not discount or negotiate our rates."

That was one of the first rules Pete and I had set after buying the place. We wanted to keep things simple and we loathed haggling. We'd since run it by the Monahans and while they agreed with our logic, they themselves had a least eight different rate schedules at their Best Western.

The man's face was growing red with anger. "Look, Madam, seniors get discounts everywhere and that certainly applies at dinky motels like this! My wife and I travel to different parts of the world every year and stay at fine hotels when we go to shows in Toronto and New York, and we always get discounts. You have absolutely no right to deny seniors their discount! It's discriminatory! I think you'd better get the manager, right now!"

I smiled: "I am the manager, Sir, and one of the owners, too. And our rates are the same for everybody. We don't play favourites."

Well, he went ballistic after that. He yelled that there should be a government regulation mandating that seniors get a discount. The CARP card should be honoured at every motel. In fact, all motels should have the same price for seniors right across Canada! He said that as soon as he got home, he would e-mail the Chamber of Commerce, Better Business Bureau, Lodging Ontario, the Premier, the Minister Responsible for Seniors, the Mayor of Wackimac and anyone else he could think of. He stormed out of the office and drove off in his shiny new Lincoln.

All that just to save $6.50 off a $65 room!

After I told Pete of this incident, he reflected a while, then announced that CARP could stand for something else for those seniors who insisted on CARPing about everything: Crabby Arrogant Reluctant Payers.

Saturday:

A horde (pod? school?) of SCUBA divers had descended on

the inn last night. The local Wackimac dive club ("The Wacky Muskrats") had organized a big gathering today at a nearby lake, and invited clubs from around the province. Many of our rooms were taken by divers from a club called "Neptune's Numb-Nuts", a reference to the frigid waters of Georgian Bay where they usually dove.

Pete was thrilled. In the early years of his high school teaching career, he had also taught SCUBA diving on weekends. Long since retired as an instructor, he still dove occasionally for recreation. So having an inn full of divers was a great opportunity for him to catch up on the latest equipment.

This morning, the divers were sorting out their gear on our big front lawn, before leaving for the first of several dives. It looked like Jacques Cousteau's yard sale! Walking among the clank and clatter of tanks, regulators, back packs, weight belts, vests and other underwater equipment, Pete eventually located the Divemaster responsible for the group: a tall, gruff guy named Steve.

Pete quickly discovered that Steve was one of those rare individuals blessed by God as all-knowing. And supremely devoted to the sound of his own voice. You didn't so much talk with Steve, as listen to him spout off. Occasionally, he'd let you get in a sentence of your own, but he'd cut you off if you had the temerity to start a second sentence. Pete soon tired of the one-sided conversation with The Great One and started to leave. Then Steve dragged out his red neoprene dry suit.

"Just got it back from having some special modifications made," he boasted, fussing over it. "Also had new boots put on; original ones wore out. No other suit like this one, fella!"

Pete looked at the suit and smiled. "You're right about that. I think you're going to have problems with that suit."

"Problems? You're nuts! This is a special custom job!"

"You checked over your suit after you got it back?"

"Yes, of COURSE. I check over all my gear; I'm a Divemaster!" Steve glared at Pete, then turned away in contemptuous dismissal. He folded up the suit and replaced it in his car.

Pete shrugged and walked away grinning. He came up to where I was standing.

"What was that all about?" I asked.

Pete replied: "God's gift to diving over there is one of those people you hope meets a Great White shark some day! Know-it-all jerk! I can't believe that arrogant moron is leading this club on their dives today! Well, wait'll he gets to the dive site and puts on his newly-modified dry suit. Heh. Is he going to be surprised!"

"Oh? Why?"

My hubby let go with a deep belly laugh: "The feet are on backwards!"

Sunday:

The Good Lord declared Sunday to be a day of rest. Motels didn't exist when the Good Lord said that.

We had been going flat out since we bought this place, so we promised ourselves that today we'd take a break. I planned to get caught up with this Diary. Pete was going to attack our growing reading pile.

Then Angie called in sick. So Pete and I had to clean the rooms ourselves, just like we did every Monday and Tuesday. There went our day of rest!

However, there was one bright spot this morning. A police cruiser delivered a tired, dishevelled, and hugely-embarrassed Divemaster Steve.

After first cutting off his boots so he could put them back on the right way, seems Steve had gone missing during last evening's night dive. He'd been bragging about his new high-tech underwater compass. Showing off how well it worked, he'd become separated from his dive buddy and ended up clear across the lake from where the club was diving. The OPP Marine Unit, called in by frantic club members, had finally found Steve this morning, huddled on shore in a patch of bulrushes.

After finding out about this, Pete had a spring in his step for the rest of the day as he went about his chores.

Our Eighth Week

In Which Our Pool Explodes

Dear Diary:

Monday:

During my early morning walkabout today, I stopped by the shoulder of the highway at the edge of our property and took a good look at it. After only two months, our place was already looking very different from when we had bought it. A freshly paved parking lot, neatly-mowed grass, colourful flowers around a massive pile of pink-white-grey boulders (titled *Pete's Folly* by yours truly) in the centre of our front lawn, a crisp new roadside sign, tinkling wind chimes in some trees, and a huge white 'H' on our side lawn (that was different, all right!).

Overall, it had a tidy appearance. Except for the building itself, which was still crying out for a coat of fresh paint. We'd have to tackle that this fall.

Besides our new name and gradually-improving new look, a strong draw for customers was the large UNDER NEW MANAGEMENT sign that Pete had erected during our first week. The inn's previous reputation being what it was, that sign was one of the most effective things we'd done.

According to the Monahans, all our changes, combined with our friendly customer service, should pay off in increased occupancy. It worked; we definitely had more guests each night now, than when we started here. Owens' records of previous years, which he had grudgingly turned over to us, were very spotty.

However, from what we could make out, we were already achieving higher occupancy than he had. (Not surprising, considering how he had run the place!)

It was very satisfying to see our efforts paying off. It made our hard work worthwhile and compensated for all the trials and tribulations we'd gone through. Plus we'd met some really nice people among our guests, many of whom said they'd stay with us again. That was the best praise of all!

When Pete was cleaning Number 21 with me today, he stopped vacuuming and entered the bathroom I was washing. (An aside: Though we changed the beds together, we divided the rest of our housekeeping duties when we did the rooms on Angie's days off. Pete vacuumed while I cleaned bathrooms. Many guests were amazed to see a man doing vacuuming!)

"Y'know that cesspool of a swimming pool out back?" Pete asked. "Well, we've had a lot of people ask why don't we fix it up so they can use it. It IS a scorching-hot summer, after all. And though it's mid-August, there's still a chunk of summer left and they're predicting a warmer-than-normal fall. So I was thinking – maybe we should clean out that old pool. We'd still get about six weeks use out of it this year. Whaddya think, El?"

Pete always picked weird times for weighty discussions. Here I was with my rubber gloves on, dripping brush in hand, standing over a toilet bowl!

"Oh, I don't know, hon," I said. "Owens hadn't opened that pool in years. We're still awfully busy – that's why we left it the way we found it when we took over. And what about the cost? We've got to watch our renovation fund; it's been hit with some unexpected expenses, y'know."

"Aw, it wouldn't take much to bring 'er back into service, El. I know it looks crummy now; it's got years of stagnant water in it with lots of leaves and crap. But I could clean 'er out quickly. And I bet it's still in good shape under all that smelly sludge. It's a good old-fashioned cement pool; I understand they really built 'em solid back then! And just think how happy our guests would be if we had a pool to offer 'em, in this heat! That rainstorm last week did nothing to break this heat wave; if anything, it's now more humid than ever."

That did it: Pete mentioning our guests. I really enjoyed giving them the best possible stay here. A sparkling swimming pool would certainly add to their positive experience!

"Okay, go ahead," I said. **(Diary**, you'd think I would have learned better by now!) "It'll be a great addition to our amenities."

We had no idea of what we had just let ourselves in for.

Tuesday:

Pete wasted no time on the pool re-birth project. As soon as he got up, he was off to the Rent-All for a big suction pump to empty the pool. I had asked Angie to come in a day early, to help with the rooms so Pete could work on the pool. Luckily, she'd recovered from her illness of last Sunday.

Draining the pool took a lot longer than Pete thought. The pump kept clogging with all the stuff in that stagnant water: waterlogged leaves, twigs, drowned field mice, and so on. Yuck! And the smell! It'd choke a sewer worker!

But Pete remained optimistic. Once it was drained, he figured a good power-washing of the insides followed by a fresh coat of paint, was all it would need.

"You'll see, El. It'll be ready by the weekend! I've got a pool company coming Thursday to check out the mechanical stuff, and to show us how to run the pump and filter and things."

I left him to his noisy and noisome task.

Today's mail brought a real treat: a letter from Mrs. Litresits, that charming elderly lady who'd stayed here two weeks ago, to whom I'd loaned the stuffed bear. She warmly thanked us for our hospitality and again stated that we were "The Caring Inn". How nice!

This afternoon, I got a call from the Regional Health Centre administration office. Mrs. Litresits had sent them a letter thanking them for their successful treatment of her husband. She'd also enclosed a copy of her letter to us.

"Did you really go out and buy a stuffed bear so she could have something to comfort her?" asked the hospital official.

"Yes," I replied, self-consciously. "I felt it'd help her get through the rough patch she was in."

"Why, that was very sweet of you. I can see why she calls you 'The Caring Inn'. And she writes that your rates are reasonable and your rooms are very clean. It's obvious you're running a very different place than the previous owner did. Listen, may we add you to our list of recommended places to stay, that we provide the families of our out-of-town patients?"

I was flabbergasted. "Why ... why yes, of course. Please do! Thank you very much!"

"No, Mrs. Tomlinson, thank YOU. It's rare to find someone so compassionate about strangers. You'll be getting a fair bit of business through us in future, I expect. Around here, you're going to become known as The Caring Inn."

I floated out on Cloud Nine and told Pete the good news.

"Wow, El, we never thought of that angle!" he said, taking a break from his stinky chore. "Y'know, this'll be year-round business for us, since folks need surgery anytime, rain or shine. And it's all because of you and a stuffed bear! You're a real gem!"

Now I was on Cloud Ten! Thank you hubby! (I promise not to call you a Pompous Idiot until at least next week.)

Wednesday:

Around mid-morning, Pete finally finished draining the pool. He spent the rest of the morning shovelling out the remaining sludge on the bottom, carting it out by the bucketful. He was done by lunchtime. Though the walls and bottom still reeked, at least all the water and crud were gone.

I took pity on the poor man and brought out a nice picnic lunch. I carefully placed him downwind of me under a nearby shade tree and we ate together.

"You're doing a great job with that pool, hon," I said. "It was a real mess, but I'm proud of you that you've stuck with it." (And no disaster has happened. Maybe Handyman Pete's bad luck was changing!)

Pete smiled and took a huge bite from his sub sandwich. *KRAK!* Startled, we both looked at the sandwich. "Pete! Did you bite on something hard in there?" I said.

"No," he replied, gulping it down. He took another bite. *KRAK!*

He put the sub down on his plate and stopped chewing while he stared at it. Then our eyes met, mirroring each other's surprise.

KRAK! KRAK! KRAK!

We both realized it wasn't the sandwich at all. The sounds were coming from the pool!

We ran over just as another loud *KRAK!* sounded. Then we got the first of three major shocks:

Shock #1: The whole pool was rising out of the ground! The sides were about two inches higher than the tiled patio that surrounded it. As we watched, the pool rose up another inch! Under our feet, the ground was trembling.

"Damn!" exclaimed Pete. "We've got a haunted room; do we have a haunted pool, too? Is this place built over an old Indian burial ground, or something?"

Shock #2: We looked into the pool and were horrified to see several long cracks splitting the cement bottom. With a deafening *KRAK!*, another tear appeared in the bottom. The pool rose a bit higher. "This ... this is totally unbelievable!" I stammered. By unspoken agreement, we slowly backed away. Good thing we did, too.

Shock #3: With an awful grating screech, like hundreds of fingernails scraping on blackboards, the bottom of the pool exploded! Chunks of concrete flew upwards along with a great fountain of water! Pete and I both screamed and ran away as concrete and water sprayed a wide area all around the pool.

Attracted by the commotion, Angie came running into the backyard, trailing a cloud of dust. She took one look at the pool, spun on her heel, and pelted back the way she'd come. (Amazing how fast a big woman like her could move when she had the right motivation.)

From a safe distance, we watched as the geyser of water slowly subsided. By this time, the pool was filled to overflowing. The water poured down the lawn to the dried mud flat of the Woebegone River that bordered our backyard.

"What ... what happened?" I finally managed.

"Dunno. I just dunno. I've never heard of, or seen, ANYTHING like that!" Pete paused and his face slowly went white. "Ellen, if you hadn't fetched me out of there to have lunch, I'd have been inside when it exploded!"

That made me go white too.

Angie hadn't run off and quit, never to set foot around here again. Actually, she'd called the police. They arrived and assessed the situation. When they realized it was beyond their jurisdiction, calls were made. A city engineer would visit tomorrow.

Shaken, Pete and I were a long time getting to sleep that night.

Thursday:

The engineer from the city arrived at about the same time as the guys from the pool maintenance company that Pete had called earlier this week. They discussed our exploding pool for over an hour. The engineer made several phone calls. Soon, members of his staff arrived, with charts and books. About thirty minutes later, officials from the Ministry of the Environment drove up, to join the conflab in our backyard. (Who next? An exorcist?)

Finally, in late afternoon, they presented us with their explanation.

Several years ago, a large factory and warehouse complex had been constructed on wetlands upstream. In draining the wetlands, one of the underground streams feeding the Woebegone River had inadvertently and unknowingly been diverted.

The diverted underground stream had carved a new channel – right under our pool! The downward weight of water in the pool had offset the upward pressure of the stream beneath it. When

Pete had drained the pool, for the first time in years, the counter-weight had been removed and the underground stream had burst through the cement bottom.

But there was more bad news:

"Waal, folks," said the engineer as he sucked noisily on a candy that seemed permanently lodged in his cheek, "I hate to tell ya, but I'll bet you'll find that your insurance don't cover this. You'll obviously not be able ta use that pool again; fixing it won't solve the problem. Y'see, th' stream'd just burst through again, every time you'd drain it for maintenance."

"Yep, yep. You'll need a complete new pool installed somewheres else an' that's big bucks. Mebbe around $60,000, though we could probably give yous a better deal if yous had us do it come fall," added one of the pool company men cheerfully.

"Oh, lovely." said Pete flatly.

With a heavy heart, I called up Dave Matthews, the insurance broker who had signed us onto the Lodging Ontario program last week. I poured out my story and he interjected questions at various intervals. Then he gave me the fourth shock of this incident:

"Don't worry. Your new policy covers this damage, Mrs. Tomlinson," he said.

"WHAT?" I blurted.

"Oh yes, that's one of the little-known features of the association insurance program that I designed. We insure cement pools! We sometimes take flack for it; operators say what the heck can go wrong with a cement pool that's been there for 20 years? Why should I pay for that kind of coverage? But we pride ourselves on how comprehensive our policy is. We insure the things others never think about – until it's too late."

That really perked up our spirits! Dave promised to have an insurance adjuster visit us within a day, to start the claims process. The policy would pay for a new pool, located well away from the underground stream, and also pay to have the old one filled in and landscaped over.

Pete was ecstatic at the news. When he'd calmed down, he said: "We really owe the Monahans, El! They told us to join

Lodging Ontario, which then got us the specialized insurance policy. Can you imagine if we still had the old policy? We wouldn't have been covered!"

Pete was right. I rooted through our desk and found the old policy. Not a word about covering pools.

Friday:

With the stress of this week's Pool Incident, we felt we really must take a break to restore our sanity. We now realized that it was almost impossible for the two of us to take off together; the inn was a demanding mistress. We had to take separate breaks. So I took today off and Pete would get tomorrow.

These days off would become known as our Sanity Days. We promised ourselves we'd take one a week from now on. We had come to understand that operating an inn would suck the life right out of you, unless you made some time for yourself, preferably away from the place. And separate Sanity Days would also give us a better relief valve from being together 24/7, than a few hours of Personal Time grabbed here and there.

I mean, we still love each other very much – that hasn't changed – but every couple needs some time apart. If only to prevent one from shooting the other on certain occasions.

Today, Pete oversaw the clean-up of the pool mess, including arranging for a temporary fence to be quickly constructed around the area, to protect our guests from injury.

Meanwhile, I enjoyed my first full day off since we bought the inn two months ago. It did wonders for me! I spent the morning shopping at Wackimac's one-and-only mall, followed by a delicious lunch. In the afternoon, I drove through the pastoral countryside around the city, exploring pretty country lanes and quaint villages.

In early evening, I returned to the Windsong Inn refreshed, but with mixed feelings. Part of me felt guilty leaving Pete by himself all day to run the place, and part of me wondered what new disaster awaited me, because I'd left Pete by himself all day to run the place.

But everything was fine. Pete gave me a big hug and a kiss, then treated me to a supper that he'd cooked himself. (And it was mostly edible, too.) What a great inaugural Sanity Day!

Saturday:

Today was my day to run the place. Pete drove off to do some fishing.

Mid-morning, Angie alerted me to a situation in Number Nine, when she went in to clean. There was dog hair all over the room, even on the bed quilts! I was furious; we had a strict No Pets policy.

The guests, a young twentysomething couple, were staying for two days. When they returned from sightseeing later today, I confronted them as they walked from their car to their room. Their dog, a big Golden Retriever, was with them. The couple was bold as brass; they made no attempt to conceal the dog. (They must have kept it in their car during check-in yesterday, because Pete wouldn't have rented them a room if he'd known about the mutt.)

"Why in heaven's name did you bring your dog into your room? We don't allow pets here!" I said.

"You don't? Well, we didn't know," the guy replied. Their beast strained against its leash trying to approach me, tail wagging furiously. (In friendliness, or because I looked tasty?) I wasn't feeling very friendly.

"You didn't know?" I retorted. "Look at the entrance to our office there. There's a huge sign in the window that says, in big red letters: NO PETS. You can't miss it!"

"Yeah, we saw it when we checked-in yesterday. We thought it meant no pets in your lobby."

I resisted the urge to strangle the jerk. I figured if he had logic like that, he had enough problems without me killing him.

I took a deep breath and said: "It means no pets at this inn! There's also a letter in your room that outlines our house rules and half-way down it states no pets please."

His wife sniffed: "We never saw any letter."

"Isn't that strange," I said. "It was sitting in its usual position on the dresser next to the vase, in plain sight, when my housekeeper went in to clean this morning!"

"Nuh-uh. We never saw it," the woman repeated. "Besides, we couldn't leave Gnasher in the car overnight; he's one of the family! We didn't think you'd mind; we're only here two nights."

"Didn't think we'd mind? That means you must have realized we don't allow pets!"

The couple looked at each other guiltily. I'd caught them in their lie.

As nicely as I could, I told the dog-lovers that I'd have to charge them extra to cover our cleaning costs to restore the room. When they gave me a blank look, I said:

"You must realize it's going to take a lot of extra effort and expense to completely clean the room to get rid of all the dog hairs. We'll even have to send the bed quilts out for dry-cleaning. We provide pet-free rooms and many people rely on that because they're allergic to pet hair. It was very inconsiderate of you to bring your dog inside!"

The couple just shrugged. They had become bored by this conversation.

"Yeah, whatever," said the guy.

Infuriated by their attitude, I said: "Whatever! Well, I'm charging you an extra $100 to cover our cleaning expenses and, on top of that, you're NOT staying here another night! I want you packed up and out of here within 30 minutes, or I'm calling the police to have you evicted!"

That got their attention. Both of them went nuts on me, yelling and swearing that I had no right to charge them $100 more and no right to have them evicted. But I had been talking with Bert and Madeline Monahan at least once a week since we'd met them and taking notes on all their advice. I knew I was on solid ground here.

"Oh yes, I DO have the right!" I snapped. "The $100 is a charge for damages; you've damaged the room with your animal's hairs and I cannot re-rent it unless it's thoroughly cleaned. And I have the right to evict you, because you broke our house rule about pets. When you agreed to stay here, it was with the understanding that you'd abide by our rules!"

With more colourful language, they paid up and packed up. As they left, they drove their cherry red BMW across our nicely manicured lawn, spinning their tires and leaving two deep ruts. The woman stuck her hand out the window and gave me the finger. They roared off down the highway.

As I stood there fuming, Angie ran up and said the couple had flung the TV to the floor, shattering the screen.

But I had the last laugh (not that I felt like laughing). I knew what to do about this too. I quickly called the police and gave a full description of their car with their licence number (guests had to write their licence number on the Registration Card). I said I wanted them charged with wilful property damage and that I had witnesses (some guests had seen the spoiled brats' departing tantrum).

The cops caught the couple soon after, then charged them.

I decided that, upon his return from fishing, if Pete was stupid enough to ask me how my day went, I'd smack him upside the head with whatever he had caught. But when he returned, he took one look at my face and wisely didn't ask.

Besides, he hadn't caught anything.

Sunday:

Tonight, after another long day, we took stock. It was the end of our second month as innkeepers. Did we feel like celebrating? Did we feel that we had made the right decision buying this place? Wasn't this a great semi-retirement project?

We still weren't sure about the first two questions. A definite no to the last one. We popped the cork on a bottle of wine anyway.

We'd earned it.

And lo! Wonder of wonders! We were able to cuddle up and leisurely drink the bottle dry.

WITHOUT INTERRUPTIONS.

Our Ninth Week

In Which Sex, Drugs, And Rock 'n' Roll Take Their Toll

Dear Diary:

Monday:

"Excuse me, are you the owner or manager here?"

I looked up – waaay up – into the eyes of the man towering over our front desk. Hard eyes, that had seen hard things. The rest of his face was equally grim.

"Yes, I'm one of the owners," I said. "How can I help you?"

He reached into a rumpled windbreaker and tugged out what looked like a wallet. He flipped it open to reveal a gold badge and ID card. "Detective Ben Rosen, Ontario Provincial Police Anti-Drug Task Force. You're new owners, right?"

"Yes, since two months. What's the problem?"

"You aware of this motel's reputation, ma'am?"

"We found out after we bought that it was known as a seedy place. But my husband and I have been working hard to change that. You've hopefully noticed the improvements we've already made outside."

The tall cop looked at me with those cold eyes for a long moment. Then he said:

"Yeah, it's nice. But I was talking about the type of clientele this place gets. Like hookers and drug dealers."

"WHAT? No sir, we don't cater to those types here! We're a family inn!"

"Uh-huh. Well ma'am, you've got a known drug dealer in Number 18 right now, a guy we've been tracking for months."

I felt light-headed. "We do? Look, we certainly didn't know! He checked-in late yesterday and seemed like a regular guy. Paid cash, too. We'll evict him immediately!"

"No, we'd appreciate it if you'd just leave him be, ma'am. We've been building a case on him for some time and we're close to an arrest. We want to catch him in one last major deal, then we'll collar him. We'd like your cooperation on this."

"Of ... of course," I said. "Whatever we can do to help. Just as long as you know we had no idea he was a drug dealer!"

Another long calculating stare. "Yeah, I believe you. We've checked you and your husband out. You're not like the former owner. But you've got an uphill battle to change your motel's rep. Take our friend in Number 18 there. He's been coming here once a month, regular, for over a year. Local dealers know when he comes and visit his room to buy their stuff."

"So this has happened twice now, since we took over here?"

"Yep."

At this point, I fetched Pete and brought him up to speed. He was as shocked as I and the infamous Pompous Idiot temper started flaring. He insisted on evicting the dealer right away, but Detective Rosen stood firm. He wanted us to carry on as normal. He and his task force would continue to watch the suspect, secretly. Pete eventually calmed down.

The task force was composed of officers from all three levels of law enforcement: city, provincial, and the federal RCMP. Rosen said shutting down this major drug supplier would clean up much of this area's drug use. At least for a while.

Tuesday:

Since yesterday's dialogue with the police, we went about our business like we were walking barefoot on sharp gravel. Detective Rosen had rented a room in the long section of our L-shaped motel, with a good view of Number 18, which was located on the shorter arm of the L. He or his partner were always at the window of their room, watching through a small gap in the curtains.

We tried not to pay attention to the cops' room as we passed it. It was hard carrying on our chores as if nothing was amiss. Talk about tension! I'd have to make sure I briefed Angie first thing tomorrow.

Something else I didn't need: A family showed up today looking for Ellen's Fubar Motel. They had a copy of that cursed brochure. An elderly WW II vet was part of the family and he cackled with glee as he showed it to me.

"Can't wait to see this place!" he chortled.

I tried hard to keep my cool (Damn you, Sarge!), but my face flushed and irritation showed in my voice.

"There's no such place," I said coldly. "That brochure was printed as a malicious joke. But if you want to stay at the inn it describes, then you've come to the right place. That's us."

The old gent was very disappointed. But they decided to stay the night with us.

"*Where* did you get that brochure?" I pleaded. "*Please* tell me!" All the family could remember was that they got it at "some gas station outside of town". Oh, I'd definitely have to track that place down!

(Was this an elaborate practical joke of Sarge's? He'd *know* how much this would upset me.)

An unforseen side effect of having our parking lot paved had started. Several times a week, sometimes as often as once a day, we noticed new cars enter our lot, swing around and drive back out. All the cars bore dealer plates and did their entrance and exit quite fast. By the models we saw, it was obvious different local car dealers were involved.

Pete and I didn't want this practice to continue. We were worried about our guests' safety.

I called the sales managers at each of the city's car dealers today, after we'd finished the housekeeping chores. I found out that, since we were now the only motel on this side of town with a paved lot, sales reps taking customers on a test drive used us as a convenient turn-around spot that wouldn't get their cars dirty.

I explained that our lot was private property and was not there for the dealers' convenience. I stressed that we were concerned someone crossing our lot may get hit, especially children running to our shady front lawn. All the managers promised to tell their salespeople to stop using our lot, although some seemed annoyed that I had made the request.

Wednesday:

Today was my Sanity Day and I spent part of it visiting Madeline Monahan. I told her about the police anti-drug unit camped at the Windsong. She said we'd done the right thing cooperating with the law and advised that, in return, we must ask the officers to keep our inn's name out of their statements to the media if they made an arrest there. Otherwise, that would really put us in a bad light. We hadn't thought of that!

"Oh my dear, you've already seen that running an inn means many things happen that you'd never thought of!" Maddy said. "It was the same with us, too. Why, when Bert and I bought this place almost 26 years ago, our first-born was only 18 months old. We had no idea we'd be so busy operating the business. (I could relate to that!) I found myself working the front desk, with my baby sleeping on a blanket on the floor behind the counter. Our guests never knew he was there, except for those times he cried out or woke up.

"And doing the rooms was quite the challenge, too. I'd put little Andy in his playpen on the lawn opposite the room I'd be cleaning and I'd leave the door open so I could keep an eye on him. Well, he'd just stand there and cry and cry for his mommy – especially when he'd catch sight of me through the door! It was heart-breaking!"

"Wow, that sounds awful," I said. "What did you end up doing?"

"Well, after several weeks of that, I insisted we get a housekeeper to help with the rooms. That let me spend more time with Andy. When he had his nap, I put him back in the playpen and dashed around doing my part of the housekeeping." Madeline took a long drink of her coffee. "Then I got pregnant again."

"Oh! That must have been even more stressful for you; running a motel while carrying a baby."

Maddy smiled. "You have NO idea."

"Well, I'm glad I'm past *that* stage. We've had all the kids we're going to have."

"Don't be so sure, my dear. You never know."

Thursday:

Fall was fast approaching and we knew from the Monahans that our summer glut of tourist business would fall off after Labour Day. It was time to start planning our exterior painting project.

Pete took part of his Sanity Day today to visit the hardware store's paint department. He returned with many paint colour cards, so we could choose our new look. I remembered the Monahan's advice several weeks ago about going with warm colours that complimented each other and I quickly made my choice.

It didn't work that way with Pete. He installed himself at the table behind our front desk, where he fiddled and fussed with the colour swatches for over an hour, getting more and more frustrated with selecting "just the right look". Meanwhile, I was taking reservations and paying bills. Finally, I had enough of his constant interruptions and shooed him outside.

Around 9:00 this evening, three nondescript cars pulled in and parked next to our rear apartment, out of sight of our rooms. Ben Rosen slipped into our office, as quiet as a panther despite his great height.

"Tonight's the night," he said. "We have 12 officers outside. There's a big buy set and we want to catch him with his main customer from this area; the scum that works the local high schools. Please just stay inside here and let us do our job."

Of course, we agreed. Time crawled by. I was so nervous, I stayed up past my normal bedtime, drinking tea by the potful. Pete paced restlessly around our office, like a vacationer anxious for the all-you-can-eat buffet to open.

Suddenly, a thunderous *SHRAKT* split the night quiet. The air was filled with the tortured sounds of tearing wood, loud shouts and angry curses.

TEARING WOOD?

Pete and I ran outside. The cops had smashed in the door of Number 18 with a huge black battering ram!

"COPS!" wailed the criminals.

"OUR DOOR!" wailed the Tomlinsons.

An officer intercepted us and kept us well back as his colleagues arrested the dealers. They were carted off and their room was sealed with bright yellow "police – do not cross" tape. Ben Rosen came over and thanked us for our cooperation.

"Ah, you're welcome," said Pete. "But my God! Did you have to break down our door? You never told us you were going to do THAT! It's an old style solid wood door; I don't know if they even make them like that anymore."

"We decided it was the safest way for our officers. We needed the element of surprise, to prevent any shooting."

"Yes, but why not just use our master key to unlock the door and fling it open?"

"Element of surprise, Mr. Tomlinson. They'd have heard the key in the lock. And it turns out they had fastened the door security chain."

Pete sighed: "Okay, so how do we go about getting reimbursed from you guys for the door?"

Rosen's dour face almost broke into a smile. "Oh, we won't pay for the door, Sir. We don't pay for any damages caused by a drug arrest. Federal law. Contact your insurance company and tell them the door was smashed in a police drug raid. They'll pay."

"But ... but that's UNFAIR!" Pete sputtered. "You guys caused the damages, so why should WE have to go through the hassle of claiming it on our insurance? It'll likely affect our premium, too!"

"You'll find your insurance will pay without a hassle, because this was a police raid and you folks were not implicated in the crime. And I promise not to make any mention of your motel during my press conference."

Pete opened his mouth for another outburst, but I grabbed him by the arm and pulled him away.

"Thank you, Detective Rosen. We appreciate your keeping our name out of this," I called out as I dragged Pete away. One arrest was enough for tonight.

Friday:

We anxiously read the big front page article about the drug bust in the *Expositor & Chronicle* today. There was no mention of our inn by name. It just said "at a local motel." We made a point of catching the radio and TV news; likewise no mention of us. We heaved a sigh of relief. Ben Rosen had been true to his word.

He was also right about the insurance. Dave Matthews said we'd be paid promptly and there'd be no adverse effect on our premium next year. Pete was still upset about the unfairness of it all. It wasn't our fault the drug dealer chose our motel to transact his business, we had cooperated fully with the police, yet we were left to clean up their mess and get payment for the door.

Pete called up an old friend who was a law professor at the University of Toronto. He verified that there was indeed a federal statute that absolved law enforcement officials from paying for damages while working on a drug warrant.

Today was Constituency Day for our local MP. Pete went down to her office and introduced himself. He insisted she lobby to change the law, to make the police accountable for their actions. In that polite non-committal way that long-time politicians have mastered, the MP smiled sweetly and told Pete to take a hike.

Early this afternoon, there was a horrible screech of tires in our parking lot, mixed with a terrified scream. A child's scream.

I ran outside from the laundry room, as did Angie and Pete from the rooms they were in. A car had stopped just inches from a young boy of about five, who stood crying in shock. The driver had almost hit him, as the boy was running across our lot. It was a new car – with a dealer plate. They were doing it again: using our lot as a turn-around zone, at high speed. The very thing we'd been most afraid of, had almost happened.

While I comforted the child, Pete exploded on the driver and the sales rep. Then the child's mother ran up and added her screams to the scene. I slipped away from the commotion and called the police. When they arrived, we had them charge the car's occupants with trespassing. The officer added reckless driving.

The mother swore she'd never stay here again. Lovely.

Pete and I were furious. After all my phone calls earlier this week and all those promises from the sales managers! Not only had a child almost been hit, but we just lost a customer!

We contacted a local lawyer recommended by the Monahans and had him send a stiff legal letter to every Wackimac car dealer, to cease and desist using our lot. We also had a sign erected at our front entrance: "Private Property. For Registered Guests Only."

Hopefully, all that would work. This had to stop.

Saturday:

I was de-weeding *Pete's Folly* boulder garden flower bed late this afternoon, when a taxi drove up. Two attractive women got out and went inside Number Six. As he was leaving, the cabbie noticed me and stopped. He beckoned me over.

"You're the new owner here, yah?" he said.

"Yah ... er ... yes," I replied. "Why?"

"Don' you know who dose ladies are, that I just dropped off?"

"No, but we're new here and don't know many locals."

The cabbie clucked his tongue. "Well, ya'd better know dese two. They're hookers!"

"Hookers? Quaint little Wackimac has prostitutes?"

"Hah! Lady, everyplace gots hookers! Anyways, at least now ya knows about dem two."

I thanked him and he drove off. I went into our front office and checked the register. The room had two telephone linemen in it. I was at a loss. What to do? I decided not to call Pete, who'd probably want to storm in and evict them all. My gut told me this was a delicate situation. So I called the Monahans instead.

They were away for the weekend.

I was flustered. The Monahan's daughter was unavailable; their desk clerk said she was overseeing final preparations for a big wedding there. Who else could I turn to for advice? The Lodging Ontario association office was closed on weekends, of course, and I had only met one of our innkeeper neighbours so far, who left his inn in the care of a barely-experienced college student on weekends.

But I couldn't just let this slide – we certainly didn't want the Windsong Inn to become known as Hooker Haven!

I returned to *Pete's Folly* and kept watch on the room, as I continued my de-weeding. About an hour later, the door opened and the women came out. I stood up and went over to them. Warily, they watched me approach: a short woman in dirt-streaked baggy overalls with a sweat-stained kerchief above her eyes.

I had to admit they were quite well-dressed. Expensive clothing, though the skirts were very high and the half-open blouses were much too tight. Beautiful hairdos. And their leather shoes probably cost more than any of the outfits in my wardrobe. These women didn't look like the cliche of cheap hookers. I felt self-conscious. Next to them, I looked like a cliche myself: country bumpkin.

That didn't stop me though.

"Hello ladies. My name is Ellen Tomlinson and I'm one of the owners here. I would appreciate it if you did not return to these premises, please."

The two women looked at each other, then back at me. One said: "What do you mean, honey? We were just visiting our boyfriends. Haven't seen them in a while."

"Boyfriends, eh? By the hour, maybe. Look, cut the B.S., okay? Your cab driver tipped me off. I know what you're up to and there's no place for it here. This is a family inn now."

"Well, the guys in there called us; we didn't call them. We were invited over, as their guests."

"That makes no difference. Our property is for the use of registered guests only and it is certainly not for the purposes of prostitution!"

The other hooker popped a wad of gum in her mouth and smiled. "Oh yes," she said as she chewed, "you're new owners here. Well, we had an ... understanding ... with Hal when he ran this place."

"Obviously we can't have the same type of 'understanding' with Ellen here," said her companion. Both women giggled. It made my skin crawl.

The gum-chewer stepped closer and said: "So look, dearie, let's make our own arrangement, okay? Let's say we'll give you a percent of our fee, each time we come here to entertain your guests. We've got arrangements with some of the motels along here, like your neighbour across the street. Why should you be any different? And what's the harm with what we do anyway? It's all consensual."

I stood up to my full 5'2" height (I had an extra inch thanks to the heels on my work boots) and said:

"No thanks, 'dearie'. I don't care what the other motels do. I want you and your friend off our property right away and I don't want to ever see you here again. Are we clear on this?"

Both hookers stared at me. "Crystal," said one finally. They both stalked off towards the highway. Just as they reached it, their cab arrived to take them back to town.

It was only after they were out of sight that I allowed myself to relax. I was bathed in sweat and it had nothing to do with the heat.

Sunday:

I told Pete about the hooker incident yesterday. He complimented me on how I handled it, which lifted my spirits a little. But I still fretted about whether they'd return, or others like them. How could we keep them away – especially if our guests invited them? We couldn't watch our parking lot 24/7.

Pete resolved to call Bert for advice next week.

Sunday afternoons were usually quieter than the rest of the week. We found that Sunday was the day of lowest occupancy and we didn't mind. It gave us a breather.

Today was sunny, hot and breezy. The wind rustled the leaves on our many shade trees, adding nature's music to the soft tinkling of our three wind chimes. A wonderful atmosphere to relax in and Pete and I took full advantage. We planted ourselves under a towering oak, each with a pile of newspapers and a nice cold beer.

BAOM! BAOM! KRUMP! THUMP! THUMP! WRAAANG!

The deep pounding beat of punk-rock music shattered the peaceful afternoon. One of those bands whose lyrics were liberally spiced with enough cursing to make a trucker blush. Their screaming 'song' blared from the largest portable CD player I'd ever seen, placed outside of Number 21. The teenaged son of the family that rented the room lay sunbathing on the lawn nearby, twitching in time to the 'music'. The parents were gone for the afternoon.

Pete and I had just gone through one hell of a week. Drug dealers, a police raid, hookers and a little boy almost run over. Our patience was shot.

My hubby stormed over and bellowed at the teenager to please turn his 'music' down, in consideration of others. The kid just stared at Pete, mouth hanging open.

"Aw, the hell with it!" said Pete. He walked over to the CD player, yanked its electrical cord out of the exterior wall socket, grabbed the machine and lugged it away.

The teen came alive.

"HEY! HEY! What are you doing, Grampa? You have no right to take that! Give it back! It's private property! HEY!"

"I'll give it back when your parents return and not a second before!" Pete yelled over his shoulder as he walked away. He placed it inside our office and came back out, locking the door behind him. The kid swore long and loud at Pete, but stopped after Pete promised to repeat every word of his colourful language to his parents.

Blessed peace returned to the Windsong Inn.

Our 10th Week

In Which I Meet The Neighbours
And
Pete Goes Colour-Blind

Dear Diary:

Monday:

"Forest green with light grey trim? Tan with green trim? Sand with dark brown trim? Light blue with royal blue trim? Yellow with purple polka-dot trim? El, you even listening to me?" Pete asked.

"Yes, hon, but it's the same things you said an hour ago. Just make up your mind, please!" I looked at the jumble of paint swatches surrounding Pete on the floor of our apartment. The man had been trying endless combinations of colours for days, whenever he got a spare moment. He was trying to decide on the "perfect" colours to repaint the outside of our inn. It was driving me crazy; I thought the cliche was that it was women who could never make up their minds!

"Look, Pete," I said, "Any one of your finalists would be nice. Anything will be better than the flaking grungy blue paint we have on there now. My own vote is for the forest green and light grey, which you know was my choice last week when you first brought these swatches home. Forest green will make our building blend in beautifully with our acres of trees and lawn.

"Now, I've lined up a company to do the painting. You know that it took me a long time to find painters that could do us right away – most of them are booked solid until the snow falls. We're lucky this company had an unexpected opening in their schedule.

They start next week – but they need to know the colours this week so they can order the paint."

"Ah, so you feel it should be the forest green here, for the walls, with this light grey trim for the door jambs and around the windows, eh?" Pete looked at the colours as if seeing them for the first time (instead of the 201st). "Well then, my sweet, make it so! Call the painters and tell them."

He gathered up all the other colour swatches and dumped them ceremoniously into the garbage can. "It is done!"

Wow! The male had finally made a decision!

Later today, we took delivery of 25 compact micro-wave ovens; one for each of our 23 rooms plus two spares. Thumbing through the Buyer's Guide of Lodging Ontario two weeks ago, I'd come across an ad from a supplier member of the association, that sold mini-fridges and micro-waves for motel and hotel rooms. I thought they'd be great amenities to add to our rooms; a number of guests had been asking for them. Pete had agreed with me.

The machines looked great: cute, efficient-looking little boxes, all in white, with simple controls. Only one problem: The mini-fridges were back-ordered.

"Could be in next week, could be next month," said the company sales rep when I called her. Great. The micro-waves were supposed to go on top of the fridges. Now we had to find some other place in the rooms to put them. We didn't have a lot of furniture in our rooms and what we did have already had most of its available space committed.

We finally decided to place them on top of the dressers, on the right side. (Except in Number 11; Brenda had made it quite clear that the vase was to be on the right side. So the micro went on the left side in there.)

Tuesday:

When I stumbled into the kitchen at the crack of dawn this morning, I was stunned to find the table covered with colour swatches. PETE!

After he awoke (hours later), he mumbled that he had to take another look last night "just to be sure". But he did say that he was sticking with our decision of yesterday. Definitely.

"Although," he said, stroking his chin stubble while looking at the swatches, "I've been wondering why we should limit ourselves to just two colours. Why not use several? Y'know, maybe have the doors in a third colour, the gutters and soffits another colour – and even paint our end walls in a different colour!"

"Aw, c'mon Pete! FIVE different colours out there? Are you serious? It'll look like a carnival! Besides, you had me call the painters yesterday, remember?"

"Right, right. But I'm sure there's still time to change our order."

I gave up. I had rooms to clean – and so did he.

That nice lady from the administrative office of our Regional Health Centre called me today. She was concerned about a complaint she'd received.

"Complaint? What kind of complaint?" I asked, worried that somehow our service had been found lacking. We had been getting many guests that were family of patients undergoing treatment at the hospital, all of whom called us "The Caring Inn."

She cleared her throat. "Well, that you're a drug haven and that yours was the place where that big drug bust happened last week. Is that true?"

"We are NOT a drug haven! It is true that the police arrested the drug dealers here last week, yes, but we had no knowledge whatsoever that the guest was a dealer until the police told us. We're working hard to be a reputable family place."

There was a pause at the other end of the line. "Well, it is true that until now we've only received positive reports about you," she said finally. "But you must understand that we have our own reputation to consider. There are also legal implications. We must be sure we're not recommending an unsavoury place to relatives of our patients."

"I assure you that we are certainly not an unsavoury place. In fact, I'll send you copies of the cards and letters we've been receiving all summer, thanking us for a great stay."

I finally convinced her that the complaint was unfounded. Then I asked who had made it.

"Your neighbour across the street, the owner of the Big Eagle Inn."

I was, to put it mildly, a tad upset. After Pete and I finished our housekeeping chores, he started the laundry while I went over to have a talk with our fellow innkeeper at the Big Eagle Inn. It was the first time we'd met.

He was an Asian gentleman, several inches taller than me, with jet black hair slicked back severely over a round face. His dark eyes were piercing, yet he greeted me warmly when I introduced myself.

"Ah, a very great pleasure to finally meet you, Mrs. Ellen! You have a very nice establishment over there – not as nice as mine perhaps, but very nice all the same! I am Surinder Patel. So wonderful that you finally took the time to come over and say hello."

(Yeah, like you couldn't even cross the highway to welcome us to the area like the Monahans had done, and they crossed the whole city!)

Mr. Patel stuck out his hand and I shook it. He went on:

"I've been noticing all the improvements you and your husband – I am correct in assuming he's your husband? – have been making. It is looking most wonderful! Especially that very large rock garden and your lovely paved parking lot. Are you trying to put the rest of us to shame?"

"No, no," I said. "To each his or her own. Your place has things we don't; you're twice our size for one. We each have our own special features."

"Perhaps, perhaps. But I do notice that your lot is quite full of automobiles most nights. It was rarely that way with the previous owner."

"Well, we're doing things a lot different than he did. Anyway, your place is usually very busy too. I'm just happy all the hard work my husband and I have done, and all the problems we've wrestled with, are paying off in increased occupancy."

"Ah, problems indeed, Mrs. Ellen. I could not help but notice how many times the police have been over there. That crazy lady shooting guns in her room, that exploding swimming pool, those hooligans who tore up your front lawn with their car, and that horrible drug arrest just last week!"

I took a deep breath. "Now look, Mr. Patel, we had nothing to do with that drug dealer. The police said so themselves. They didn't even mention our inn in their press conference. We were innocent victims."

"Oh yes indeed, you certainly were. Most unfortunate."

"So why, then, did you feel it necessary to call up the Regional Health Centre and complain about us?"

"Oh it was nothing personal, I assure you. Just business. We too are on their list of preferred accommodation for patients' families. It seems to me that they are referring far too much business to you. That is why your occupancy is so much higher than before. Most unfair. My business is suffering. So I merely sought to re-balance the scales."

"Really? Pardon me, but that's nuts! It's the *families* that decide where they want to stay; the hospital doesn't make that decision. They just provide the list. Our occupancy is high because of all the improvements we're making and our customer service. I treat families of patients very compassionately and give them a special treat. And how dare you tell the hospital that we're a drug haven, when you just admitted you knew it wasn't true? You've slandered our inn's reputation!"

"Mrs. Ellen, your inn already had a very bad reputation. Surely you know that."

"Yes, but Pete and I are trying to change it. And we're succeeding." This was getting confrontational. I wondered if I should leave and let Pete handle this, mano a mano. Then I remembered Pete's temper. And I thought: No, I can handle this by myself. I refuse to be intimidated!

I looked Patel right in the eyes and said: "Maybe what's really bothering you is that you haven't had serious competition right across the road before."

"I am not afraid to compete with you, or anyone! As long as it is fair! People like me have to work so very much harder to succeed in this country – you westerners are quite bigoted against Asians! People from India, Pakistan, or Hong Kong, we never get a fair chance!"

"Oh PLEASE! Don't play the race card with me! Growing up, my best friend was Asian. This has nothing to do with your race. It has everything to do with the way you do business! How can you talk about fairness? It was completely unfair for you to lie about us to the hospital, to drag our reputation through the mud! Your own reputation is not so clean – I know that you have a certain arrangement with the local hookers to let them use your motel!"

That got him. He stammered denials, but his eyes told me I'd hit home. Finally, his voice rising in volume, he said:

"You are being very, very unreasonable! My poor heart cannot take any more of this stress! I regret meeting you! Just get out! Go! You stay on your side of the highway and I'll stay on mine!"

"That's just fine with me! But you stop telling lies about us!" I retorted and left. *Jerk.*

Wednesday:

I took today as a Sanity Day. I decided to visit the rest of our neighbouring innkeepers along the motel strip, to make their acquaintance and see if our reputation needed burnishing.

Besides Patel's place and ours, there were five other inns in our area. One was run by a couple from Eastern Europe (whom I'd met in Week Three; it was they who had advised us to call our place an inn, not a motel), and three others were run by Asians.

As I called on each one, I discovered that they basically wanted nothing to do with us.

"We are all in competition with one another. It is a cut-throat business. No place for friendship!" said the Eastern European couple with thick accents.

However, I was very impressed when I visited one of our other

Asian neighbours. Her name was Shamim, a divorcee, and she was completely different from Surinder Patel, both in temperament and operating style. She had a cheerful, engaging demeanor and was very professional. A refugee immigrant herself years ago, she had taken in two families of refugees from Afghanistan and put them up at her property. Shamim felt it was her duty, as a human being and as a devout practitioner of her religion. Her humanitarian service was partly funded by a charitable foundation set up by her religious order.

She taught the refugees about shopping and cooking in Canada, how to bank and apply for a job. Her children coached them in English and social skills. All that effort would be quite a burden for any family, never mind a family that also had a 37-room inn to run, but they took it cheerfully in their stride.

The other two Asian couples were similar: outgoing, hard-working and professional. Both men had full-time jobs in the city, one as an engineer and the other taught at the college, while their wives ran the motels and raised their families.

Yet they all had one thing in common with the Eastern European couple: They didn't want anything to do with the Tomlinsons; we were the competition.

So I was feeling pretty depressed by the time I dropped in on our sixth and last neighbour, the Wackimac Rest Haven, run by a Canadian-born couple. He was the only neighbour who had phoned us after we'd taken over, to welcome us. He had invited us to visit him anytime; he said it was difficult for him to come over to our place.

A slim middle-aged man came out from the apartment behind the front desk, in answer to the door buzzer that announced my entrance. He moved with a particular slowness. His manner reminded me of a collector whose treasures must always be meticulously placed in a certain order. He looked right at me with pale grey eyes set in a serious, tanned face and said:

"Yes, can I help you?"

"Hi, I'm Ellen Tomlinson, one of the new owners of the Windsong Inn down the road. You're Graham Sparrow, right? We talked on the phone almost three months ago – wow, how time flies, eh?"

"Oh yes, the old Pleasant Holiday Inn! Welcome! I"m glad you could come over." He stuck out his hand, smiling. I put my hand out, but he made no move to meet it. I moved my hand closer. He just stood there, still smiling. Finally, I placed my hand in his, whereupon he gripped it strongly.

"Pleasure to meet you, Ellen. Let me call my wife, Patricia. She's cleaning rooms." He released my hand and pulled out a cell phone from a pouch on his belt. "Pat? Could you come to the desk, please? Our new neighbour is here!"

He replaced the phone and said: "Please, come through the door here into our home. Do you have a jacket? If so, let me take it." He held out his hand, aimed slightly to one side of where I stood.

It suddenly dawned on me: Graham was blind!

"Oh, I ... I just realized that you can't see ... er, I mean that you're visually impaired," I said.

He chuckled. "Please, you can say I'm blind, because that's what it is. Yes, I'm tracking you by your voice – which may I say sounds very nice. You sound to be about my age and judging by where your voice is coming from, I'd say you're shorter than me, right?"

"Ah, right. That's amazing! But how on earth can you operate an inn being blind ... oh, I'm sorry, that was rude of me." I was suddenly embarrassed.

"Not at all. But you'd be more comfortable hearing the answer if you came in and sat down. Oh, I hear Pat now."

His wife entered, a tall thin woman with much gray in her dark brown hair and a careworn face. Pleasantries were exchanged. She had a lovely British accent and a lively manner despite her wan appearance. We all went into their apartment, where I heard Graham's story.

He had started losing his sight in his late teens. By the age of 28, he was blind. He then went through two years of therapy and training, to handle his loss of sight. That's where he met Patricia;

she was one of his volunteer helpers.

"After all my training was over, I decided I had a choice. I could sit around home collecting a modest disability cheque from the government, or I could get into a business with Pat and stand on my own two feet and be a productive member of society," Graham said.

They bought this motel. With only nine units, it is the perfect size for them to handle, they said. They've been running it for 18 years now. Graham shares the duties equally with Pat, despite his disability. He navigates by knowing exactly where everything is. Each morning, Pat checks the sidewalk and the vacated bedrooms, making sure there are no obstructions and that everything is in its proper place. Then Graham does his rounds: stripping off the bed linens, taking the towels, emptying wastebaskets and so on. Pat does the vacuuming, cleans bathrooms and does the laundry. They remake the beds together.

Graham also runs the front desk. He has some amazing machines to help him, purchased with financial assistance from the government. His computer is hooked up to a scanner and a pair of speakers. Any letters he receives, he puts on the scanner. Once scanned, the computer reads the letter aloud using specialized speech software. It does the same thing with any e-mails or faxes it receives. Using a special braille keyboard, Graham types and sends replies. His computer lets him register guests and do the bookkeeping.

Among his other gadgets is a money-identifier, that reads out the denomination of the bills placed in it. His adding machine has a braille keypad and a voice box that reads the totals aloud. His desk and cell phones also have braille keypads. The desk clock announces the time at the touch of a button.

Graham does the gardening; they have an extensive flower and vegetable garden in back of the inn. Pat does the planting in spring, in neat rows with the plants in a specific order, which Graham memorizes. He tends them as they grow, including de-weeding.

"He's very good now at identifying plants just by their smell, but it was quite a challenge the first year," said Pat, chuckling. "He had a hard time telling the difference between plant and weed! We lost many perfectly good plants that year."

I laughed. "That's a problem even sighted people have! My husband often lets weeds grow, especially if they're flowering, and pulls up plants that should be left alone!"

We chatted for over an hour before I insisted on leaving. I felt guilty about keeping them from their chores – I well knew that you only had so many hours for housekeeping before the next batch of guests arrived.

Talking with the Sparrows, I realized they had gone through some of the difficulties we'd faced – although their incidents had been spread over several years, instead of several months like us. Maybe one reason was that Patricia was quite the handyperson; she said she could even repair their balky furnace when it refused to start on cold winter's days.

"You just have to know where to hit it!" she laughed.

I found their can-do attitude so inspirational. As I left, Graham said: "Despite all the ups and downs, attitude is everything. I have had a positive attitude all my life and the success of our business proves it pays off."

When I returned home, Pete dragged me into our living room. Crayons lay strewn over the carpet. Taped up on the walls were over three dozen sheets, each with various combinations of colours. Each sheet represented a proposed colour group for our exterior. Most sheets had four or five different colours! He wanted to lead me through the combinations, to select just the right one for our inn.

I said I'd already given him my decision on colours and he had now crossed over the border of indecision into the land of pure obsession. I kissed his fevered little brow and went to bed.

Thursday:

We had the Monahans over for dinner this evening. It was our thank you for all their patient advice over the past several weeks.

We told them of my encounter with the hookers last week.

Bert said I had handled them just right, which gave my ego a boost. To prevent future visits, he said our best tactic was to be vigilant and try to intercept them before they went into a guest room. He cautioned that we must be absolutely sure the women were hookers, otherwise we'd be liable for a hefty lawsuit. And under no circumstances must we ever lay hands on them; this could encourage an assault claim.

He suggested we contact the police, who had more tips on how to deal with hookers and descriptions of the city's known call girls. This would also let the police know we were serious about not being a "hooker motel"; that we wanted to change the situation that had existed under Owens.

"It's very hard to change a bad reputation, but stick with it. It can be done," Bert said. "Eventually, prostitutes will know your place is one where they are not welcome and they'll just refuse to come here when a guest invites them."

Several times that evening, Pete tried to involve the Monahans in his quest for the perfect exterior colours. Each time I deflected the conversation onto another topic When he tried it for the fifth time, I kicked him under the table. He gave me such a look, but he stopped.

Later, over dessert, I told them about my visits to our immediate neighbours. Bert and Madeline weren't surprised that most of them wanted nothing to do with us.

"That's very common in our industry, dear," said Maddy. "Don't take it personally. Many innkeepers are just focussed on their own operation and are not interested in anything beyond their property line. Everyone is fiercely competitive and suspicious of other operators. In fact, some will go out of their way to sabotage their competitors."

"Yeah, we've already encountered that," I said and told them about Patel across the highway.

"Ah, that's Surinder all right," Bert snorted. "He's quite the character. Now, bear in mind that most Asians are not like him at all. Broke the mold when they made him. Why, I remember one Lodging Ontario convention where he got up at the Annual Meeting and urged the association to lobby for legalized prostitution! Said it would greatly boost our revenues. No one took him up on it, of course."

"Well, it seems he went ahead on his own, anyway. I've heard from a friend in the police that he's basically running an escort service over there," said Madeline. "If a guest asks for female companionship, Surinder provides a phone number for the guest to call. Within thirty minutes, a limo pulls up and the girl gets out and goes into the room."

"Yes, we've noticed those limos over there, from time to time," I said. "So that's what they're for. And he had the nerve to cast stones about our reputation! Why don't the police shut him down?"

"Oh, they've tried a few times, but nothing stuck in court. It's not that easy. He's very careful."

Changing neighbours, I told them about my chat with the Sparrows. "Oh, such a courageous couple!" Maddy gushed. "Especially Graham, doing what he does despite being blind. I mean, we too face the same challenges each day, but for him, on top of all that, he has to operate sightless. Yet you never hear either of them complain.

"You already know how hard it is to get mortgage financing from the banks; you went through that when you bought here. Bankers are very reluctant to lend to tourism businesses. Well, the Sparrows ran into an additional hurdle – when the loan managers found out Graham was blind, they refused them a mortgage. Oh, the managers never admitted his disability was the reason, but the Sparrows knew it was. Every single bank turned them down. Finally, they had to use a mortgage broker, with a higher interest rate."

As they were leaving, the Monahans dropped a bombshell. They were off in two weeks for their condo in Arizona, where they would stay for five months. They had done this for several years now, ever since their daughter had assumed responsibility for running their inn.

We wished them well and made them promise to send us a

card.

GAH! We were losing our sources of reliable advice!

Still, as I think about it sitting here writing this Diary, maybe it'll be okay. After all, I did figure out how to handle the hookers by myself. Patel too.

Friday:

Start of a long weekend today. Our third since purchasing the motel. But we'd been warned this one was usually the worst. Labour Day weekend. Last blow-out of the summer.

We were extra vigilant with every guest at check-in. We stated that all alcoholic beverages must be consumed within their rooms and that parties must be kept low-key in consideration of other guests. We emphasized that quiet time started at 11:00 pm and that loud noises would not be tolerated after that.

People seemed quite agreeable to these house rules. We had no incidents tonight.

Had a phone call around dinnertime, interrupting our supper (as usual; we'd learned to bolt our food since becoming innkeepers). Caller wanted directions to Ellen's Fubar Motel. I hung up on her. Didn't feel like finishing my dinner.

Pete spent over two hours tonight fretting over the damn paint colours. I refused to get involved. He sulked until bedtime.

Saturday:

When I woke up, I gathered every paint swatch I could find, placed them in a paper bag and went to a far corner of our property with a shovel. There, I buried the bag. I said a few words over the grave; none printable here.

A sunny uneventful day today. Lots of happy families enjoying our lawns. Squeals of playing children amidst the hum of adult conversation. Barbequing. Frisbee games and a very earnest football game. Sunbathing (the ladies kept their tops on, much to Pete's disappointment). Reading. Good cheer all round.

Pete spent forever looking for his paint swatches. I wore my most innocent look. He knew I'd done something to 'em, though.

Twenty-one years of marriage. I admitted nothing.

Late in the evening, after I'd gone to bed, Pete was finishing up some paperwork at the front desk when a bed sheet floated by the window. Then a naked man raced by in hot pursuit. He was closely followed by a giant beer can on two legs.

Pete pinched himself to check if he'd fallen asleep. Ouch. Nope.

Going outside, he saw the trio disappear around the side of the building. The bed sheet was not moving supernaturally; a laughing woman wearing only bra and panties was flying it behind her as she ran, like a giant white cape. Naked man was shouting for her to give it back. The beer can said nothing.

Pete looked back and saw a group of revellers outside Number 22. Loud music pulsed from inside the room. It was after eleven. As he walked across our parking lot toward the room, Pete saw the Sheet Man Can Trio race up and disappear inside. It took two tries for the beer can; the guy wearing the big inflatable thing ran into the door jamb the first time and fell down. Helpless as a turtle on its back, he had to be helped to his feet.

Putting on his most stern face and armed with a righteous air, my Pompous Idiot waded into the party and finally succeeded in calming it down. Everyone promised to behave. Someone even offered him a beer.

Twenty minutes later, Pete had to do it all over again. Then again thirty minutes after that. Each time, our phone jangled with complaints from guests trying to sleep. Finally, after Pete threatened to call the cops, the party folks shut down. Or passed out.

Exhausted and irritated, Pete tumbled into bed.

Sunday:

Pete said not a word about paint colours today. Tough love worked!

Graham Sparrow phoned me just after lunch, asking how our long weekend was going.

"Not too bad so far," I replied. "Had a wild party last night, but Pete eventually succeeded in closing it down. No damages, thank God, except for some frayed nerves. And massive hangovers today. How about you guys?"

Long pause. "Not so good, Ellen. A group of bikers decided to paint all the walls in their room with Worcestershire sauce. They also smashed the custom-made desk in there. They left this morning; that's when we discovered the damage."

"Oh my God! Graham, that's awful! You called the police, of course."

"No ... no we didn't. We think these guys are gang-related. They seemed decent when they checked-in, but Pat says they painted some gang insignia on the walls with that sauce. It's going to take us days to clean those walls."

"No, it will not, Graham. Pete and I will be right over, with buckets and sponges. Trust me, we have *lots* of buckets. Our housekeeper can keep an eye on the place while we're gone."

He protested, saying he had only called to see if we had any bikers staying with us and, if so, to be wary.

We went anyway. It took the four of us all afternoon and most of the evening to clean the walls of the pungent brown liquid. Yuck.

For most folks, it was holiday Labour Day weekend.

For us innkeepers, it was Days of Labour.

Our 11ᵗʰ Week

In Which We Encounter Painters That Won't And Players That Will

Dear Diary:

Monday:

Today was the day our team of painters was due to arrive, to do our exterior. Their first task was to scrape off the loose flaking paint and prime any bare areas. They said they'd show up first thing, to get an early start. They promised we'd have a completely-repainted inn by the weekend. That was great news; the weather was supposed to be sunny all week.

8:00 am: no painters.

10:00 am: no painters. I called their office. Was told they were "just finishing another job and they'd be over by noon."

Noon: still no painters.

2:00 pm: definitely no painters. Pete: losing patience.

The Monahans had been right; our occupancy did drop off sharply after Labour Day weekend. Kids were back in school; family road trips were over. But they said we'd gain a new type of clientele to make up for the lost business: sports teams.

"Though they do help pay the bills, be careful! Teams bring their own special headaches," advised Madeline. "Noise, underage drinking, room damages, early check-outs if they lose the first game of a two-game weekend. Make sure you get a hefty damage deposit on check-in and have the coach sign a letter that she or he's responsible for the team."

With Maddy's advice in mind, I booked our first sports team today, for this Friday: a senior high school boys' hockey team.

5:00 pm: no hope of any painters. Pete: no patience. Increased muttering about "what kind of clowns had *I* chosen?" Muttering stopped when I retorted that they'd come highly recommended and if it had been left up to him, we'd still be arguing over colours.

5:05 pm: I called painters' office and complained about their broken promises. Was told they were sorry – complications at previous job – and they'd be here tomorrow before 9:00 am for *sure*.

Tuesday:

Mail arrived. I added the latest batch of magazines, plus another hardcover book, to the piles on our small coffee table. The piles now covered the entire table top and were well on their way skyward. Note to self: Check strength of table's rickety legs, sometime soon.

1:00 pm: no painters. Despair setting in.

Mid-afternoon: loud crash. Surprisingly, not at our place! Across the highway. Running out, we saw that a dump truck at the Big Eagle Inn had just off-loaded a pile of large rocks on the front lawn. Another dump truck was pulling up, full of top soil.

"That Patel is copying our rock garden!" I said, hands on my hips. "How dare he! That was our idea!"

Pete said: "Humph. Well, at least OUR rocks are bigger." Smugness tinged his voice.

Later on, a 50ish suit-and-tie businessman drove up, with a much younger woman in the passenger seat. He came into the office and asked what our hourly rate was.

"I'm sorry, we don't have an hourly rate," I said. "We only rent rooms by the night."

"Yeah, yeah, but I only NEED it for an hour. Or less," he replied, grinning. "Look lady, I know all about this motel. I don't have to spell it out for you, surely!"

"Sir, we are a family inn. We don't rent by the hour, we're not a place for 'quickies' and we don't allow prostitutes!"

The would-be Lothario reddened."What? Oh, she's no hooker! She's my secretary! Not that it's any of your business. And what do you mean 'family inn'? Everyone around here has known for years that this place is great for quickies. Hell, I saw that picture in the paper several weeks ago; that councillor and his mistress caught in the hole right here at your so-called 'family inn' after their afternoon love nest! So c'mon, rent me the damn room or I'll take my business elsewhere!"

"Then you'll take your business elsewhere. I'm sure the motel across the street will be happy to accommodate you." I smiled. "And the gentleman in that picture had rented the room for the night." He left, fuming. I could see it was indeed a long road to change our reputation.

5:00 pm: no painters. Despair so well rooted by now, it was staying for dinner.

Wednesday:

Today's mail contained a wonderful surprise: A former guest sent us a gift! It was a cute hand-painted ceramic statue of a robin. It came with a note thanking us for our hospitality during their five-day stay here last month.

Pete and I were blown away! We'd been receiving an ever-increasing number of cards and letters thanking us for a nice stay, but this was the first time we'd been blessed with a gift. So we must be doing something right! We put it in a place of honour on the small shelf behind our front desk.

The guys that had installed our new Windsong Inn roadside sign several weeks ago returned this morning to add a large reader board beneath it. I'd ordered it last week; I got the idea from my visits to our neighbouring innkeepers, most of whom had reader boards. They used them to advertise rates and amenities. Heck, if people stole our ideas, we could steal theirs. (Didn't this make me as bad as Patel copying our rock garden?)

The new reader board was bolted to the existing sign pole, just below the Windsong Inn sign. The board had two sides, so messages could be read by traffic travelling in either direction on the highway, and was a good 20 feet above the ground. To apply the large plastic letters, we bought a telescoping pole with a suction cup on the end.

With the box of letters that came with the sign, I wasted no time putting up our first messages. One side read: REASONABLE RATES. CLEAN ROOMS. The other side read: NEW! MICROWAVE OVENS IN EACH ROOM.

This morning, Pete performed his least-liked duty: plunging a foul, clogged toilet. My man had come a long way since he first did this chore, during our second week. By now, he'd had lots of practice: on average, a toilet needed plunging once a week. We'd been told this was a normal routine at motels; it was amazing (and sometimes disgusting) what some guests insisted on flushing down.

What made this morning's odious task different was that Pete was whistling as he did it. Angie heard him when she came in to clean the room. The Human Dust Mop immediately ran out and dragged me in to hear for myself. She was convinced the Pompous Idiot's frail mind had finally snapped. She knew Pete loathed this chore.

"Are you okay, hon?" I asked from the bathroom entrance, interrupting his whistling. Angie stayed behind me, hovering by the phone, ready to dial 911 should Pete turn violent.

He stopped plunging the smelly, repulsive mess and looked at me, puzzled. "Sure, El, never better. Why?"

"Well, er, you're whistling. You're happy doing that chore now?"

"Nah, still *hate* it. But I've gotten used to it. I've accepted it as part of my routine. So what the hell – might as well be cheerful about it." He returned to his plunging and whistling.

My worst fears were realized. His mind had definitely snapped. Either that, or he was on some drug.

Actually, **Diary**, kidding aside, this marked quite a change in Pete. Maybe there's hope for him yet! (In hindsight, considering what happened a few weeks later, I was tragically naive.)

High noon: painters finally showed up! Looked over the job,

nodding and murmuring amongst themselves. Then promptly left. Lunch break.

One hour later: The Return Of The Painters! Spent the rest of the afternoon furiously scraping and priming our entire exterior. Place looked like hell when they finished: faded blue paint with great splotches of bright white primer scattered all over. Ugh! But it would only be for one night. They promised to return first thing tomorrow to put on the first coat. We were so excited – this was the last major step of our exterior make-over!

(Well, except for needing a new roof – I dreaded what would happen when the November rains arrived – but for that we'd need some serious financing.)

We had reached the end of our renovation fund. It hadn't lasted nearly as long as we'd hoped when we took possession here. Expenses had been higher than we'd figured and some of those expenses had been unexpected. We would need a bank loan for future renovations, like the room interiors and the new roof.

I visited a local bank and obtained a how-to guide on preparing a business plan. We'd need all our ducks in a row when we went to ask for major renovation money.

Thursday:

Around noon, the man in Number Six came to check out. He'd been staying there with his seven-year-old daughter, visiting his wife while she was in the hospital undergoing treatment. As usual with certain guests whom I thought it would help, I'd loaned the daughter our stuffed bear to hug for solace, when they'd arrived five days ago. (We'd come to call it the Comfort Bear.) Thankfully, the mother had survived her serious operation and was being released today.

"Um, Mrs. Tomlinson, I'm kinda embarrassed to say this, um, but there's a problem with that nice brown bear you gave my Ashley," the father said, eyes flicking from my face to the walls nervously.

"Oh? Something wrong with it?"

"No, quite the opposite. She's grown too attached to that bear.

She's even given it a name. I really can't get her to part with it."

I laughed. "That's quite understandable! It's helped several people since I bought it, though this is the first child I've loaned it to. I've seen how much she likes it. Now I wouldn't have the heart to ask her to give it up. Look, she may keep it, with our compliments."

"Why, that's very kind of you, thank you! But at least let me pay for it, so you can get another."

"No, I won't take any money for the Comfort Bear. Consider it our gift to Ashley. And I'm SO glad everything went well with your wife. By the way, what did she name the bear?"

"Hope."

The painters did not return today. Maybe I could use a bear named Hope.

Friday:

During my Sanity Day today, I purchased four more of the supremely-hugable Comfort Bears. I'd decided to automatically place one in the room of each guest visiting family at the hospital from now on, accompanied by a welcome note on crisp parchment, advising that they should feel free to hug the bear when necessary.

Then I had another brainstorm. I went to a store supplying engraved plaques and trophies and ordered four silver medallions, one for each bear, to be hung with ribbons around their necks. Inspired by young Ashley, I gave each bear a name: Hope, Love, Strength and Courage. The front of each engraved medallion bore the name of the bear that wore it. The backs read: "On loan from the Windsong Inn, this Comfort Bear has unlimited hugs."

When I told Pete of what I'd done, a funny look flitted across his eyes, then he gave me a monster hug of my own.

No painters showed up today. Pete called their office to tear a strip off them. No answer. The inn really looked awful. I changed the "reasonable rates" side of our reader board to read: PLEASE PARDON OUR LOOKS. WE'RE RENOVATING!

"First thing Monday morning, I'm driving down to their

office and pounding a counter until we get some action," Pete vowed.

To add to our frustration, this week we had not one, not two, but THREE phone calls from tourists wanting to book rooms at Ellen's Fubar Motel. "And no SNAFUs, y'hear?" laughed one caller. With the first caller, I snorted and hung up. With the second, I snapped "this is NOT funny!" and hung up. With the last caller, I screamed into the phone and hung up.

(Yeah, I'm getting really wound up about this!)

In early evening, the senior boys' hockey team checked-in. With the players, coaching staff and assorted parents, the group took most of our rooms. They were in Wackimac for a weekend-long tournament. We were very nervous; this was our first time dealing with such a large group and the Monahans' warnings about sports teams heightened our anxiety. But aside from a huge commotion as they sorted out rooms and roommates, then moved their luggage in, there were no incidents. In fact, Pete reported that most of them had lights-out fairly early, around 10:30 pm.

"That certainly wasn't so bad," he said.

He should have kept his mouth shut.

Saturday:

Fairly quiet during the day. Hockey team and hangers-on were gone very early; off to the Wackimac Memorial Arena and Farm Implement Museum for the first of their series of games. We had a few families in, on weekend getaway trips, and they had all left by mid-morning to sightsee around the area.

Angie asked how the team had behaved last night. "Just fine," I replied and related what Pete had told me. "Pete and I are wondering what all the fuss was about."

"Oh, yous may find out soon enough, Miz. Tomlinson," Angie said, stuffing a mass of her unruly grey-blonde hair back under her kerchief. "But I hopes fer yore sake that yous don't. My sake too – I hates cleanin' them rooms after a team's abused 'em."

"How did Hal Owens handle sports teams? Did he have a special tactic?"

"A-yep. Baseball bat. Big 'un."

The team returned in late afternoon. They were in a foul mood. Their games had not gone well; they were dead last in the tournament. The late afternoon air was punctuated with loud arguments sprinkled liberally with swearing. And that was the parents. Cases of beer materialized from car trunks and all the adults started drinking.

A massive delivery of pizza arrived around 6:00 pm. The group heard that Wackimac's restaurants were jammed with hockey players, so they'd ordered out. Pete and I cringed at the thought of all that food being scarfed down in our rooms – we hoped they'd keep it off the furniture.

The drinking continued after supper. The doors to their rooms propped open, many adults and players lounged outside on lawn chairs or chairs they dragged out from the rooms. Arguments as to what went wrong with their playing grew more heated. Pete and I started doing regular patrols around the parking lot, making sure the group saw us and knew we were keeping tabs on them.

Around 8:00, Pete came into our office and said: "I just saw several boys drinking beer, right beside some adults. Parents are giving beer to the kids! There may be the odd boy who's 19, but most are 17 and 18 year-olds. I've gotta go talk with them."

"We'll both go, hon."

We went up to the biggest group and picked out the coach. Tall, grey-haired, with a slight paunch, he had a huge beak of a nose on a narrow face, perched atop a spindly neck. A vulture with a beer bottle.

"Excuse me, coach," said Pete, "but these boys with a beer, are they all of legal drinking age?"

The man, well lubricated, fixed Pete with a predatory look that matched the bird he resembled and said: "Yeah, you bet, buddy. All 19. Don't you worry now."

"Well, we are worrying," I said. "Underage drinking is illegal. In fact, we'd prefer it if you did your drinking inside your rooms."

"Aw, ma'am, it's a lovely night out. We're just enjoying it an' havin' a few brews. Hey – ya want one?"

I declined. A big-bellied mountain of a man wobbled up to us. His face was so red , it was almost purple. A mean, violent face. "Problem here, coach?" he asked and let go with a gut-wrenching belch.

"Oh, these folks own the motel an' they're just concerned that some of our boys who're drinking, are underage. One of 'em's your son, Rod. But I said they were all 19."

"Damn right!" barked the mountain. "All 19, definitely." He glared belligerently at Pete, then at me. "Look you two, we've had a helluva day, okay? We're just havin' a little social drinkin' here, doin' no harm. Nuthin' to be concerned about."

"Well, don't get too rowdy and remember we have a no noise policy after 11:00. And we'd really appreciate it if you drank inside your rooms, please," said Pete. "It's for your benefit; the rooms are considered your private domain, while out here's public. The police sometimes cruise through our parking lot and you don't want any trouble with them, right?"

Mountain looked at coach. Another primordial belch erupted from mountain. "Oh, alright," said the coach, wincing in disgust as the stench of the belch wafted over him.

The drinkers slowly migrated inside.

I tried to stay up as late as I could, to support Pete in his patrols, but by 10:00 I had to hit the sack. Just couldn't keep my eyes open any longer. Early to rise means early to bed.

About 10 minutes later, the hi-jinks started. Groups of boys racing from room to room, grabbing someone's stuff and being chased for it. Water fights outside in the parking lot, using balloons that some twit had thoughtfully packed, filled with water. A few balloon ballistic missiles were lobbed into rooms, to explode on the chest or back of some unfortunate watching TV. Mayhem ensued as those soaked unfortunates sought dire revenge.

Pete tried to ride herd on the worst of the pranks, but he was outnumbered 20 to one. He finally threatened to call the cops if the kids didn't settle down and that worked – for a while. Then more tomfoolery started. The coach and parents were nowhere to be seen; they were drinking together in two of the rooms.

Around 11:15, the fighting started. Among the adults! A heated shouting match escalated to shoves, then punches, then a wrestling grapple of flailing fists and snarled curses. As soon as Pete got wind of it, he made one of the wisest decisions of his life: He did not attempt to break it up himself. He called the police. They arrived and stopped the combat, but by then blood had been spilled and furniture broken. Charges were laid.

About an hour later, another fight started. Cops returned. More damaged bodies and furniture. This time, one of the scrappers needed stiches at the hospital. The hi-jinks didn't stop. While everyone was distracted by the fights, some boys raided the rooms taking all the sheets and blankets. They hid them in a car trunk and refused to give them back until the coach threatened them with a slow bloody death that would make what Braveheart went through seem like a spa vacation.

While all this was going on, the night was alive with another sound of music: people retching miserably. The joys of over-drinking. Finally, at around 2:00 am, silence reigned. Everyone was blessedly unconscious.

Pete, feeling like he had just lived through the D-Day beach landing, collapsed into bed. I woke briefly to hear him mutter: "In future, the only sports teams we're accepting will be grannies in wheelchairs."

Sunday:

Our non-hockey guests, when they checked-out, complained about last night's noise. Though I apologized profusely, many vowed never to stay here again.

The hockey team checked-out late this morning. They were very quiet, many were hung-over, and a few had bruised faces. No-one apologized for the previous night's ruckus.

We refused to return the large damage deposit of $100 per room that we'd collected in advance (thanks Maddy!), until we inspected the rooms. Good thing we did.

If Pete had felt like he'd gone through a D-Day landing last night, the rooms looked like the Normandy beaches. The best of them were filthy; the worst had broken furniture and vomit. Despair numbed us; this must be how people in war-torn countries felt, to see their home and possessions destroyed by uncaring combatants. We angrily told the coach that we were keeping his entire damage deposit. We would need every penny to clean up the mess and repair the broken furniture. The coach nodded silently; he was more concerned with keeping his head from exploding.

Angie, bless her, surprised us by bringing along her sister today, to help clean the rooms. Angie'd been through this before, so she knew what to expect. We realized it would take the four of us all day to set things right. Some rooms were so bad, it'd take two days to get them back into service.

We prided ourselves on our clean rooms. To see them treated like this drove me to tears and Pete to profanity.

Angie took it personally too; after all, she'd been cleaning these rooms far longer than we had. But she hid her emotions much better than us. Her face just got more dour; a feat I wouldn't have thought possible.

About 45 minutes after the team's departure, our phone rang. It was a family that had just passed us in their car, en route to Sunday services. The mother was calling us on her cellphone to complain about our "highly objectionable reader board".

Pete and I went outside to look at it. We had been so busy with the team's check-out and cleaning the rooms, that we never noticed our messages had been changed. The kids must have done it late last night, after Pete went to bed, altering the letters already on the board. Since the telescoping suction cup pole was still safely locked away in our shed, the boys must have formed a human pyramid to reach the letters.

Pete smiled in spite of his anger. "Gotta admire their tenacity in getting up there and their inventiveness reusing those letters."

One side read: NEW! SEMEN IN EACH ROOM.

The other side read: PLEASE PARDON US. WE'RE REVOLTING!

Our 12ᵗʰ Week

In Which Two Guests Depart Involuntarily And Our Banker Smiles

Dear Diary:

Monday:

It was 3:12 am. Night's peace snuggled around the countryside like a big comforter. The sleepy moan of bullfrogs was the only sound, save for the occasional whine of tractor-trailer rigs rocketing by on the highway.

Silent night. All was dark (we had turned off our sign and our lights). Twinkling stars above.

A car gliding up to our front door. The imperious pounding of fists.

The staccato roar of machine gun fire.

The squeal of tires as the car bore its passengers away, terror in their eyes.

The satisfied sigh of Peter as he returned to bed, resuming an interrupted sleep.

Night's peace descended again.

Tuesday:

True to his vow, Pete had gone to the office of our alleged painters yesterday and raised a ruckus about their slowness in finishing the job. He refused to leave until he'd pried a promise out of the owner that a crew would be at our place first thing today, painting.

His efforts paid off. A crew did indeed arrive early this morning and set to painting with a vengeance.

Unfortunately, they used the wrong colours.

We noticed it after the first few roller strokes and called a halt to the endeavour. After some argument and phone calls to their boss, the painters left, promising to return tomorrow with the right colours.

So the blue and white-speckled Ugly Duckling Inn stayed on display for another day.

"We're definitely in the wrong business," muttered Pete. "With what they charge and considering how much in demand they are, you'd think these painters would at least have the courtesy to stick to a schedule!"

Because of last weekend's horrible experience with that hockey team, I called the Lodging Ontario association to see if they had any advice. They said much the same things the Monahans had said and added that they had a generic Sports Team Agreement form, which we should get coaches to sign beforehand when we obtained the damage deposit. The form made things more official and drove home to coaches that unruly behaviour would not be tolerated. They promised to email us a copy.

They also said we should carefully choose the types of teams we booked.

"And how do we do that?" I asked, with a tinge of despair in my voice. "Ask them at check-in if they intend to trash our rooms?"

"No, no of course not," answered Brewster, the association's Executive Director, with a tinge of exasperation in his voice (I could almost hear his thoughts: *Oh God! Another new owner!*). "Only accept certain types of teams, like girls' teams, women's leagues, seniors' teams, figure skaters, chess players, like that. They're generally much less trouble and kinder to your facilities. Stay away from boys' and men's teams. And bear in mind that you're not obligated to accept any team at all."

I thanked him for the advice.

When Pete came in from mowing the lawn this afternoon, his

face was grim. "Come take a look at Patel's reader board across the street," he said.

I did. It read: NOW MICROWAVES IN ROOMS.

"There goes that copycat, again!" I groused. "Well, we'll just have to stay one step ahead of him. Anyway, they say imitation is the sincerest form of flattery, right?"

Pete muttered something decidedly unflattering.

It was only days later that we discovered, from a guest that checked-in after first visiting Patel's inn, that he did not have a microwave in each room, as we did. He only had two or three of the appliances and he would deliver one to a room on request. A cheapskate copycat.

Wednesday:

Yes! Yes! Yes! The painters returned and with the right colours this time! Oh frabjous day! Callooh! Callay! We chortled in our joy. (With apologies to Lewis Carroll; I've always loved his poem *Jabberwocky*.)

Our exterior walls became a soothing rich forest green. The door jambs and window trims became a restful pale grey. These were the colours we had agreed-upon weeks ago. But, in a concession to Pete, who REALLY wanted a third colour, the doors became a deep burnt yellow. The painters suggested the door hue; they said the latest trend in exterior painting called for bold colours.

With the Pompous Idiot anxiously supervising every brush and roller stroke, I continued working on our business plan and other documents that we would need when we went to the bank to apply for a loan to do our massive interior renovations and get a new roof. We had an appointment with the loans officer this Friday.

I did take time out from my paperwork to call Madeline Monahan, to wish her and Bert a wonderful time at their Arizona condo. They were leaving tomorrow and would be gone for five months. Maddy said I could call their daughter for advice if we were really stuck and added that Lodging Ontario was always helpful as well (except on weekends and holidays when they were closed – which was when innkeepers most often needed advice).

But I still had a lump in my throat as I hung up. We had come to rely so much on the Monahans over the past weeks. For the next five months, we wouldn't have the opportunity of calling upon their decades of innkeeper experience, as the need arose.

By suppertime, the painters had finished applying the first coat on everything. Our inn looked awesome! Dressed in its new colours, surrounded by our large lawn and towering trees, and fronted by the crisp black of a freshly-paved lot, the Windsong Inn presented a striking image to passers-by. To say nothing of our dramatic boulder garden and new sign.

Pete and I went to bed happy tonight.

Thursday:

The painting platoon arrived promptly at 8:00 am and started on the second coat. Wonderful!

During lunch, Pete announced he'd dreamed up something to make extra money for us.

"Y'know how we sometimes find stuff left behind by guests after they've checked out?" he asked around a mouthful of sandwich. "Well, why don't we set up a small gift shop in a corner of our lobby, to sell all these left-behind items? We could call it 'Finders Keepers'. I checked with Bert before they left and he said these forgotten items are ours to dispose of as we see fit, unless it's something valuable, like jewellery or a watch or a fur coat. So our little shop could sell that stuff we've been piling into boxes all summer: toys, dolls, frilly undies, half-packages of gum and condoms, single socks, sweaters, t-shirts, pocket books, whatever! We'd price 'em low, so they'd be real bargains. Whaddaya think?"

I sat there, mouth open, staring at him.

"I mean, we'd obviously wash the clothing first," he went on. "And there's some stuff we wouldn't try and sell, like half-full bottles of wine or the sex toys we sometimes find. So, good idea, or not?"

I cleared my throat and said: "Or not. Pete, that's gotta be one of your silliest ideas ever. And it's also gross. I mean, really! No one would be interested in buying that stuff! I think we should simply donate the clothes, toys and dolls to the Salvation Army or Goodwill, and chuck the rest."

"Seriously?"

"Seriously. Now finish your lunch. Towel rods in 12 and 16 need fixing."

"Yes, ma'am," he said, crestfallen. "But don't you think ..."

"Eat!"

In early afternoon, we were surprised to see Pete's father drive onto our lot. This was his first visit since his Fubar practical joke, ten weeks ago. As usual, he had not told us ahead of time that he was coming.

Pete looked at me nervously as Sarge heaved himself out of his car, extracted his cane and hobbled over to our office. He knew that I considered the Fubar prank to be a worsening of the long-standing Cold War between us.

"You ... ah ... you're gonna be civil with Pop, right, El?" he said. "He is 83 years old, after all, and he did loan us a chunk of money to help buy this place."

"Peter, dear, don't you worry. I shall be sweetness and light! I shall *kill* him with kindness."

Pete regarded me dubiously, like a sick child asked to drink some juice that he just *knows* has sour medicine lurking within.

But I surprised him – and REALLY shocked his old man – by giving Sarge a great big hug and a kiss on the cheek as he entered the office.

Sarge hastily extricated himself from my grasp, stepped back and stared at me. "What was that for?" he asked suspiciously. "I didn't figger you'd be happy to see me, after my l'il joke."

"Nonsense!" I replied laughing. "You're always welcome here! I admit that I was quite upset about your prank and we wasted over two thousand dollars in printing costs, but let bygones be bygones, I always say."

"Actually, El, I've never heard you say that," said Pete.

"Well, you just haven't been listening, dear! Now you and Sarge go into the kitchen, make a nice cup of that paint remover he calls strong coffee and have a chat. I'll just go out and make sure there's a suitable clean room for him to have. Oh, give me your car keys, Sarge, and I'll put your bag into your room."

Sometime later, I returned to our apartment. Pete and Sarge were still talking away (guys are just like us gals). I cooked dinner and we all passed a fairly pleasant evening. With sporadic interruptions to rent rooms, resuscitate comatose TVs and supply more towels. And with a father-in-law who must have been Walt Disney's inspiration for Grumpy in *Snow White*.

The whole time, the old codger never said a word about the Ellen's Fubar Motel brochures that were circulating around. Finally, I couldn't stand it any longer. I asked him point blank if he was responsible. He retorted sharply that he had nothing to do with it and how dare I suggest it. Though, on reflection, he did admit it would be a nice practical joke.

(He's obviously lying through his false teeth.)

Finally, around 10:00, both Sarge and myself could hardly keep our eyes open.

"Well, I gotta hit the sack," Sarge announced and lurched to his feet. "Fair chow, Ellen, thanks. Tomorra I'll give this place an inspection, to see all these improvements you've been yakking about. What I seen so far, as I came in, looked okay."

Pete and I each gave him a hug, which he grumbled about, then I gave him his room key.

"See you here for breakfast tomorrow then," I said. "Have a very pleasant night."

"Humph."

After he was gone, Pete looked at me with admiration. "You were great to him, El. I'm impressed! And it sure surprised him, too. Thank you!"

I smiled. "Oh, you're most welcome, honey."

"By the way," Pete asked as he picked up empty drink glasses, "What room did you put Pop into?"

My smile had grown broader. "Number 11."

The glasses crashed on the floor.

Friday:

When I got up, before the sun as usual, Sarge was gone. All of his things were out of the room, the key was on the dresser and his car was not in the lot.

After Pete awoke and I'd told him of Sarge's mysterious departure, he called him on his cellphone. Sarge answered and said he was half-way home. He said he suddenly remembered an urgent commitment and had to leave very early.

He never told us what happened in his room that night.

Pete glowered at me for days afterwards, convinced I had encouraged our resident ghost to terrorize his father.

Honestly, **Diary**, I did not encourage Brenda to terrorize Sarge. However, I'll admit that when I placed his bag in the room, I did announce who'd be staying there and what he'd pulled on us and that if she felt like spooking the crusty old warhorse just a *little* ...

(I could play nasty practical jokes too.)

Mid-morning found us sitting in front of Cathy, the loans officer at our local bank. We presented her with our business plan, financial statements and the increased occupancy statistics since we took over the inn. We outlined all the improvements we'd already done. Then we requested the money we'd need to continue our renovations. We showed how we'd repay it out of cash flow over the succeeding years.

I'd worked hard on our presentation and it showed. Cathy was quite impressed.

Pete said: "And once we've completely renovated our 23 rooms, not only will we be able to more easily attract the nice family clientele we want, but we'll be able to raise our room rates, too. That'll help pay off this loan even faster."

After more discussion and some tap-tapping by Cathy on her computer keyboard, she sat back in her chair and smiled.

"Folks, this looks do-able, as far as I'm concerned. It's a great plan. I'm happy that one of Wackimac's institutions is getting the

TLC treatment. You two are the best thing that's happened to that tired old motel in years. And I heard what you do for family members of patients at the Regional Health Centre; my sister works in the office there. You're good people.

"I'll send this loan request to our Toronto head office this very afternoon, with my personal recommendation that it be approved."

"Oh?" I said, a little concerned. "You don't have the authority to approve our loan?"

"Not for this large an amount. Haven't for years. Only small loans can be approved locally. Anything else must go to head office, or to a regional loans centre. All the banks work that way now. It's really too bad, because local managers like me know the area and the businesses and the owners. But, that's the way it is, these days."

"Do ... do you foresee any problems?"

"Oh no, not at all, Ellen. It's just a formality. In fact, we should have approval as early as next week."

Pete and I looked at each other and grinned like we'd just won the lottery. (Which is ironic, considering we were digging ourselves deeper into debt.)

On the drive back to the Windsong, Pete could hardly contain his excitement. "This is great, El! You did a wonderful job on that business plan and it paid off! I don't understand why the Lodging Ontario association put an article in their newsletter about tourism operators having a hard time getting financing. We got our loan easy as pie!"

"Maybe that's because we were so well prepared," I said.

"Anyway, we're off to the races, El! You know that while you were working on those financial documents these past weeks, I've been calling construction companies. Well, I found one that can start on Monday: Hermann Van Hooydonk Construction. I'll call them right away and we'll sign the contract this very afternoon."

"Now honey, don't you think we should at least wait until the loan is officially approved?"

"Nah! You heard Cathy; it's just a formality. Besides, we

can't risk losing that construction company. We were lucky to find one that could start so quickly. We gotta lock 'em in before they commit elsewhere!"

I smiled. "And besides, Pete, they're willing to let you help with the demolition, right?"

My hubby grinned sheepishly. I'd agreed to this days ago. It was a no-brainer: Pete had proven he had a knack for destruction, so he'd be a natural helping the crew tear down the rooms.

Phase Two of our Motel Make-over was starting!

Saturday:

During my early-morning walkabout, I couldn't help marvelling at how sharp our inn looked in its new coat of paint. Now that the outside looked prestigious, our next task was to do likewise to the inside. The contract had been signed late yesterday, and the Van Hooydonk construction crew would start Monday.

I spent a very pleasant morning checking-out our guests, many of whom had nice compliments about our friendly hospitality and our spacious grounds. I thanked them and said "just wait 'til you see what we'll do to our rooms! You must come back to see them; this'll be a completely different place in a few months."

After lunch, I went to speak to the woman in Number Five: Nora Latimer. She was a shy, mousy person, as if she was afraid of bringing too much attention to herself. About my height and pudgy, she had lank brown hair surrounding a pale, almost chinless face. Her eyes reminded me of a deer caught in a car's headlights.

She'd been staying with us for four weeks now and I'd given her a special weekly rate. She had travelled to Wackimac by bus and needed a place to stay while her husband finished up with his job in Moncton, before moving here to a new job. She said she'd gone ahead to scout apartments.

Nora was supposed to pay us every Saturday, but she'd missed the last two Saturday's payments. Now she was three weeks behind. I'd learned from the Lodging Ontario newsletter that you must not let long-term guests get behind on their rent. Something about not being able to evict them easily under the

Innkeeper's Act if they were significantly in arrears.

She had lots of excuses, but no money to give me. She said her husband was arriving soon with money, but when she tried to call him on his cellphone, there was no answer. He was living in a Moncton motel, as they'd moved out of their apartment.

"Now look, Nora, I'm sorry you can't reach him, but you have to realize that we're not running a charity here," I said. "You owe us for three weeks rent already. How much longer until your husband gets here?"

"Two, maybe three weeks," she replied, fidgeting. "Depends on how long it takes him to finish up the contract he's got."

I was starting to get a funny feeling about this. "Look, do you have a credit card you can give me?"

"Oh ... ah ... sure." Nora fished one out from the depths of a purse large enough to swallow a pillow. "Here."

We both went to the office, where I ran the card through our electronic terminal. It was denied. So were the other three cards she gave me to try. My funny feeling had intensified.

"Look, I'm very sorry, but you've no money and no credit and no idea when your husband's coming, supposedly with some cash. I can't run my business that way. I'm afraid I'll have to ask you to leave. I can give you cab fare to the YWCA downtown, they've got some nice rooms there, I'm told."

I braced myself for a flood of tears, but Nora surprised me. The shy mouse became angry and abusive, insisting I had no right to evict her. She stormed back to her room and slammed the door.

Pete was off on his Sanity Day today (just my luck!). So I called the police. When the officer arrived, I asked him to evict the woman for non-payment of rent. He grimaced and we both went to Number Five to talk with Nora.

"You have NO RIGHT to evict me!" she yelled. "I've lived in Ontario before! I know MY rights! I've been here one month and that makes me a tenant and you a landlord and landlords can't just kick tenants out THAT easy! No way!"

The cop looked at me and nodded. "Mrs. Latimer is right,

ma'am. Under the Tenant Protection Act, you can't evict just like that."

"Excuse me, but you're both wrong," I said. "This is an inn and we're under the Innkeepers Act. That gives me the right to evict for non-payment of rent. It also gives me the right to seize her goods and hold them for up to three months until I get what she owes me and if not, then to sell her goods at public auction. (Thank God I'd been talking to the Monahans all these weeks and reading the Lodging Ontario newsletter. That newsletter was about the only thing we ever had time to read.)

"Now I've no interest in seizing her goods – I'm not some mean ogre – and I even offered to give her cab fare to the YWCA. It's just that I can't have her stay here for free – she already owes me for three weeks and she has no prospects of any money for two or three more weeks. Frankly, I'm worried this is a scam and I don't want to get stuck with a large bill if she takes off in the middle of the night!"

The officer had never heard of the Innkeepers Act. He asked if I had a copy. I did not.

While he tried to contact Nora's husband by phone, I called the Monahan's inn. The daughter was away for the weekend and the front desk clerk did not have a copy of the Innkeepers Act either. Lodging Ontario was, of course, closed until Monday.

I called Graham Sparrow and got lucky. Years ago, he had scanned a copy of the Act into his read-aloud computer. He emailed it to me and I printed it out.

Triumphantly, I gave it to the cop. "There! Told you! Just read it; you'll see it gives me the right to do what I said."

The policeman read it and admitted I was right. He'd also been unsuccessful in reaching the husband (I was starting to wonder if there even WAS a husband). He turned to Nora and instructed her to pack up her things and leave. Fuming and swearing, she did as she was told. I called a cab. I told Nora that she could pay me for what she owed when her husband finally arrived, but she just snarled a curse in response. The cop stayed until the cab came and took her away. She stuck her hand out the window and gave us the finger.

I thanked the officer for his assistance and he replied that he'd learned something today. I said I felt awful turfing out that woman, but I really had no choice. The cop said I'd done the right thing; he'd seen many cases of deadbeats using the legal system to stay in an apartment despite being months behind in the rent.

"It's very hard for a landlord to evict, Mrs. Tomlinson," he remarked as he got in his cruiser. "You're lucky your industry has that Innkeepers Act to protect you."

When he returned in early evening, Pete said I'd done the right thing too. But I still felt like Scrooge.

Sunday:

I continued to feel crummy about yesterday's incident.

Just before lunch, a lady named Lorraine Sulieman, who was staying in Number 17, came in with her daughter in tow. Lorraine was thirtyish, about a head taller than me, with a trim body and coiffed blonde hair. She dressed very well, in a businesslike manner. Something about her face, with its steady blue eyes and thin lips, looked familiar. I felt that I should know her. But I drew a blank.

Her young daughter, who looked to be about nine, was carrying Love, the Comfort Bear I'd placed in their room yesterday when they'd checked-in. She was hugging the bruin for all she was worth; if it had been alive, its eyes would have been bulging from its sockets. Lorraine's husband was in for a heart operation at the Centre.

"Thank you VERY much for your thoughtfulness with this bear," Lorraine said. "What a wonderful idea! My little Sydney here took to it right away."

"Oh, I'm glad you like it," I replied. "I feel it's the least we can do, to help guests like yourselves get through a very difficult time."

"I gather from that nice note you left with the bear, that he has three brothers?"

"Or sisters, if you wish. Yes, their names are Hope, Strength and Courage."

"That's just wonderful! You're REALLY a saint, you know that?"

I blushed and shrugged my shoulders. "Not at all, please! I'm just trying to help out, to make your stay here a little more homey and a little less stressful."

"You're much too modest. I'm going to tell all my friends about you after we return home. These bears are SUCH a clever idea!"

Sydney looked up at me and announced importantly: "And Mom has many many friends, you know."

Lorraine chuckled and patted her daughter's head. Then she said:

"Umm, Ellen, one thing though ..."

"Yes?"

"Could ... could I possibly have a bear for myself? If you have one to spare, that is."

"Sure," I said and went to fetch Courage from its perch on our hall closet shelf.

Our 13th Week

Disaster

Dear Diary:

Superstition.

It's why high-rise hotels have no 13th floor and motels have no 13th bedroom. The public simply won't stay in a room or on a floor numbered unlucky 13. (That's why our 23-unit inn has rooms numbered to 24.)

I wish this Diary had no Chapter 13, either. Even more, I wish we could have skipped Week 13 of our new life as innkeepers.

Superstition? Or coincidence?

(You know my vote, **Diary**. I talk to a ghost.)

As I sit here on Sunday, recording the events of the past week as I've faithfully done every week for over three months now, I'm in a state of despair. My confidence, my enthusiasm are badly shaken.

But I'm getting ahead of myself.

This week passed with a minor assortment of incidents, and some good stuff too, like more thank-you notes from satisfied guests. Oh yes, on Monday morning, the mini-fridges that had been back-ordered finally arrived, so we were able to set the micro-waves on them as originally planned.

I put up new words on one side of our reader board: NOW MINI-FRIDGES IN EACH ROOM.

Pete and I agreed that it wouldn't be long before the Big Eagle Inn across the street had the same sign.

"Maybe we should throw that copycat for a real loop," suggested Pete. "Maybe we should put up a sign that announces something outrageous for a motel, like valet parking, gold washroom fixtures, or five-star French cuisine for room service. Then let him spend big bucks to copy that!"

"No, Peter. Our potential clientele will read it too, then we'll have problems with false advertising."

"Aw, phooey."

At 1:00 pm, on Monday, Van Hooydonk Construction showed up, on time, as promised. What a refreshing change from our experience with the painters! Hermann Van Hooydonk himself came out with his crew, "just to start things off right" he said.

He was in his mid-thirties, with a tangle of unruly black hair that looked like it hadn't seen a comb since grade school. Tall and thin, his eyes constantly flicked from object to object, and he had the annoying habit of spitting at regular intervals.

Pete greeted him like he was a long-lost college buddy.

"Hermann! Good to finally meet you! Y'know, I've heard a lot about you and your team here!"

Hermann let go a long white ribbon of spit and passed a hand through his briar patch of hair. His fingers got stuck halfway through.

"Nah, that was my dad ya heard about. He's retired now. I'm Hermann Junior. Took over the business a year ago."

"Oh . Sorry. I didn't know that when I signed the contract last Friday with your office manager. Well, no problem, eh? Let's get down to business!"

With the highly-skilled assistance of Pete the Destructor, the crew started gutting guest rooms with abandon.

We had decided to renovate half our rooms at a time, Numbers 12 to 24, leaving the other 11 open for business as usual. Then when those 12 were done, we'd re-open them and close Numbers One to Eleven for their make-over. This would let some rooms remain open throughout the construction period, giving us much-needed cash flow to pay bills and the bank loan.

While the first batch of rooms were being done, we'd have roofers in to re-shingle The Sieve, protecting the new inn being created below.

On the other side of our reader board, I put up: WE'RE BUILDING SOMETHING NEW FOR YOU.

Pete was in seventh heaven. He was now officially allowed to wreck things. He joked that instead of dealing with the trauma of guests wrecking our rooms, he now got to do it himself. It gave him an odd satisfaction.

He got on well with the construction crew, though he resisted wearing a hard hat and steel-toed boots, at first. But Ernie, the foreman, was intractable: Pete had to wear proper safety gear, or he'd be booted off his own job site.

Pete finally agreed to wear the gear. One hour later, when he dropped a heavy load of drywall scraps on his feet, he was grateful for the protection.

Pete also grudgingly recognized that his specialized assistance would end when the demolition ended. He would have no involvement with the construction phase. Both I, Van Hooeydonk, and foreman Ernie had been emphatic about that.

The rooms were gutted right down to the support studs. They would be completely rebuilt with all-new materials, including soundproofing, thermal windows, electrical wiring, plumbing pipes, and bathroom fixtures. In fact, we would enlarge the bathrooms, making a welcome change from the existing cramped 1950s motel bathroom. In some of the bathrooms, we would install whirlpool tubs which, the Monahans assured us, were in demand by the public, who were willing to pay a higher rate for rooms with them.

There would be a total change to the room decor. The walls would have real knotty pine wood wainscotting from the floor to waist-height. Drywall covered with restful wallpaper would complete the rest of the walls. The ratty old carpeting was ripped out, to be replaced by new broadloom.

The renovations would not stop with the rooms themselves.

All the old tired 50s-era furniture was carted out and donated to local charities. We'd be putting in all-new quality furniture, including large flat-screen TVs with remotes.

We would even have wireless Internet installed in each room, plus a new phone system with voice mail and data ports. This would make us more attractive to commercial travellers, though I suspected our main target market – families – would really appreciate the high-tech stuff too. Especially the kids! (We'd heard a number of youthful wails during the summer: "Aw geez! No internet here!")

All this was quite expensive, of course, which was why we'd arranged for that hefty loan last week. But it would certainly pay off in increased occupancy and a better class of clientele – and the ability to charge higher rates.

While Pete was happily trashing rooms, and collecting a host of new cuts and bruises, I was pouring over catalogues to select fixtures, wallpaper, ceramic tiles for the bathrooms, new furniture, carpet, and much more. I asked Angie for her input, and she provided suggestions about materials that would be easier to keep clean.

* * * * * * *

Wednesday morning, as I was driving back from the decorating store with more catalogues, I noticed the reader boards of two neighbouring inns.

The inn run by the Eastern European couple had a sign boasting: MICROWAVES IN EVERY ROOM.

Graham and Pat Sparrow's place sported a sign announcing: ENJOY OUR NEW BACKYARD ROCK GARDEN WATERFALL.

My God! The Windsong Inn had inspired an entire row of copycats!

When I returned and told Pete, he grimaced through the dust caking his face, then barked a short laugh. "Well, they'll have a ways to go to copy us on THIS project!"

We returned to our tasks with renewed energy.

Then, on Thursday afternoon, I got The Call.

It was Cathy, the loans manager from our bank. Our loan application had been denied by their Toronto head office.

"But, but that's impossible!" I blurted over the phone. "We've signed a contract with a construction company – hell, we've already started gutting rooms! All the furniture in those rooms is gone! You said approval would be just a formality!"

"Yes, that's what I said," replied Cathy with a heavy sigh. "But I was overruled by the Bay Street Boys in Toronto. And my God, Ellen! You should never have started the project until the loan was official!"

Within 15 minutes, I was in Cathy's office. I had not told Pete; besides being buried under several layers of plaster dust, he was armed with hammer and crowbar.

Cathy was very apologetic. She said that the reason our loan was turned down had nothing to do with us or our project. The bank had a strict quota of various business sectors that it granted loans to; our sector – tourism – had reached its quota for this year. Cathy admitted that tourism had one of the bank's smallest quotas; all financial institutions wanted to limit their exposure to tourism businesses, because so many motels, hotels and resorts had gone bankrupt in the last recession.

"Well, you certainly didn't tell us all this when we came in last week!" I said. "You said we had a great project and that we'd get the money."

"Yes and I still feel you have a great project. I honestly didn't know that our tourism quota for the year had already been reached. The e-mail alerting me to that, never made it to my computer. Ellen, I feel so horrible about this, but there's really nothing I can do. My hands are tied."

"Well, I feel horrible too, but unlike you, it's OUR livelihood that's on the line here! Pete and I are really out on a limb now – we've got a signed contract and a crew on site and roofers coming next week – and you guys can't help us just because of some stupid bean-counter's QUOTA!"

"Now Ellen, please understand the bank has an obligation to its shareholders. We can't over-extend ourselves in any one sector."

"Oh PLEASE! Excuse me, but the bank also has an obligation to its customers! Without customers, there'd be nothing for your precious shareholders to buy stock in! You've got all our business and personal banking. It's painfully obvious that doesn't count for much at your head office!"

I stormed out and drove back to the Windsong in a state of shock.

As I approached our property, the sight of its sparkling new exterior brought a sob to my lips. It looked so different compared to when we first arrived! We'd already done so much to it. And we'd sunk everything we had into it, including our entire retirement fund.

Then I set my jaw. I would not – could not – give up now. There were other banks.

I went to our office and dug out that much-praised business plan I'd created. I fired up our computer and printed off three copies, each with the name of a different bank on the cover. Then I hit the phone and made appointments with the loans manager of each, for tomorrow.

By the time I'd done all that, it was suppertime. Pete clomped into the apartment, shed layers of dusty clothing like a snake squirming out of too-tight skin, and took a long shower. I wished it lasted longer. Because when he emerged, I told him the news.

As I expected, he was furious. It helped that I'd made those appointments for tomorrow, but Pete still spent the entire evening raging against Cathy and her bank. I didn't blame him.

There was a further worry: We had been required to pay a substantial deposit when we signed the contract with Van Hooydonk last week. With our reserve fund exhausted, we used this month's mortgage money, and the GST and PST funds we had put aside to remit to the governments at the end of this quarter, plus any other cash we could scrape together. Even the money to pay Angie next week. We had figured there wouldn't be a problem replacing this money, because we expected our loan to be in place within a week.

If we didn't secure a new loan soon, we'd have no money to pay our mortgage to Sarge this month, not to mention our other bills! And we'd just cut our cash flow in half, by taking half our rooms off-line.

We passed a mostly sleepless night.

* * * * * * *

On Friday, Pete and I met with the loans officers of the three other banks. This time, before we wasted any time presenting our business plan and filling out reams of forms, I first asked the key question:

"Has your bank reached its quota for tourism loans yet?"

The answer was "yes" at every bank. None of them could loan us a cent, no matter how solid our proposal was. All because we were a tourism business. In fact, one surly manager asked us what kind of business we operated as soon as we sat down. When we told him it was an inn, he promptly showed us the door!

In early afternoon, dejected and demoralized, we drove to Van Hooydonk's office. He was in and we told him of our financial difficulties.

"We just wanted to be up front with you, Hermann," Pete said. "We'll get the loan, I'm sure of that, but it'll take a little while. We won't have the money to pay you in regular installments until then."

Van Hooydonk looked at us a long time, then leaned to one side and drooled spit onto a potted plant next to him. (The thing looked well-watered.) He cleared his throat and said:

"Huh. Well folks, I thought your loan was a done deal, that you were signed and sealed on the dotted line."

"Yeah, so did we, Hermann," I said.

"Huh. Well, I really can't continue until I'm sure you can pay me and my crew. They're expensive, and I ain't got deep pockets to pay 'em if you can't. I appreciate you bein' honest with me about your money problems, though."

"But surely that large deposit we paid covers us for a while?" Pete asked.

"Oh, the deposit ain't for that. It's to tell me you're serious about this job, and to protect me from breach of contract if you suddenly decide to cancel. It's held in trust by my lawyer; I can't use it to pay my crew."

When we returned to the inn at 2:30 pm, Ernie and his workers had already packed up their tools and left.

Pete hardly spoke for the rest of the day – a dangerous sign.

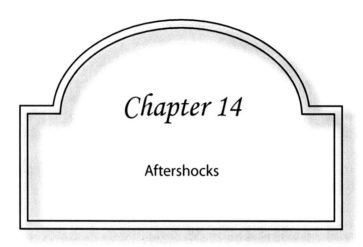

Chapter 14

Aftershocks

Dear Diary:

Yes, I know it's been a little while since I've written. Three weeks, in fact. So sue me. It's been a helluva three weeks.

During the first week following that shocking 13th week, when our "sure-thing" loan was denied, we made the rounds of every single financial institution in Wackimac. And some that weren't in Wackimac – we accessed banks over the Internet and even went to Toronto to see others. But the results were all the same.

No one would lend us the money.

It didn't matter how thorough our business plan was, or how promising our renovations were, or how much equity we had in the place, or how good our cash flow was, or how our personal credit history was spotless. We were a tourism business, and the small quota open to tourism businesses was full for this year. "Sorry. Try us again next year."

Thanks a lot. We couldn't wait until next year. Half our rooms were ripped apart and our roof leaked like a colander.

Some of the banks added insult to injury by insisting we provide a "professional" business plan, done by an expensive consultant, as part of our loan request. The consultant must be chosen from a list pre-approved by the bank. I thought that stipulation was outrageous. No one knew our business better than we did, and many loans officers told me my business plan was as good as any done by a pro. And so it should be; I'd crafted it using guidelines published by the Canadian Bankers Association.

Anyway, we didn't have to meet their demand for a consultant's business plan; when I asked that key question about their tourism quota, they'd already reached theirs.

So we were not only up a creek without a paddle, but somebody had sunk our canoe too. We were operating at half cash flow. Our contractor refused to start work again until we could prove we had the funds to pay him.

As that 14th week dragged on, as we went through rejection after rejection, Pete became more and more depressed. Each door that banged shut in our face sucked another piece of enthusiasm out of him. Me, I refused to give up. As long as there were financial institutions with doors to knock on, I was there knocking.

* ** *** ** *

During the following week, after I'd gone through the last of the major banks and those few trust companies that were still around, I started on the second-stringers: credit unions, mortgage brokers, venture capitalists. The size of our loan was too rich for the small credit unions, and the interest demanded by the mortgage brokers was too rich for us. None of the venture capitalists were interested in a tired old unbranded inn on the outskirts of Boondocks, Ontario.

By the end of that second week, Pete had become quite withdrawn. He was convinced that we were just steps away from ruin (he might be right about that!), and there was nothing we could do about it. His one or two beers during the evening became four or five.

The one piece of good news was that we had succeeded in getting this month's mortgage payment to Sarge deferred. I really didn't think he'd do it, considering my practical joke when he last visited us. But "for my son's sake", he agreed.

That mortgage deferral really helped our cash flow. Even Angie helped. When she heard how we'd used all our money for the construction deposit, she said we could pay her next month for what we owed her. Bless her!

We told our kids about what had happened to us. Well, at least I did. Pete was too embarrassed to talk about it with them. Dawn and Clint's concern was evident over the phone. Both offered to lend us money, but Pete would have none of it.

"There's no way we're borrowing money from our kids!" he stormed. "It's supposed to be the other way around, dammit!"

Dawn, our sharp lawyer daughter, offered to help us sue Cathy and her bank for misrepresentation and incompetence. I said no; it'd been an honest mistake and we shared part of the blame, by starting the project before funding had been assured.

Clint, our non-conformist son, had made over a million dollars as a software designer before cashing out and buying a huge sailboat to cruise the world with his lady. He offered to hack into the bank's computers and cause havoc.

"No," I said. "We Tomlinsons don't work that way."

"Well, can I at least frag their web site, or tie it up so badly that no one else can use it for days?" he pleaded over the satellite phone link between his yacht and Wackimac.

"No."

"Aw, c'mon, Mom. How about I start nasty rumours in blogs visited by stockbrokers, about the bank's bad loans to Third World countries, so their stock'll plummet?"

"No!"

"Create a nasty virus to eat up their credit card client files?"

"NO!"

"O-kay, muh-ther."

* * * * * * *

This past week, the third since the disaster and week 16 in our new life as innkeepers, we rented enough rooms to make ends meet – barely. There was a big convention in town, and if we'd had all 23 rooms available, we could have rented every one for four straight days. But we didn't have 23 rooms. Still, we made enough to at least pay Angie, and I was glad for that.

Luckily for our nerves, we had no major incidents during these past three weeks. There was one person who went temporarily blind when he passed our large NO PETS sign in our front office window, and tried to check-in with a dog.

Dog? The beast was large enough to throw a saddle on it. I sent him and his hairy pony packing.

A cheque arrived in the mail from the husband of Nora Latimer, that lady I had evicted a month ago. It paid for the three weeks we were owed, and came with a nasty note about how cold and mean I was. If I wasn't already feeling down about our financial situation, that would have made me feel miserable.

I called the Sparrows, to see if they had any leads or advice about bank loans. But they couldn't suggest anything that I hadn't already tried. I contacted Lodging Ontario, and they suggested one avenue that I'd never thought of: the federal government's Canadian Business Development Bank, or CBDB for short. It was considered the "bank of last resort". We certainly fit that criteria.

I tried to get an appointment all week with our local CBDB branch, but I only got voice-mail. No one returned my messages. Finally, I showed up in person, was forced to fill out 15 yards of paperwork, then was kept waiting for over an hour before being permitted to see a bored-looking loans officer.

My spirits soared when the sleepy-eyed functionary drawled that the CBDB still had openings in its quota to lend to tourism businesses. In fact, since tourism was a special interest of the Prime Minister, they had a separate half-billion dollar fund just for tourism projects. God bless our Prime Minister!

Then the bureaucrat yawned and said the fund was for major projects of five million dollars and up, preferably to construct new resorts and hotels in rural areas. Our project was too small.

Pete swore mightily when he heard this news, cracked open another beer, and almost drained it in one swig. Then he said:

"I've got some bad news of my own, El. My dad called today. He says we should cut our losses and sell the place."

"What?" I said. "No way! Certainly not!"

"We don't really have a choice." Pete drained his bottle. "Ellen, he wants his share of the motel investment back. And you know how big a share that is."

My world started spinning. I sat down. Hard. That was because there was no chair behind me, so my butt crashed to the floor. I hardly felt it.

"He ... he can't DO that, Pete! He just loaned us the money four months ago! He can't want it back so soon! Our agreement was five years – we'd pay him back over five years! That's what the mortgage papers state!"

"Well, he wants it now. There's a clause in our agreement that says he can do that."

"But ... but WHY? It's not retaliation for my ghost prank several weeks ago, is it?"

"No, honey, it's not that. He feels we've made a bad mistake and he wants his money back." Pete opened another brew, took a long drink, and continued: "Y'know, El, maybe Pop's right about selling. I mean, look at us. We've worked ourselves ragged for four months, sunk everything we had into this place, and look where we are today. We've got half our rooms ripped to hell, and no one'll lend us a penny!

"And what kind of a life IS this, anyway? Look what we've been through since we arrived here. The pain, the worry, the stress – not a week's gone by without some incident to bedevil us! And we're on call 24/7 – we live right behind the front desk and that gives us the honour of being disturbed at any hour of the day or night, seven days a week! We're slaves to this place, El! SLAVES! None of this is what we expected!"

"No, Peter, it's not. But we've never run from anything in our lives. Why start now?"

"Because we've never had a life like this! It's inhuman! And some of those people we've encountered!"

"Pete, you're just dwelling on the bad ones. We've met far more nice folks than nasty ones. Remember all the compliments we get, the cards and letters we've received, even that gift? And isn't it exciting to meet people from all over Canada, the States, and even the world, who have been our guests? I know we're always on call here, but that's what lets us provide the level of personal service that gets us those compliments. Admit it, doesn't it give you a real good feeling to serve the public?"

Pete took another long pull from the bottle, finishing it. He glared at me.

"No, Ellen, it doesn't. I just don't feel the same way you do about all this anymore. I see everything that's gone wrong, all the disasters, and I'm scared to think what new trials and horrors await us if we continue with this insane business venture! We should have done what Clint did – buy a boat and sail away!"

"But Peter –"

"No buts, El! Pop wants his money back, we have no funds left, no one'll lend us a cent, half our rooms can't be rented – we're finished here! I mean, not only can't we get money to do our renovations, but now we have to find money to buy my dad out! There's no way! Wake up and smell the coffee, woman! We've hit rock bottom! We're finished!"

He stomped out of the apartment. I felt tears welling up, but stubbornly blinked them away. Sarge had just kicked us hard while we were down, and that had been the last straw for Pete.

NOW what would happen to our little enterprise? United, Pete and I have always been able to face anything. But divided? I couldn't carry this burden on my own.

I went out to our back lawn and sat beneath a stately maple, whose leaves were blazing yellow and red. I hardly noticed the brilliant canopy. Angie found me there, an hour later.

"Here, Miz. Ellen. Looks like yous kin use it," she said and gave me one of my own Comfort Bears. I looked at its medallion; it was Strength.

"Why ... why thank you, Angie. Thank you very much." I suddenly felt like crying again. But crying wouldn't solve anything.

I just have to keep fighting, that's all, **_Diary_**. Pete may have given up, but not me. Not yet.

A new week starts soon. There's gotta be an answer out there somewhere.

Right?

Chapter 15

Never Say Die

Dear Diary:

Yeah, it's been awhile again. A whole month, this time. But what a month!

The week following Pete's crash-and-burn in mid-October, I did something I've never done in 21 years of marriage to that man. (No, I didn't shoot him. Couldn't find the bullets for the gun.)

I lied to him.

In view of his unwillingness to carry on, and Sarge's demand for his money, Pete asked me to engage a real estate agent to put the Windsong Inn up for sale. We agreed on a price that reflected the exterior upgrades we'd done and the fact that half our rooms were currently unuseable. Then Pete went back to his moping – and seeing how many beers he could consume before falling down drunk – leaving it up to me to do the necessary.

Except that I did not. Sell? Like hell. There was no way I was throwing in the towel just yet.

And therein was the lie: I told Pete I'd engaged an agent, who said that it'd take several months – at best – to sell the place at the price we wanted. Pete groused, but when he informed Sarge, the old grump seemed satisfied.

"At least you now have a light at the end of the tunnel," Sarge told his son. "You'll be rid of that damn place soon enough, and can get back to a normal life. You're supposed to be semi-retired, y'know. There's always consulting. And that wife of yours can always go back to being a secretary."

When Pete related this conversation to me, I was ... mildly perturbed:

"Tell your dad: thanks. For NOTHING! Did it ever occur to that miserable father of yours that maybe I like this new life, where I can interact with lots more people than if I was stuck in some stuffy office? I'm different from him; I actually LIKE people!"

Pete suddenly remembered a sports event on TV that needed watching.

I threw myself into the task of finding financing with fresh, desperate energy. I figured I only had about a month before Pete found out that I hadn't listed the Windsong. Far as I was concerned, a month's delay in listing the place wouldn't make that much difference – and it just might be enough time for me to pull a rabbit out of a hat.

Except I never trained as a magician.

I revisited all the local banks and tried to get one of them to budge. I discovered that once you've been turned down, it's hard to go back to the same bank. They simply don't want to see you.

But I refused to take "no" for an answer. I flung myself against their wall of indifference for an entire week: pushing, prodding, cajoling, arguing – yes, even begging. I refused to go away.

Nothing worked.

The answer was still "no".

One day during that frustrating week 17, I chanced upon a notice in a bank about a financial seminar coming up in Toronto the following Tuesday, dealing with the availability of commercial loans. Senior loans managers from the head offices of all the major banks were scheduled as panellists. I registered myself for the seminar, being careful not to identify my business type

* * * * * * *

On Friday, as I was walking in downtown Wackimac en route to yet another bank appointment, I passed a couple walking in the opposite direction. The woman stared at me as we passed, and I was just placing her face when a hand grabbed my shoulder from behind. I was roughly spun around and found myself face-to-face with an angry male. Built like a football linebacker, he towered over me. He had an unkempt red beard framing a slash of a mouth, and a dirty ball cap squashed on his head.

"You!" he barked. "D'you know who I am, eh?"

"Hey, hands off! I've no idea who you are! I just recognized that lady; she's Nora Latimer, who stayed at our inn several weeks ago," I said, squirming in his powerful grip.

"Right! And I'm her husband, Frank. And YOU are the little turd what threw my Nora out on the street!"

"Look, mister, you let go of me RIGHT NOW, or I start screaming for a cop! How DARE you manhandle me!"

He released me and I stepped back, readjusting my coat. I looked around. Just my luck, we were the only ones on the sidewalk for at least a block in either direction.

"You've got one helluva nerve treating me like that!" I said.

"Yeah? What about how you treated someone new to your city, eh? Wouldn't even show her a little compassion, a little kindness –"

"Excuse me, fella! Don't talk to me about compassion! I let her stay three weeks without paying, and only asked her to leave when it became obvious she had no prospects of getting any money. I even paid her cab fare to the Y. Neither she nor the police could reach you –"

"Oh yeah, the police," he snarled, and took a step toward me. Involuntarily, I stepped back. "Real nice of you, calling the cops on my poor Nora! Scared her half to death!"

"Oh really? Was that before or after she blew up and swore at me and slammed the door in my face? And what about YOUR responsibility towards your 'poor Nora'? How could you send her half-way across the country with hardly any money?"

"I had to wait until I got paid for that contract I was doing!"

"Well don't put the blame on me! You had not made any arrangements with me, no one could reach you, she had maxed-out credit cards, so I thought she was trying to scam me into letting her stay for free. Then, in the middle of the night, she skips out and I"m left holding the bag for five or six weeks' rent! That's something innkeepers always have to watch out for."

The man took another step towards me and raised his hand as if to slap me. "Don't you dare accuse my Nora of being a scam artist, lady!"

"Well don't you dare accuse me of not being compassionate! And you'd better not touch me again, or you'll find yourself on the ground in considerable pain, mister! I've taken self-defence."

We stared hard at each other, then he blinked, lowered his arm, and backed off. Quickly, I turned on my heel and walked away, wincing as he shouted vile words after me.

Creep!

Nora The Mouse had said nothing throughout the entire incident.

That encounter really rattled me. Several blocks away, when I was sure I wasn't being followed, I went into a café, sat down, and ordered a large tea.

Like I needed that little scene, on top of all the other stress I was going through right now! And after me feeling so crummy about having to evict her, too!

I hoped Frank wouldn't come out to the inn to continue the discussion. It would be a real horror show when he ran into my man, likely well-lubricated by Molson's finest.

As I nursed my tea and calmed down, doubts assailed me. Was Pete right? Did the few jerks like the Latimers outweigh all the nice folks? Should we just cut our losses and sell?

No, I decided. No, no, no. I'll not go down THAT road; I'll run into my husband.

* * * * * * *

Speaking about jerks, I must tell you, **Diary**, that my Pompous Idiot was currently wearing that label. With the apparent end of his dream of operating our own business, he had become a changed man. He had no interest in running the Windsong any longer; he spent his days lying around watching television, or crying in his cups about how unfair life was. In fact, I found him one day in one of the gutted guest rooms, sitting on the floor drunk and sobbing over and over: "The dream is dead, the dream is dead."

His drinking had become much worse. Although we were tight on money, he still scraped up enough to buy beer. Each day, he started drinking earlier and each night he passed out later. Finally, I banished him from our apartment and insisted he stay in Number One. I realized this deprived us of another precious rentable room, but I refused to live with a drunk.

Pete then spent most of his days holed up in that room, watching TV, only emerging to get more beer. Angie and I did our best to avoid him. I certainly had little time for him while he was in this state; the operation of the inn was now solely on my shoulders (perhaps it was a blessing that we only had 10 rooms for rent), plus the many hours I spent trying to find financing

* * * * * *
** ** ** ** **

The following Tuesday found me in Toronto at that financial seminar, wearing my best business outfit. (Angie covered the front desk while I was away.) The speakers, mostly bank vice-presidents and senior managers, outlined financial programs and loans that were available to commercial businesses.

Government officials were there too, including the federal Cabinet Minister responsible for small business. The bankers boasted of the high percentage of their recent loans that went to "small business", an area the federal government had identified as needing more financial assistance. The Minister and her bureaucrats nodded approvingly. Bobbleheads.

They were all SO smug.

During a question period, I asked the panellists to describe what types of small businesses they were lending to. Their reply covered a range of enterprises, mostly in the high-tech and life sciences fields, though some were light manufacturing and retail.

But no tourism businesses.

When we broke for lunch, I made sure I sat beside John Oliver, a senior loans manager from the head office of the same bank that had been the first to reject our loan request.

John didn't look like any cliche of a banker. Tall, tanned and looking very fit, he had an easy smile and friendly manner. His brown hair was carefully styled, and his suit impeccably tailored. But his eyes were piercing; they seemed to look right through you. I suspected that behind his sociable demeanor, was a sharp no-nonsense brain.

Revealing exactly what kind of business I ran, I poured out my frustrations to him. I said that I'd been dealing with his bank all my life; I was so brand-loyal that we had chosen his bank when we bought our inn. I lamented it was too bad that my loyalty wasn't returned in kind.

I went into the details of our business plan, our favourable prospects once we got the place renovated, all the exterior work we'd already done, how we'd sunk everything we owned into the place, and how we'd run into a brick wall just because of a stupid quota.

By dessert, the poor man had received quite an earful from me. He had also received a copy of my business plan, which I insisted on giving him.

"Well, Mrs. Tomlinson," John said. "You've certainly made one thing very clear: how passionate you are about your business. You believe in it 100% and that counts for a lot."

"So you'll at least review our business plan?"

"Yes, I promise. I've an hour before I'm scheduled to speak again, so I'll do it now."

At the end of the afternoon, as the seminar was wrapping up, I buttonholed John Oliver again.

"Well? What did you think about our plan?" I asked.

He looked at me with those laser-beam eyes, then looked away.

"Ah ... it's a very good plan, Mrs. Tomlinson. Excellent, in fact. But as you already know ... um, I'm afraid that we've reached our –"

"No! Don't say a word about your tourism quota. Not until you've seen our place. You've read our plan, you know about our prospects, now you must come out and see our place for yourself!"

"Oh no, Mrs. Tomlinson. I simply couldn't –"

"Couldn't what? Have a legitimate excuse to get out of your downtown high-rise Toronto office for a day and drive through some of Ontario's most beautiful countryside? Walk around a unique hospitality business located on just about the prettiest site you'll ever see? Inspect the potential of this business for yourself? Oh please, Mr. Oliver, I'm sure that you meant to say you could."

He smiled. "You've got quite a fire in your eyes when you speak of this Windsong Inn, you know. Yes, I'll come up next week. But I make you no promises. I'm just coming to have a look."

"That's all I ask."

** ** ** ** **

Three nights later, it was Hallowe'en. Not being in a residential area, we didn't get many trick-or-treaters; just a few kids from the neighbouring inns. By 7:00, it was all over. I was very disappointed. When we lived at our condo in Toronto, answering the door on Hallowe'en had been one of my favourite events. I missed seeing hordes of kids in costume.

Then I had an inspiration. Hallowe'en. All Hallows Eve. Walpurgis Night. According to ancient myth, the time when ghosts and goblins could manifest themselves and roam the earth freely.

Hmmm. What about ghosts that were already here? What would this National Spook Holiday do for them?

I made myself a big mug of tea and went into Number 11.

I felt positively mischievous.

Actually, I really needed to talk to someone. Pete was in a drunken stupor again, Madeline was in Arizona, Angie and the Sparrows had their own families tonight, and I'd not made any other new friends around here, yet. My old friends in Toronto were too far away to visit on impulse.

So that left Brenda Ames.

I only switched on one light, a small corner lamp. I left the rest of the room dark. I made myself comfy in the easy chair and started talking. About everything that had happened over the past several months. About how I felt, and how Pete had fallen apart. I just went on and on.

Eventually, I ran out of things to say and stopped. The room was silent. Nothing moved.

Then I said: "Y'know, Brenda, this IS Hallowe'en. Doesn't that give you special powers, like making you stronger, or something? Well, it's just occurred to me that I've been here almost six months and I've never seen you. Oh, I've seen you move things, but I haven't seen YOU. So I was wondering, it being Hallowe'en and all, could you ... ah, make yourself appear? I'd really like to see who I've been talking to all these months. I think of you as a friend now. So c'mon – show yourself, lady."

No mournful dirge of wind. No eerie howl of wolf. No creaks, moans or wails. And the room stayed warm.

"Please?"

Nothing.

"Oh! Wait! You're probably totally gross or something, what with that shotgun blast that killed you, and I'd have nightmares for the rest of my life if I saw you, right?"

Nothing.

Boy, was I feeling foolish again. Then I had a thought: Maybe she wasn't even here. Perhaps if there really were special powers granted by this night, it enabled Brenda to leave the room and roam around, maybe to visit childhood places or family members or her old boyfriend. If so, I couldn't blame her, what with her being cooped up in here the rest of the year.

Good grief: I'm applying logic to supernatural stuff! Maybe, with all the stress, I'm losing it, like Pete. Still, it did me good to talk about my problems out loud.

Back in our apartment, as I was dropping off to sleep, a random thought flitted across my brain: Maybe I should have asked Brenda to appear at the stroke of midnight, the witching hour?

What would have happened then?

* * * * * *
** ** ** ** ** **

The next week, true to his word, John Oliver visited the Windsong Inn. Though it was now early November, and all the leaves had fallen, it was still a beautiful fall day with blue sky and bright sunshine. The mighty Woebegone River had even reappeared, thanks to all the rain we'd had in October. It provided a sparkling border to our back yard.

I made excuses for Pete's absence, saying he was off on his Sanity Day, which I then had to explain. (Actually, Pete was on site, holed up in Number One as usual. But I didn't want him around while I was showing John the property. If Pete noticed me and John walking around, I'd tell him later that it was a prospective buyer.)

I gave John the grand tour, emphasising our exterior improvements. As the real estate agents say, the outside of our property "showed very well." (Well, except for the roof.) The fresh paint job gleamed in the sunlight and we were still the only inn along this "strip" with paved parking.

John was quite impressed with the size of our acreage, remarking that it was much bigger than a typical motel lot, where there is usually just enough room for the building and parking.

"You've got huge lawns all around your building. Looks very inviting; must be wonderful in summer. And gives you lots of room for future expansion," he said with a twinkle in his eye.

"Oh PLEASE! Let us just get through upgrading what we already have, first!" I replied with a laugh.

Then I showed him the interior, including the gutted rooms. "You see, we're going to be rebuilding from the studs out with all new materials and fixtures and furniture. This will become a brand-new, thoroughly modern inn when we're done."

He nodded, but said nothing.

Then I drove him up and down the "strip", showing him our neighbour inns. This let him see how unique our site was compared to our competitors. I said:

"Now just imagine the edge we'll have once our renovations are complete. Our occupancy will be much higher than our competition, because we'll be the nicest inn on this side of town."

Finally, over tea in our small living room, I reviewed highlights of our business plan, showing how the increased occupancy resulting from the renovations would be more than sufficient to cover the loan payments.

"So now you see why I'm so passionate about this place," I finished. "We see its potential and we have a vision about what it can become. All my husband and I need now is for someone to believe in that vision."

John sipped at his tea for several long minutes. I felt like I'd burst with the suspense! Then he cleared his throat. (I thought: *Oh no, please no! Not another refusal!*)

"Mrs. Tomlinson – Ellen – you've convinced me. My bank should be a part of your vision. I'm going back to head office today and schedule a meeting with my superior. I'm making no promises, but I'll go to bat for you and see if I can convince her to make an exception to our tourism quota. This Windsong Inn – love that name by the way – deserves to grow."

I was speechless (unusual for me!). John rose to leave. I snapped out of my shock, and pumped his hand furiously, thanking him for his support.

As I opened our hall closet to get his coat, he noticed the row of Comfort Bears peering down from the top shelf.

"Bear collector, are you?" he asked with a grin, shrugging into his coat.

"Not at all; they're for our guests," I replied. He looked at me with surprise, so I told him all about the Comfort Bears.

When I had finished, John whistled softly and said:

"What a kind thing to do, Ellen. I've never heard of that being done by any motel – or hotel, for that matter. You know, it's said small motels take on the personality of their owners. Well, I haven't met your husband yet, but you're a remarkable woman, and this place reflects a lot of you."

He left, promising to get back to me soon with the result of his meeting with his superior. I felt like doing a jig, but made myself a cuppa instead. I didn't want to jinx the deal.

* * * * * *
** ** ** ** ** **

The following week (this would be just days ago, as I write this), John did not call me.

He did something better. He came in person, with Cathy from our local branch in tow. Their eyes were shining, and Cathy was grinning like a cat left alone with a room full of uncaged budgies.

I couldn't contain myself and blurted out: "We got the loan?"

"Yes," John replied. "Actually, YOU got the loan. It was your drive, your passion, that won the day. I was really impressed with your commitment."

"Mr. Oliver is being modest here," said Cathy. "I heard that he really worked hard convincing the vice-president to relax our quota just for your project. But I'm so happy for you! I always said it was a great project."

Then John delivered his other bombshell: "In fact, Ellen, we're prepared to loan you more than you were asking for, in case you want to expand your business now by adding more units – say another ten? Your business plan shows your cash flow can cover the increased payments, and shows how consumer traffic will support a bigger inn on this side of town. And you do talk about expansion in the future projection section of your plan."

I was overwhelmed. Two shocks at once! Then I remembered Sarge.

"Why, thank you for that offer. I'll take you up on it, but instead of expanding, I'll use the extra money to buy out a major shareholder: my father-in-law. Then my husband and I will be sole owners – and we'll be free of any outside interference! Well, apart from you guys."

The bankers nodded. Cathy opened her briefcase and hauled out a huge pile of paper – the loan documents. They reviewed them with me, and noted where Pete and I, as co-owners, had to sign. I said that Pete was away on a Sanity Day again (true this time; the local pub had two-for-one beers today), but that I'd get him to sign tonight, when he returned. I'd deliver the papers to Cathy tomorrow.

After John and Cathy left, this time I DID do a jig. Lots of hooting and cheering, too. Then I ran out, found Angie, gave her a surprise hug, and did an impromptu dance with her too, heedless of the dust cloud it raised. She was so excited about the news that one of her eyebrows rose.

I could hardly wait until Pete returned. Too bad he hadn't taken his cell phone with him. This wonderful news would surely break him out of his blue funk!

I did my front desk work with one eye cocked at our parking lot. When our battered old station wagon finally limped in, I ran out to meet it. I was yelling before Pete even parked it.

"WE GOT OUR LOAN! WE GOT OUR LOAN!"

Pete got out of the car and used the male animal's time-honoured expression of instant comprehension:

"Wha – ?"

"Our bank loan, ya big goof! I got approval for our bank loan!"

"Wha – ?"

I babbled out the whole story of the seminar and John Oliver, and finished by saying: "Isn't that GREAT, honey?"

Pete gave me a long look. "But we got this place listed for sale. What about that?"

So I had to tell him about my little lie, that I'd never really listed with an agent.

"It's because I truly believed that we could find a solution if we just kept at it," I said at the end.

A great hurt expression settled on Pete's face.

"You ... you lied to me?" he choked out. He looked so mournful, like Eeyore in *Winnie The Pooh.* All he needed was a little black rain cloud over his head.

"It was for your own good, dear. You weren't thinking straight;

you were too busy drinking and alternating between being angry and being a martyr."

"And we'd get enough money to pay off my dad and do all our renovations?"

"Yes, yes, yes!"

"Huh. Well, bring me the papers and I'll co-sign 'em. Let the farce continue."

Pete didn't hug me. He didn't congratulate me or thank me for all my hard work and perseverance. He didn't even apologize for being a drunken slacker these past several weeks.

He just turned and walked off to his room, closing the door behind him.

I couldn't believe it. What a JERK. Sometimes, I just can't figure men out! I said as much to Angie the next day.

She nodded agreement, then said:

"Y'know they has this course at th' farm college called Animal Husbandry? Well, I's always thought it should be about what us wimen has ta learn so's we kin manage our husbands."

"Hah! Too true! You're a wise lady, Angie."

"A-yep."

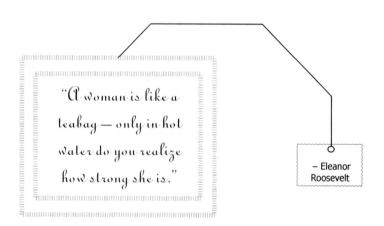

"A woman is like a teabag — only in hot water do you realize how strong she is."

– Eleanor Roosevelt

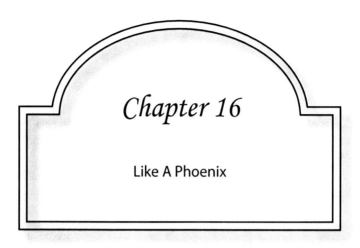

Chapter 16

Like A Phoenix

Dear Diary:

Well, it's now the end of January, two and a half months since my last entry. But things have been so hectic, it only seems like last week. Life in the fast lane. Anyway, I'll try to catch up.

The day after our bank loan was signed, I visited Van Hooydonk Construction, to get our massive renovation project rolling again. Satisfied that we now had sufficient funding, Hermann reinstated us on his schedule. Foreman Ernie and his crew were back at our inn two weeks later, at the end of November, as soon as they had finished another job.

The air sang again with the whine of power tools, the pounding of hammers, and the shouts and guffaws of workmen (and workwomen – Ernie had two). They were great sounds, and I found them stimulating.

Unfortunately, Pete did not. He and his blue funk stayed in his room. I was totally mystified. Not even the opportunity of doing more demolition attracted him. And he had been so excited tearing rooms apart before.

One day, I couldn't stand it any longer. I marched into Number One and said:

"C'mon, Pete! Enough of this sulking and drinking! Stuff the self-pity! We've got the money, we're back on track, we're building our dream, and Ernie says he misses – as he puts it – 'the best damn room wrecker I've ever seen'.

"And I could certainly use your help around here, honey. I'm doing everything – yet we're supposed to be a team!"

Pete turned his head away from the TV and looked at me. "You got us the money, Ellen. You have the drive to continue with this farce. I don't. I thought we had decided to sell and that's what I came to accept. Now we're not selling, but getting deeper into hock.

"Well, I'm not a yo-yo. I'm not getting sucked into another set of false hopes. I just know that something bad is gonna happen again, that'll wreck our plans once more. I'm just gonna sit here and wait for it. Then you'll see that you should have listened to me; that we should have cut our losses and sold, just like my dad recommended."

His sermon finished, Pete returned to watching the exhilarating sport of grown men harassing a tiny white ball.

I couldn't believe my ears. What a miserable, pouty little BOY!

I thought of another use for a golf club. But this place had already seen one murder.

* * * * * * *

The first week of December, our long-delayed new roof was installed. Thankfully, we had sunny days with no rain or snow, and the roofers made great progress. We'd have no further use for those dozens of pails!

Meanwhile, the construction crew soon completed the gutting of rooms 12 to 24. Then Team Van Hooydonk started on the re-building. They were like an army of worker ants swarming all over the place: hammering, drilling, cutting, welding and swearing (at times). They worked FAST. Every time I checked the rooms, another part had been rebuilt.

All of this construction cacophony took place during the weekdays, so it did not disturb our overnight and weekend guests in Numbers Two to Eleven. Which was good, because we needed the cash flow those ten rooms generated.

I was so busy during those weeks! Not only did I have to

supervise the construction and run our half-an-inn, but I had to specify the materials for the rebuilding, plus select and purchase the new fixtures and furniture. Every night, I fell into bed exhausted. But every morning, I was up bright and early. With a good breakfast in me (pear slices smothered in molasses, on toast) and a happy thought, I was ready to tackle another long day.

Since I was running the place by myself, I closed it at 10:00 each night. As an early-riser, I simply couldn't stay awake any longer than that. I turned out the office lights and our roadside sign, and put our FULL HOUSE placard in the window, so I (hopefully) wouldn't be awakened by late-night door-pounding.

I realized after several weeks, that I avoided a lot of troublesome clientele by closing early like that. Going back over our records, I discovered that many of our problem incidents came from guests who had checked-in very late. I didn't have nearly as much hassles from folks that checked-in at a decent hour.

Live and learn.

During that hectic time, I failed to notice that the number of guests related to patients at the Regional Health Centre had sharply increased. It only hit me when I realized that our four Comfort Bears were always in use. One day, the reason for this increased occupancy revealed itself.

"I'm pleased to discover that this place is every bit as nice as that article said," announced a man on check-out. "And these bears of yours are really helpful. The one you loaned us certainly got its share of hugs from my wife and daughters; we were so worried about Grandpa's operation. It's so nice of you to think of us this way."

"Why, thank you," I replied. "Hold on – what article now?"

"You didn't know? There was a write-up about you in that magazine three or four weeks ago. Lorraine Sulieman's column."

A light bulb in my brain clicked on. THAT'S where I'd seen her face! The woman who had stayed with us during Week 12 – she was a regular columnist for Canada's national weekly newsmagazine! Her photo was always at the top of her articles.

I went into our living room and gingerly sifted through the

towering piles of books and magazines on the small table, until I found it. My gosh! Lorraine had written an entire column about her husband's heart operation – and there were two paragraphs about the Windsong Inn and our Comfort Bears! Nation-wide publicity!

Wow!

I ran into Pete's room, waving the magazine.

He didn't share my excitement. He continued sucking on his beer and watching the serious sport of greased-up men in outrageous costumes supposedly pummelling each other into submission.

Hurt, I left, thinking darkly about how a small bomb could fit under his easy chair. That would get him moving again.

While on the topic of miserable grumps, I took great satisfaction in sending a certified cheque by courier to Sarge, paying him back in full, with interest, for his investment in the inn. He was stunned to get it, knowing that we had not sold the place yet. He called his son, and after Pete told him of my accomplishment with the bank and refusal to list with a real estate agent, the two of them commiserated about headstrong women who would not follow orders.

Poor babies.

Deal with it.

I sent Lorraine Sulieman a nice letter, thanking her for mentioning the Windsong in her article.

Not only did Lorraine's article result in increased occupancy, but it got us some local publicity too.

A reporter from the *Wackimac Expositor & Farmers' Chronicle* showed up unannounced several days after I had discovered the article, and interviewed me for the paper. (Of course, the Pompous Idiot refused to participate.) Though she focussed mostly on the Comfort Bears and our relationship with the Health Centre, I took the opportunity to talk about all our improvements, including our current interior make-over project.

The resulting article appeared under the headline: CARING INN PROVIDES THE BEAR NECESSITIES. It was on the front page – of Section D: Local News, Farm Auctions and Stud Animals Available/Wanted. Still, the story was well done and showed us in a good light. I hung framed copies of it and the Sulieman article in our lobby.

In the weeks following the *Expositor & Chronicle* story, our occupancy grew even more, because local Wackimac residents started recommending our place to visiting friends and relatives. That was the best kind of advertising: word of mouth.

Every bit helps!

* * * * * *
** ** ** ** **

We received lots of Christmas cards, not just the usual number from family and friends, but many from people who had stayed here since we bought the place in June. What a nice thing to do! I bought several boxes of Christmas cards and made sure every former guest that sent us a card, received one back. I made a note that, for next year, we should get cards specially printed for this place; something unique, perhaps with a sketch or photo. I would send them to all past customers that indicated they might return. I thought it would be a nice gesture – and good marketing!

About three days before Christmas, around 7:30 pm, there was a big commotion in Number Seven. A couple ran out into the freezing night air, coughing and swearing. I saw them through our office window. They looked like someone had attacked them with a spray can of black paint! Their faces and clothes were black, making the white of their eyes and pink of their lips look comical in contrast, like an old-time "blackface" movie.

"What is it? What's wrong?" I asked, running out of our office.

"The room heater just blew up!" exclaimed the man. "There's soot all over!"

I dashed into their room. Ugly black soot was everywhere.

The room's elderly gas heater had chosen this evening to expire. Instead of going quietly into the Great Unknown, it had blown up, spewing a great quantity of soot into the room. Not only were the furniture, drapes, carpet and bed linens covered, but the clothes and possessions of the guests too.

The room would need a complete redecoration. Since it was slated for a total gutting and renovation, it made no sense to redecorate it now. I'd just have to close it off until it was re-built. That meant I was down to only nine rentable units now.

I put the guests in another room (luckily we weren't full that night), and said our insurance would pay for the cleaning or replacement of all their soot-damaged possessions.

What a mess! Thank God we were installing new energy-efficient gas heaters in our renovated rooms.

Our Christmas celebration was very unusual this year. For one thing, Pete and I were not really together. For another, it was our first Christmas at the inn. Tourist traffic was almost non-existent during the holiday season, since most travellers stayed with the family and friends they were visiting. Our place was almost deserted.

I joked to Angie that we had lots of room to put up our own family and friends when they came to visit. So what happened?

Hardly anybody came.

Son Clint, enjoying his first full year living aboard his boat, refused to leave the sunny tropics to celebrate Christmas with us in frozen Canada. I couldn't blame him. I found the older I got, the more the cold affected my bones. Clint invited us to join him on his yacht, but I said we couldn't get away, what with all our construction and tight money.

I didn't tell him the real reason was that his dad had devolved into a drunken jerk.

And this was the year for Dawn, our daughter in Calgary, and her husband, to spend Christmas with his folks in B.C. They alternated between them and us, every year.

Most of our Toronto friends, and our other relatives scattered all over Canada, had their own family commitments.

So: no kids, no relatives, no friends. And us with lots of room to accommodate them!

Actually, I did get one visitor who spent several days at the Windsong: my oldest and dearest girlfriend. We had grown up together and knew each other better than we knew ourselves.

A single mother, Catherine was a big woman with a big laugh and a bigger heart. Her kids were spending Christmas with her Ex, so she trekked from Montreal to Wackimac to see what foolishness her old friend had gotten into.

We passed a wonderful four days together. Catherine was quite impressed with our new enterprise – especially all the work we had put into it.

"Whaddya mean, 'we', Ellen?" she said. "It's YOU. That louse you married is doing bugger-all to help!"

Catherine was a little negative towards men. Nowhere near as bad as Aunt Ginny, but no great fan of them either. Still, in this instance, she had a point.

Pete spent the entire holiday season closeted away in Number One. Wouldn't even come out for my Christmas dinner. Just made himself some sandwiches, and continued drinking beer by the caseload. And this used to be the happiest time of the year for him. That really depressed me; even Christmas couldn't snap him out of the black hole he'd dug for himself.

"So, why don't you just divorce him, El?" asked Catherine suddenly on her last evening with me. "You're doing everything by yourself anyway – it was you that rescued this place – it's you that's keeping it going – so why put up with Mister Moody? In fact, without him, you'd have one more room to rent!"

"Oh no, Cath, I couldn't do that! We've been married 21 years, plus those years we lived together before we got hitched. You don't throw all that away just over a snag like this."

"This ain't no snag, girlfriend. This is a man whose controls are set on self-destruct, and I'm worried he'll take you with him when he blows!" Catherine took a long sip from her wine glass. "How long you gonna put up with him being like this, anyway?"

"I don't know, Cath. I just don't know."

"Humph. Well, enough about that loser. It's Christmas! Lets have some fun, eh? I read in your local rag that tonight is Ladies Night at your one-and-only strip club, and they've brought in those Chippendale studmuffins. In honour of the holidays, they're gonna be wearin' red ribbons – and guess where?

"But first, lets go visit this ghost of yours!"

(No action from Brenda. Lots of action at the strip club. Big hangover and hoarse voice – from cheering and whooping – next morning. Ouch.)

After Catherine had returned to Montreal, I related the conversation to Angie, and finished by asking:

"So, what do you think? Should I divorce Peter? Or at least threaten him with divorce, to shake him out of his mood, his drinking? Or maybe I should just drag him to an AA meeting?"

The Human Dust Mop stopped her cleaning, gave me a look, then cleared her throat. It sounded like an old Chevy backfiring.

"Miz. Ellen, what's happin' to yore man, well, I seed it before. This new life yous chose ain't fer everybody. Take that motel across the street here. Before Patel bought it, th' couple that ran it, well, th' wife had to take on all the responsibilities, 'cause th' husband jest started drinkin' more an' more. Finally, he drank hisself ta death.

"An' before that blind guy Sparrow an' his wife bought the Wackimac Rest Haven, there was a young lady in her early twenties what owned it. Her father had bought it for her. She lasted only two years. Single mom, she had a baby, and couldn't cope with both runnin' th' place an' th' kid. In her final months, she was on tranqs jest ta get through th'day.

"Then I heared of a motel over in Parsimony, th' next town, where th' owners, a German couple, went through a nasty divorce 'cause of the strain of dealin' with the public. Got so bad one day, th' husband punched a hole in th' drywall behind th' front desk with his fist. After they split up, th' guy was left runnin' the place. He became convinced that space aliens were listenin' in on him an' controlin' his life, so he covered th' walls of their apartment and th' lobby in aluminum foil. Guy wuz nuts. Finally, one night, he jest disappeared. Ta this day, no one knows what happened ta him. Mebbe he wuz right about them aliens. His motel's an abandoned derelict now."

These were the most words that I'd ever heard out of Angie

in one shot. I felt a little scared.

"Those ... those are pretty depressing stories, Angie. But lots of people survive and do well in this business. The Sparrows have been at it for 18 years, and look at the Monahans across town; over 25 years and they grew their business from a small motel into a big Best Western."

"A-yep, true. They's two paths ta take. Some folks take one, some th' other."

"So, which path do you think we're on?"

"Well, Miz. Ellen, as I sees it, the Pompous Idiot is well on his way down one path, while yous is on th' other. An' that's the thing, ain't it?"

She stopped and the Chevy backfired again. "Yore question 'bout divorce. Yep, that's pretty drastic, but let's jest say that if yous stay together, I hopes he don' drag yous down with him. Yore one special lady. An' yous can't force him ta clean up his act; he has ta make that decision hisself, in his own time. 'Specially 'bout the booze."

She returned to her cleaning, leaving me with lots to think about.

..*.*.*.*.*

One morning, about a week later, I was walking toward our laundry room when I noticed a man crouching beside his car, wiping the slush and salt off his fancy hubcaps with a cloth. As I passed, I did a double-take. He was using one of my lovely beige face cloths from his room!

"Excuse me, but why are you cleaning your filthy hub caps with one of my face cloths?" I said.

The guest looked up at me and grinned. "Because it does such a GREAT job! Look at the shine!"

"It should do a great job! Those are expensive face cloths! They are not rags meant for cleaning cars! So please stop that, this instant! It will be almost impossible to get that cloth clean, now!"

The guy didn't look very apologetic. "Oh. Huh. I didn't

realize this cloth was all that fancy. Didn't think a little Mom-and-Pop motel would have such nice stuff. Well listen, since the cloth is dirty now anyway, why don't I just finish the rest of my hub caps?"

"Absolutely," I replied, keeping my temper in check. "Tell you what; just keep the cloth. I'll be happy to add the cost of it to your bill."

(**Diary**, I HATE the term: "Mom-and-Pop". It's like our business is second-class, somehow unprofessional. It's so demeaning! Especially now, when it's just Mom!)

After all these months, I've realized that many people treat us small independent innkeepers far different than they would treat a large downtown hotel or a national hotel chain. Many of the incidents we've experienced bear this out. Here's another:

A man came in several days later, and inquired about our rates. We were on our cheaper winter rates, and I said: "$53, including taxes."

"Okay," said he and hauled out a wad of cash. He placed $50 on the counter, and replaced the wad in his jeans.

"It's $53, including all taxes," I reminded him.

"Oh – so you want the three dollars?"

"Yes. It's an excellent rate for the quality of room you're getting."

He gave me the remaining money, in a manner that made me feel so cheap for asking for it. Then he snorted, grabbed his room key, and left.

I bet the desk clerk at the Hilton or Sheraton or even a Best Western, doesn't go through that kind of humiliation.

* * * * * *
** ** ** ** **

Several days later, Angie came up to me with her mouth more down-turned than usual.

"Yore basement, Miz. Ellen. Big problem."

The smell hit me as soon as I opened the door leading to the basement stairs. Raw sewage. I quickly descended the stairs. About three inches of sewage covered the floor!

"Oh, yuck!" I said, and retreated up the stairs. We'd had a problem with our main drain during our second week, but I was too busy rushing Pete to the hospital after his sewage bath, to find out exactly what the plumber had done to fix the problem. I did know that the problem had been localized inside the inn, and he'd been able to fix it in the basement.

I didn't have far to go to find a plumber, this time. Two were on site (a different company than the one I'd called in week two), sub-contracted by Van Hooydonk to install our new bathroom fixtures. The plumbers came running in answer to my shouts.

They sized up the situation. "Your sewer pipe is blocked tight somewhere, likely out under your lawn, ma'am," said one. "Sewage backed-up, and came out through your basement floor drains every time your guests flushed, in their rooms. You'll need a company to auger your main drain."

"But ... but what caused it?" I asked.

"Stuff flushed down that shouldn't be – or roots from one of your trees found their way into your pipe. Maybe both; the roots cause a partial blockage, then when some fathead flushes face cloths or Pampers down, it jams inta the roots and blocks the pipe up tight. Tree roots are amazing, y'know. They can force their way into the tiniest of cracks in a pipe, like where two sections are bolted together. And you must already know that people flush all sorts of things down; I'd wager you're plunging a toilet at least once a week, right?"

I nodded, and went to call the number the plumber gave me. I also called a disaster cleaning company to vacuum up the sewage from our floor, then clean and disinfect the basement. Lastly, I called Dave Matthews, who said our insurance policy covered damages caused by sewer back-ups. Thank God!

Stanislas, the drain auger man, came with a miniature TV camera and spotlight at the head of a long cable. He inserted this into the end of our basement sewer pipe, and sent it along until he found what was blocking it. The plumber had guessed right: It was a combination of tree roots and Pampers, wedged tightly in the pipe under the lawn just outside the inn.

We were lucky the blockage wasn't further along the pipe, otherwise Stan would have to dig up our front lawn to find the clean-out plug, in order to get at what was blocking our pipe. The plug was somewhere between the inn and the city's main sewer line that ran along the highway. I knew that we were responsible for any blockages on our property, before our sewer line joined the city line.

Stan sent in an auger through the end of our pipe in the basement, to chop up the diapers and the roots. But he said it was only a temporary fix; the roots would re-grow. He advised me to have the trees growing next to our sewer line cut down, this spring. Otherwise this problem would recur. If a really bad blockage or major root infestation ever occurred, an entirely new sewer line might have to be put in. He also suggested a sign in each bathroom, advising guests not to flush Pampers down the toilet.

More headaches!

* * * * * * *

But there's good news, too:

Yesterday, rooms 12 to 24 were completed! The crew did a great job!

The rooms look real sharp; completely different from before. For those 12 units, at least, the Windsong is now a brand-new inn, inside and out!

Like a phoenix rising from the ashes, our place is being re-born!

Too bad Pete didn't give a damn.

I bought several bottles of champagne, and four huge cheese-and-cracker platters, and hosted a celebration party for Ernie and his workers in Numbers 23 and 24, which had inter-connecting doors. The construction crew really appreciated the treat.

During the party, Ernie came up to me and confided:

"Y'know, Mrs. T, I usually don't like working for women. Find 'em too difficult to deal with, always changin' their minds. But you're different. It's a real pleasure workin' for you – you think like a man."

I took that as a compliment.

As the party ended, Ernie said they'd be back next Monday, to start the clean-out and gutting of Numbers One to Eleven. (Mental note: Move the drunk from unit one.)

First thing next morning, I put this message up, using both sides of our big reader board:

> COMPLETELY RENOVATED ROOMS.
> WHIRLPOOL SUITES.
> WIRELESS INTERNET. DATA PORTS.
> LARGE SCREEN TVS.
> NEW BEDS & BATHROOMS.

"There!" I muttered. "Match that, you copycat neighbours."

I took pictures of the new rooms, and sent copies to Cathy at our bank and to John Oliver at their head office. With each set of pictures, I sent a flower basket with a card that read: "Thanks for believing in us."

As I was writing those cards, I paused and wondered if I should have written: "Thanks for believing in *me*."

Oh Pete, where IS your head? Pull yourself together! I still love you. Even if you are the world's biggest jerk.

I need you.

Chapter 17

Of Swingers, Hockey Cops, And Giant Mutant Animals

Dear Diary:

Whew! February shot by, and I hardly noticed it. What a busy four weeks!

A promise: If I survive my first year in this new life, I'm treating myself to a nice long vacation. Maybe I'll take Clint up on his offer, and spend time with him and his lady on their boat, cruising the Caribbean.

(*Mental note: Oh yeah? First I have to find a live-in manager to run this place while I'm away!*)

Anyway, our renovated rooms have been very well received by travellers. We were getting compliments before, but nothing compared to what I heard now. Rave reviews about the decor, the new bathrooms, the new furniture – everything!

As planned, I raised our rates for the new rooms, but hardly anybody complained. Even when quoted the much higher rates for those rooms with whirlpool tubs, which I called our Luxury Suites. In fact, those units often rented first. So my business plan was working!

To provide more added value with our higher rates (though the new rooms more than justified the prices), I put in some complimentary amenities: two bottled waters in the mini-fridge, a basket of fruit and chips, and cozy bathrobes in the whirlpool suites. I also subscribed to an in-room movie service, but family-suitable movies only, no porno stuff.

Actually, I did encounter a new wrinkle now that we had two

classes of rooms. One day a guy came in and asked how much a standard room cost. I told him and he seemed satisfied. Then he asked if the room had a whirlpool. When I said no, not for that price, he got quite upset. He argued that the rooms with whirlpools should be the same price as the standard rooms.

"Excuse me," I said, "but upscale suites always cost more, because of the added amenities in them. In our Luxury Suites, you get a two-person whirlpool and two bathrobes."

He groused that was the norm in large hotels, "but not at a Mom-and-Pop place like this."

I bristled at the "Mom-and-Pop" reference. "Well, if you don't like our rates and you want a whirlpool, you can always go across town to the Best Western."

"Oh no! They're much more expensive than you!"

I successfully fought down the urge to clobber him.

* * * * * * *

The Van Hooydonk construction crew went at Numbers One to Ten like politicians after free food at a reception. They gutted them in just two weeks, then immediately started the rebuilding.

What about Number 11, **Diary**? Wasn't that supposed to be re-done too?

Yep. But we ran into a little obstruction.

My first inkling that we had a problem, was when foreman Ernie asked me for the key to Number 11, so his crew could cart out its furniture, as they were doing with rooms One to Ten.

"But all those rooms are open," I said. "I opened them for you this morning."

"Well, guess you missed one, Mrs. T. Door's shut tight."

I went to the door of unit 11 and tried the knob. Locked. I used my master key and tripped the lock. I turned the knob. Door wouldn't budge. I put my shoulder to it. Stayed put.

"Here, lemme at it. With this weather, it's probably warped or frozen stuck," said Ernie and heaved his body against the door. It didn't move an inch. Ernie tried a few more times, then gave up. He hollered down the walkway for Guido and Sam. Two huge men came in answer to his bellow; either one looked like he could stop a charging bull moose with one punch.

After first checking that the knob was still unlocked, Guido and Sam rammed their massive shoulders into the door with all their might. I winced, expecting the wood to shatter into a million toothpick-sized shards.

It didn't budge.

Both men tried again and again, but the results were the same. Finally, they stepped back, wheezing, their breath creating huge clouds in the sub-zero morning air.

Then, with a loud click, the lock engaged again.

"Ah," I said and turned to Ernie with a smile. "I know what it is. Look, just leave this with me for a bit, okay? Carry on with the other rooms for now."

Ernie gave me a funny look, then shrugged and walked off with his men. All three were rubbing their shoulders. As soon as they were gone, I unlocked the knob again. This time the door opened easily and I went in, closing it behind me.

"Brenda, what ARE you doing?" I asked. No reaction. "Look, honey, this is a major project here – we're renovating all the rooms. Everything will be completely new and modern. Your room here will look wonderful when the workers are through. The ones they've done already, look just great!"

The air grew chilly and the bathroom door slammed. If I didn't know better, I'd say she was mad or –

Insight flooded into me.

"Oh! I just realized! Maybe you don't want this room changed! Maybe you like it just the way it is, in this 50s style from when you ... ah ... died."

The bathroom door opened. The air got warmer. So that WAS it. Well, **Diary**, I tried to change her mind. I talked, pleaded, begged, cajoled and threatened. All the tactics I'd used with our local bankers – didn't work any better with Brenda.

In the end, I decided to just leave her alone. I figured that if I forcefully had this room renovated, she'd cause a lot of trouble. And no, I didn't want to have some cleric or shaman exorcise her;

I actually liked our resident spirit.

So the Windsong would have 22 renovated rooms – and one room left in a classic 1950s style. I'd have to be careful how I rented it, since our advertising promised modern units.

Hey! Maybe I'd market it to baby boomers as a theme room, taking them back to when they were teenagers. I recalled reading a Lodging Ontario article about the popularity of themed suites. Yeah, that could work.

I told Ernie to leave Number 11 alone, saying I wanted a classic 50s theme room. He thought I was nuts

* * * * * * *

And what about the drunk in Number One? Well, I told Pete he'd have to relocate, so the room could be redone. I said he could move into one of the new rooms – which I secretly hoped would fire up his pride and maybe break him out of his dark mood. Or, I said he could move back into our apartment with me, as long as he stopped his boozing.

In a cold tone, he said that he would "consider his options."

I walked out silently considering my own options: whether to kick him or brain him with a fry pan.

The next morning, Pete was gone. Really gone: He left the property entirely! He never said a word to me before he went away, nor did he leave a letter behind. He just took off.

I was totally shocked!

I found out a day later that he'd taken a taxi to the bus station and travelled to his father's city, where he'd moved in with Sarge. When I called there, he refused to come to the phone.

"Pete just needs a li'l time to himself," growled Sarge over the phone.

"Really?" I said. "Huh. He's had about four MONTHS to himself already. How much more time does he need?"

"Humph," replied Sarge. "Anyways, I'm sorry that damn motel of yours has wrecked your happy marriage. Shoulda sold it, y'know."

"Sarge, it was always 'this damn motel of OURS.' It's only

recently become 'of yours', unfortunately, and your son's to blame for that."

I hung up.

It hit me that we were now what folks called "separated".

My first - and second and third – impulse was to cry for days. Didn't do it. Wouldn't give Pete the satisfaction. Besides, it wouldn't have solved anything. And what would my guests think, seeing a teary-eyed sniffling woman behind the front desk?

Now I was really all alone.

I hugged a Comfort Bear for hours that night.

* * * * * *
** ** ** ** ** **

A few days later, a middle-aged couple came to the desk. They introduced themselves as Mike and Heather, and asked if we had any interconnecting rooms. I said we currently had two sets with connecting doors. They asked to see one pair, and gushed admiration as I showed them Numbers 23 and 24. They were two of our whirlpool suites. The rooms each had two queen-sized beds, and were larger than our standard rooms. Mike booked them for the upcoming weekend; Heather said it was for a couples reunion.

Come the weekend, I watched as seven late model cars arrived between 7:00 and 8:00 pm, each carrying a man and a woman. Their ages ranged from twenties to sixties. They disappeared into Numbers 23 and 24. Mike and Heather had several big boxes in their car, which they carted into one of the rooms. They also carried in several bags from the liquor store and a large case of beer.

Those were far too many people than the rooms could take for sleeping.

My internal alarm bells rang. I called Mike and Heather's room. Mike answered and I heard soft music and laughter in the background.

"Sorry for disturbing you, but I must ask what is going on," I said.

Mike chuckled. "Oh, it's just our club's little reunion, as I told you earlier this week. Don't you worry; we'll treat your nice new rooms as if we were in our own homes."

"Well, I'm concerned because I saw 14 people troop in there – and just what is in those big boxes of yours?"

"Well, that's hardly any of your concern, I should think."

I was now convinced that something was wrong. "Look, we have a policy that our rooms are for registered guests only. We also charge for extra people in a room, but you have too big a group to sleep in just two rooms. If you're having a party, you should know that we don't tolerate loud parties, in consideration of our other guests. I'm coming over there and you'd better be upfront with me."

"No, no, it's not necessary to come over. Look, I promise you there will be no loud party, and we're not going to damage your rooms."

I heard a female voice near Mike say: "Just tell her. She seems nice; I'm sure she'll understand."

Mike cleared his throat and said: "Okay ... ah, we're a club, as I've said. A swingers' club, okay? We're all consenting adults, and we've been doing this for some time. Each club member hosts the group every second week, at their homes. Sometimes, we meet at a motel or hotel in a different city, so as to ... ah ... not arouse our neighbours' suspicions.

"We're very discreet; we don't want any trouble. We'll be very quiet; you won't hear any loud noise. We promise. And we don't mind paying you for the extra people."

Trying to take this all in, I blurted: "And the big boxes?"

"That's how Heather and I make some extra money. We sell leather outfits and erotic lingerie to club members, plus ... ah ... a selection of sex toys."

That piqued my interest, but I also felt self-conscious. "So, um, this is gonna sound silly, but I have to ask. Um, exactly what do you do during the evening?"

"Oh, don't be shy. We're certainly not! Well, we only allow couples, you understand. We use one room for socializing and dancing. The other is for ... liaisons. We swap partners – and sometimes, if the mood is right, we have a great big orgy."

With a bemused cough, I wished them a pleasant evening.

Wow! What a hold-over from the Sixties! The Age of Aquarius. Peace and love.

Go to it, folks! (I was quite aware that some of us hadn't had sex in over four months.)

Swingers! Here at the Windsong!

Well, at least it wasn't prostitutes.

* * * * * *
** ** ** ** ** **

The following weekend, I allowed a men's hockey team to rent a batch of rooms. Yes, I remembered the awful experience with that hockey team in week 12, and I certainly did not want any of our new rooms damaged. So why did I do it? Because this was a team with a difference.

It was a team of off-duty Ontario Provincial Police.

I figured one couldn't get a safer, more respectable team than that! Besides, the officer who'd booked the rooms several days ago had asked SO nicely, and had been SO cute, in a rugged Sean Connery-as-a-young-man way. (Listen to me! I'm a married lady! Well, technically.)

I got to talking to that officer – Tim was his name – when the team checked-in. Our conversation got around to the swingers' club the previous weekend. (They'd been true to their word; they'd not damaged anything and were quiet as mice.)

"Swingers, eh? Oh, you want to be very careful about letting such things go on here, ma'am," Tim said.

"But why? They were very nice folks," I said, puzzled.

"Well, because swinging is against the law. If the authorities got wind of it, and as far as I'm concerned this conversation never happened, you could be charged with operating a common bawdy house."

"WHAT?!"

"Yes ma'am. The swingers would be charged for what they were doing, and you would be charged for providing the place for them to do it. You'd have to prove that you didn't know what was going on in those rooms – and you just admitted you did know."

"But ... but I didn't know it was illegal!"

Tim grimaced. "Ignorance of the law is no excuse."

I must have had a shocked look on my face, because he suddenly smiled. "Oh, don't worry – we're here to play hockey, not hassle you. Now that you know, just make sure you don't rent to swingers again."

I thanked him for his advice, and he went off with his buddies to chase a hard black rubber disk across some ice and smash people into wooden boards in a sportsmanlike manner.

Talk about a close call! Ignorance may be bliss, but it can also get you thrown in jail!

Speaking about ignorance, I made a big mistake renting to that OPP hockey team.

They won their game, and returned to the Windsong around 10:00 pm in high spirits. Their spirits soared even higher as they proceeded to consume alcohol.

They didn't damage my brand-new rooms – thank God – but they sure were rowdy! I warned them several times to keep it quiet, and each time they solemnly promised they would. But within five minutes, they were louder than ever, and my sleep was interrupted again by my phone ringing, heralding another earful of irate complaints from my other guests.

Even that nice officer, Tim, was no help; he was as rambunctious as his buddies. In fact, it was Tim who led the conga line that paraded through the parking lot. They were so sozzled that they didn't feel the biting wind and 20-below temperature.

I had a dilemma: How can you call the police to quell a disturbance, when it's cops causing that disturbance?

Who polices the police?

Finally, around midnight, in desperation, I called the Wackimac city police. A cruiser arrived within minutes, and its sole occupant eventually convinced his provincial brethren to settle the hell down. They parted on good terms and the local cop drove away. Without his pants.

(In retaliation for disturbing their partying, the rowdies had shucked off the hapless city cop's trousers, "all in good fun". They mailed them back to him the following week, cleaned and pressed.)

The next day, as Angie was cleaning one of the rooms the hockey team had vacated, there was a bloodcurdling shriek. Now remember that Angie is the most taciturn person I've ever met, so I immediately concluded that she'd been mortally wounded.

I dropped what I was doing and ran into Number 17, where I found the Human Dust Mop standing in the center of the room pointing to the floor. She was white as a sheet and shaking.

I looked where she was pointing and saw, sticking out of a tangle of sheets, a human arm on the floor!

"AAH!" I said and jumped back.

"I ... I wuz taking the bed sheets off an' this arm fell out!" Angie blurted, still staring at the appendage.

It occurred to me that if someone had had their arm lopped off last night, there'd be a lot of blood. I didn't see any blood at all.

I gingerly approached the arm and, using my feet, lifted the sheet partially covering it, so that it was fully exposed. It was a human arm, all right, pink and firm. I looked closely at the end, then burst into laughter.

"Angie! It's not real! It's a prosthetic arm, the kind worn by amputees," I gasped.

"What?" said Angie, and came forward for a closer look, still wary, as if she expected it to suddenly grab her ankle. "Huh. Why, so it is. So, um, did yous has an amputated guest las' night who fergot it?"

"No. But we did have a rowdy bunch of OPP cops, who obviously placed it here as a gruesome practical joke!"

I took the arm away and flung it into our Lost & Found box (where, weeks later, it totally freaked out a teenage boy pawing through the box for some lost gloves).

Men!

Several days later, one of my Comfort Bears went missing: Hope.

Over the months since we bought the inn, we'd come to accept a certain amount of theft as the unfortunate cost of doing business. We sometimes had a towel or face cloth stolen (one time, an entire set of towels eloped). We'd charge the cost of these items to the guest's credit card, and mail them their copy of the card slip with an explanatory note. We'd been lucky so far; nothing major like a TV had been stolen, like we heard sometimes happened.

But it saddened me that one of my four bears had been liberated. I felt almost as sad about the theft as I felt about the Pompous Idiot leaving me. The bruins were special – and not cheap, either. Still, I didn't have the heart to charge the guest for Hope. Instead, I re-wrote the parchment note that I put next to each bear when I placed it in a room, to emphasize that they were on loan.

I drove to the Giggling Squirrel, and bought another bear to become the new Hope. On impulse, I purchased two more, since the original four were in constant use. I ordered medallions for the replacement Hope and for the newcomers, naming them Brave and Resolute.

As I write this at the end of February, Team Van Hooydonk have done a month's work on the second batch of rooms. They are on schedule to finish them in another month, the same length of time it took them with the first batch.

Things progress!

* * * * * *
** ** ** ** **

One day, in early afternoon, Angie rushed up to me. I could tell she was agitated about something again: both eyebrows were raised right to her kerchief. (A record! That's twice in one month that the unflappable Angie got flapped.)

"Miz Ellen, ya gots ta come see Number 15. Monstrous beast in there."

"Beast?" I said. "What kind of beast?"

"Something that's very fast and craps pellets all over the

place."

"Craps pellets! In one of my new rooms! That's grounds for bloody murder, by God!"

I rushed to Number 15, Angie close behind. The occupants were gone, so I used my passkey to enter. I gasped in shock.

Large brown pellets were scattered all over the room! On the carpet, the chairs, even the beds! A musty, foul odour filled the air.

"AAAUGH!" I screamed in despair. I walked into the room. Something moved rapidly between the two double beds. I told Angie to close and guard the door.

Cautiously, I approached the far bed, bent down, and slowly peered underneath. A pair of beady little eyes stared back at me!

Suddenly, a large brown shape exploded from beneath the bed and shot between my legs to disappear under the other bed behind me.

"WAAA!" I yelled and jumped straight up.

"Did ... did you see what that was?" I asked Angie, as I backed away from the beds.

"A bit, Miz Ellen. Could be a giant field rat. But I don't knows 'bout wild beasts much; it's my Fred that's th' hunter in our fambly."

"Well, maybe you should go get Fred and his gun," I muttered to myself.

I took Angie's broom, and put it under the bed, moving it in a wide arc. The brown shape exploded outwards again, this time towards the wall. It left a trail of shiny brown pellets as it ran. This time I got a good look at it.

"Rabbit!" I shouted. "Biggest damn rabbit I've ever seen! Huge! That thing's as big as a cocker spaniel!"

"Right fast too," Angie allowed.

"Well, I've got to catch it. We can't leave it pooping all over the room."

In my previous life, when I had time to watch TV, I'd seen many episodes on the Discovery Channel of the late Steve Irwin, that fearless over-caffeinated Crocodile Hunter in Australia. I remembered how he subdued crocs by landing on their backs and pinning them. I resolved to use the same technique to catch this giant mutant rabbit.

I discovered that giant mutant rabbits are far more manoeuvrable than crocodiles.

Cornering the beast, I launched myself into the air with a mighty Tarzan yell ("KREEGAH!"), arms and legs spread wide. Steve Irwin would have been proud. I came down on what should have been its back. Except it moved – fast – just before I landed on it. I crashed onto the floor against the wall, getting smeared with giant mutant rabbit droppings for my trouble.

I repeated the manoeuver again and again. Crouch – leap – fly – crash. Each time, the only thing I caught were more brown pellets.

Finally, I sat there, major headache building, and tried to think of another tactic.

"Mebbe try an' throw a blanket over it," Angie suggested. "That always worked when I had ta corral one a' my young kids fer a bath."

So I grabbed one of my new blankets, cornered the beast again and threw the cloth over it, quickly landing on the blanket and pinning the animal beneath. It put up a ferocious struggle; surprisingly strong, it squirmed and kicked and clawed vigorously. Angie went to fetch a large cardboard box. Eventually, with her help, we managed to get the rabbit into the box. I closed the lid and cut air holes into the sides. The creature scratched and pushed at the box walls.

Gingerly, I carried the box into our office (it was heavy!) and placed it on the floor with the weight of five months of government forms on top. Then I returned to the room and helped Angie clean up the droppings. I drove to the local rent-all and returned with a carpet cleaner. I gave Number 15's carpet a good shampooing – twice.

In late afternoon, the room's occupants returned. Before I could go to them, they came to me, bursting into our lobby wild-eyed and frantic.

"Our rabbit! Our rabbit! Our dear Percival is gone!" they wailed.

"No," I replied grimly. "Your dear Percival is right here in this box."

The couple immediately became angry. "How DARE you! Do you realize he's a prize-winning thoroughbred rabbit with a pedigree as long as your arm? You probably traumatized the poor thing!"

"Well, your thoroughbred rabbit left his thoroughbred droppings all over my brand-new room! We had to shampoo the carpet twice! And the upholstered furniture. Now we must send out the bed quilts to be dry-cleaned. And he ruined the blanket that I used to trap him."

"See here, you let our Percy out of that box this instant or you'll regret it!" bellowed the man.

"I will not. And don't you threaten me. You only get this creature back when you check-out. See that big sign there? It states NO PETS. That includes prize-winning thoroughbred monster rabbits. Especially when they're allowed to roam free in my new guest room."

"But he's not a pet! Percy is part of our family!" whined his wife.

"He's covered in fur and has four legs. That makes him a pet in my book, lady. And I'm charging you for all our cleaning costs. I may even charge you for the pills I had to take for the headache I got trying to corral your crap-happy beast!"

Both people opened their mouths to protest more, but decided against it after taking a good look at my face. I was furious. Then the wife noticed the book that lay open on my front counter.

She went white and tugged at her husband's sleeve. They left the office, muttering softly to themselves. Within ten minutes, they returned to check-out. I gave them the box containing Percival and they drove off.

The book on my front counter was a cookbook. Open to a page with an excellent recipe for rabbit stew.

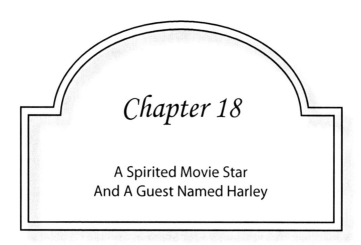

Chapter 18

A Spirited Movie Star
And A Guest Named Harley

Dear Diary:

Six weeks – March 1ˢᵗ to mid-April – have zoomed by since my last entry. Spring is here; I made it through the winter!

March did not come in like a lion or a lamb. It came in with a crash.

On the second day of March, I added the harvest from the day's mail to the tops of our – *my* – four towering piles of unread magazines and books on *my* small coffee table. Then I returned to the front desk.

Minutes later, there was a tremendous crash behind me, from within my apartment. I ran in, convinced that the ceiling had collapsed.

Actually, it was the spindly legs of the coffee table. They had broken under the weight of the written word.

I called for Angie. As we cleaned up the mess together, we both had the same idea at the same time: We used the piles of magazines and books as the table's new legs.

Quickest repair job we'd ever done.

Two days later, the phone rang. It was a bureaucrat from the Greater Wackimac and Area Economic Development Corporation and Barn Preservation Society. By some mystical incantation or overzealous marketing, he had convinced a Hollywood film production company doing a big-budget movie in Toronto, to shoot some scenes here in Wackimac. The location scout for the film was in the area this week, checking out suitable locales. A few scenes had to be set inside a 1950s-era motel room. Did I have such a room?

Does Tom Cruise have a nice butt?

I babbled that I did indeed have such a room. Very authentic. Perfectly preserved, in fact.

The GWAEDCBPS official said he'd tell the location scout and that I may get a visit.

* * * * * * *

The next day, my new laundry equipment arrived. I'd ordered it weeks ago, as part of the renovations project. It was a giant commercial washer and an equally-large commercial dryer. The huge polished-aluminum machines towered over me like gleaming silver monoliths from a science-fiction movie. The theme from *2001: A Space Odyssey* started playing in my head.

We had been using residential laundry equipment, the same type that people use in their homes. The machines had come with the motel when we bought it. It took me all day to get the laundry done. I decided that I had more important things to do with my time, especially now that I was running the place on my own. Bigger machines meant that I could do larger loads in less time.

Our gracious mentors, Bert and Madeline Monahan, returned from their five month Arizona sojourn the week of March 1st. After first assuring themselves that their daughter hadn't sold their Best Western in their absence and absconded with the money, they came over to see how the "newbies" were doing. They arrived just as my new laundry equipment was being installed.

"Good gosh," said Bert as he surveyed the silver monsters. "Ellen, you've bought equipment that's big enough to service an 80 to 100-room property – like ours, in fact!"

"That's right, Bert. I got the specs of your machines off your daughter. I wanted something that can handle huge loads, to save me time. Now I can finish all our laundry by noon."

Bert chuckled. "Well, you refute the adage that small inns can't afford big laundry equipment."

"Oh, I believe it's affordable when you consider how much

my time is worth."

We chatted about their trip and all the changes at the Windsong since they'd left. They were eager to see our interior renovations, so I toured them through the new rooms. They were very impressed, especially at my persistence in obtaining the financing. They were devastated at the news that Pete and I had broken up, and how Pete had gone into a tailspin.

Maddy gave me a long hug, while Bert muttered that maybe he ought to visit Pete and knock some sense into his fool head. They both offered to help me whenever I needed it and said they hoped Pete and I could patch things up.

"You're a real trooper, Ellen," said Madeline, as they left.

* * * * * * * *

The following day, a thin hyperactive young man presented himself at our front desk. His name was Jerome, and he was the Locations Manager for the Hollywood movie. He had a Bluetooth grafted to his ear, plus a back-up cell phone, and he was constantly having simultaneous conversations wih me and multiple callers. (Most annoying!)

He checked out Number 11, our 1950s room, and promptly fell in love with it. It was just what his director was looking for. The production was currently filming scenes in Toronto and would be in Wackimac in four weeks. When I asked who was starring in the movie, Jerome got evasive. Finally, he told me. I was quite impressed.

It starred that famous Australian-born actress who, some years ago, had the real-life role of ex-wife unexpectedly thrust upon her by her equally-famous hunk of an actor husband. Her co-star was a popular guy from a hugely-successful TV sitcom. Jerome swore me to secrecy, saying that any leak to the local media would cause great hardships for the film crew – and void any contract we might sign. He asked if our construction would be over by the time the production team arrived, and I said it would.

We returned to my office, where Jerome wanted me to sign a contract for the room right away, to book it for an entire week.

I was hesitant, until he mentioned what they'd pay me to use it. I almost fell off my chair. It was four times what I'd normally make from renting it!

I signed the contract.

It never occurred to me to tell him about Brenda Ames

* * * * * *
** ** ** ** ** **

As spring sprang and buds reappeared on trees, something else reappeared:

More of those infuriating Ellen's Fubar Motel brochures.

Of course, most people who wandered in with them couldn't exactly recall where they had picked them up. Then I *finally* got lucky. Two guys travelling together remembered:

"Yeah, we got it from Krazy Kathy's gas station out on Highway 7, on our way into Wackimac. We asked the attendant about a good place to stay and she gave us your brochure."

After they'd checked-in, I hung the "Back in an hour" sign in the front window, coaxed the old station wagon into reluctant life, and drove out to Krazy Kathy's. After I dealt with her, I vowed to call Sarge and tear a strip off him when I returned to the Windsong. Imagine! Not only was he starting his miserable practical joke again – though I don't know *how* he'd managed to get hold of the trashed brochures – but he was doing it when I was at my lowest ebb, separated from his morose son and running the inn all by my lonesome. The evil S.O.B.!

I found the place just past the entrance to Wackimac's recycling depot: Krazy Kathy's Gas Bar, Bait Shop and Imported Belgian Chocolates. I walked in and confronted the lady behind the counter.

"Are you the people giving these out to tourists?" I demanded, waving a Fubar brochure in front of her.

"Why yes," she said, taking a step back. "And you are?"

"Ellen Tomlinson, owner of the Windsong Inn that this brochure makes fun of!"

"Fun of? I thought it was a legitimate business. It seemed like a nice place, when you read the brochure. Strange name, though. And we never had anyone come back and complain."

"It IS a nice place. But it's called the Windsong Inn, not Ellen's Fubar Motel! Did you get these from a very old man with a sour face, who uses a cane?"

"I dunno. I came into work one day last year and found a pile of boxes in the back room full of them. I figgered the motel folks had dropped them off, so I started handing them out when customers asked about a nice motel in the area."

"Who was here when they were dropped off?"

"Probably the owner. I can fetch her if you'd like?"

"Yes, please."

Krazy Kathy herself soon arrived from a neighbouring house, a tall intense woman with lacquered gray-black hair and raspy voice. After the usual pleasantries were exchanged, I asked her if an old guy matching Sarge's description had delivered the boxes.

"Nope, not at all. I got 'em from a guy a little older than you, mostly bald, small beer belly, and he was driving the same old beater that you are."

"Wha-what!?" I couldn't believe my ears. She had just described PETE!

"Yeah. He asked me to please drop 'em off at the recycling across the highway when they were open. The depot was closed when he arrived. It's a city-run facility, y'know, so you have to match their hours, instead of them being open for the convenience of us taxpayers. Seems I've never gotten around to hauling those heavy boxes over there."

The counter clerk looked at her boss, aghast. "They ... they were for recycling? OhmiGAWD! I've been handing them out to tourists for MONTHS!"

Well, **Diary**, that explained that. Looks like I owed Sarge an apology. (Yeah, right. There'd be no Fubar Motel brochures in the first place if it wasn't for him!)

I left a stack of our Windsong Inn brochures at the gas bar, and carted off the offending Fubar stuff to recycling. Luckily, they were open.

* * * * * *

Since that first batch of rooms had been rebuilt, I'd noticed a disturbing side effect. My weekly plunging of the odd toilet, had become an almost daily chore of several toilets. In fact, I had to buy a second plunger, so Angie could do some too, just to keep up.

I asked the plumbers, busily installing fixtures in Numbers One to Ten, what could be causing the increased blockages. They scratched their heads (and other parts of their anatomy). Finally, one admitted that it was likely the new toilets they were installing.

"We're puttin' in six-litre toilets, ma'am. They're water-savers, using half the water of the old 13-litre toilets. While they work fine in residential homes, they often cause problems in commercial applications. Considerin' what's put down commercial toilets, these new six-litres just don't supply enough volume of water to carry things completely away."

"Then WHY in heaven's name are you installing them in my inn?" I asked.

"No choice, ma'am. Ontario Building Code requires they be installed in all new construction and retrofits."

Great. A perennial problem just got worse. Would I now have to put up a "Flush Twice" sign in each of my new bathrooms? How tacky! And no water would be "saved" at all.

I called Lodging Ontario and got hold of Brewster, the association's manager. Completely-selfishly, I asked him to drop everything and immediately lobby government to allow commercial establishments to be exempt from that Building Code requirement, permitting us to install 13-litre toilets again. I first encountered amusement, then reluctance. Finally, with a great sigh, he agreed to survey some other members that had recently completed renovations, to see if they had similar problems.

Within a week, Brewster called back, thanking me for alerting him to this problem. All the members he'd surveyed had reported blockage and overflow problems with the new so-called water-saver toilets. He said Lodging Ontario would start lobbying to modify the Building Code, although he warned me it would likely take months, if not years, to effect any change.

"Good stuff. Thank you," I said, then became inspired. "If and when you finally win that lobby, you can report it in your member newsletter under the headline: ASSOCIATION FLUSHED WITH SUCCESS."

I received a polite chuckle for my trouble.

One day, a couple in their late 40s presented themselves at my front desk, and asked what we charged for our rooms. I told them the prices for our standard and whirlpool suites. The couple settled on a standard room, then started haggling with me. I firmly stated that our rates were non-negotiable. They wouldn't stop haggling, convinced that we were over-charging for "the quality of these rooms". That got me.

"How can you say anything about the quality of my rooms, when you haven't even seen them?"

"Oh, we know what to expect in a small Mom-and-Pop motel like this," said the lady. Her husband vigorously bobbed his head in agreement. He reminded me of those decorative dogs some people put on the rear windshield platform of their cars. I wondered if his eyes would glow red.

"Do you really? Well, I've no patience for haggling," I said. "Here, take the key to this room, go check it out, then come back and tell me if you think it's worth what I'm charging."

They left, with a collective sniff, to do just that. Within five minutes, the husband returned and apologized for being so difficult. He signed the registration card and scuttled off.

I took that as a compliment.

Three days later, we enjoyed a wonderful spring day. Birds flitted about, filling the air with their music. All the snow was gone, and the grass was struggling to trade its coat of winter brown for one of spring green.

And the surest sign of spring appeared on the roads: motorcycles. In fact, we already had a biker as a guest. A clean-cut, middle-aged man, he'd arrived astride a magnificent black-and-chrome Harley-Davidson, gleaming in the sunlight.

In early evening, as I made the rounds of my property, I noticed him sitting outside his room, enjoying the setting sun while sipping a beer. His motorcycle was not in the parking spot in front of him.

"Where's that impressive-looking hog of yours?" I asked him.

"Got it put away for the night," he replied.

"Oh. Well, have a pleasant evening."

I walked on, then stopped and turned back. "Where?"

"In there." He hooked a thumb at his room.

"WHAT?"

"Oh, don't worry, ma'am. I got one of your big fluffy towels under her, so there'll be no oil drips on your new carpet."

I flung open his door and stared. The big Harley was neatly parked between the bed and the window. I tried to stay calm.

"Sir, I must ask you to please put your bike outside. It has no business being in one of my newly-renovated rooms, on top of my expensive towel."

"Oh no, I couldn't do that, ma'am. That's a limited edition Harley-Davidson Elite model. I'm not leaving an expensive gem like that outside overnight, where it could get stolen. No way. At home, I always keep it safe in my locked garage."

"Well, you can just go home and keep it safe in your garage, because you're certainly not keeping it in this room! Our rooms are not parking lots."

"Lady, either it stays, or we both go."

"Fine. I'll refund your money and wave you goodbye."

He glared at me, wrestling with the choice of exiling his beloved Harley to the cool night air, or hitting the road in that same air. Finally, with much disgusted snorting and mumbled swearing, he packed up and left.

At least he didn't fire up his hog inside the room and ride it out.

** ** ** ** ** **

At the end of the first week of April, Van Hooydonk Construction finished the second batch of rooms, Numbers One to Ten. They had taken an extra week to also do a number on our lobby. It sparkled with fresh paint, wallpaper and carpet. Ernie's team had even built me a new reception desk of real wood, which they stained in a warm shade of light oak.

(My small cramped apartment was left untouched. It needed more than a renovation; an expansion was also in order. That would have to wait for now.)

All our guest rooms were now redone (except Number 11, of course), to go with our made-over exterior. Outstanding!

I threw an even bigger celebration party for the construction crew, than the one I'd thrown nine weeks ago when they finished the first batch of rooms. I said they would get a special discount anytime they wanted to stay here. I gave everyone a huge hug, even Foreman Ernie, who squirmed and protested that this was another hazard of working for a woman.

I made a note to arrange an Official Opening of our completely-renovated inn next month. I planned to invite the mayor, other dignitaries and the media.

** ** ** ** ** **

The next morning, a small city moved onto our property.

I was interrupted from my chores by the rumble of diesels and the downshifting of gears. I came out of the room I was in and my jaw dropped.

A convoy of fifteen tractor-trailers, half-tons, and panel vans had pulled up alongside the highway. The line stretched from my inn quite a ways down the road. The trucks were all white, with no logos or signage. As I gaped, about 50 nondescript black and grey cars pulled into my parking lot. They quickly filled the lot, and spilled onto our large front lawn. An army of 65 people emerged from the vehicles.

I found it quite frightening. It looked like something from *The X-Files.* I wondered what secret government agency had descended upon me.

All of a sudden, Jerome was standing next to me, beaming. Realization flooded in: Hollywood had arrived at the Windsong Inn.

"Ellen! Ellen! How ARE you today?" he gushed.

"Uh ... fine, I thought," I replied. "What's all this?"

"Our film production crew! Quite a sight, huh? Now tell me; where can we park those trucks?"

"You want to bring them in here too? ALL of them?"

"Why yes! We can't leave them on the highway."

"You ... you need all this stuff just to shoot a few scenes in my guest room?"

"Why yes! Oh, here's the director. Ellen, I'd like you to meet Ron –"

And, just like that, I was shaking hands with a famous Hollywood celebrity; a child and teen star I'd watched on TV sitcoms, who was now an accomplished movie director in adult life. Wearing a ball cap with the name of the movie stitched on (which concealed his bald head), he had an easy smile and a casual, friendly manner. While his people bustled about like bees discovering a new flower patch, he chatted with me and soon put me at ease. I even asked for and got his autograph. (And yes, he was smaller in person.)

Before I knew it, Hollywood took possession of my inn.

Somehow, we found room to park all the trucks. I thought fast, and realized I couldn't leave their cars and trucks filling the parking lot. Otherwise, customers would have no room to park. So the cars and trucks ended up on my lawns all around the inn; thank goodness I had lots of land! Luckily, our early spring had already made the ground firm and dry; otherwise it would've been a soggy quagmire with the weight of all those vehicles.

The production crew swarmed all over Number 11, arranging furniture, props, cameras and lights. Lots of lights! It looked like a super-nova when they were all switched on.

(Thank God I'd talked to Brenda beforehand about this! I'd asked her to please accept it. Nothing moved in the room, so I'd assumed she'd agreed. It was quite an honour, after all: The Windsong – and *her* room – would be starring in a movie!)

Miles of thick black cable uncoiled and snaked everywhere: in the room and across our parking lot to where the white trucks were parked on the lawn. The crew came with their own power; one entire truck was a huge generator.

Astonished, I watched as live potted palm trees were placed outside the window of Number 11, with huge fans nearby to make them sway artfully. More lights appeared outside, to light the trees.

One truck was a mobile gym. Through its open rear doors, I saw the male co-star working out. Another truck was a make-up facility, and the cast went in to get painted and sprayed. Then they went to yet another truck, for costuming.

By late afternoon, after many hours of preparation, they were about ready to begin filming. It was only then that the star arrived.

Typical Hollywood: long stretch limo, a small army of fawning handlers, and total attention focussed on her. She was a very important person – and I could tell from the way she walked and talked that she knew it.

She had her own private trailer, into which she promptly disappeared. I was disappointed; I'd hoped she'd come over and introduce herself, as the director and the male co-star had. I was a fan and had seen all her movies. But she only emerged when it was time to do a scene, then returned to her trailer immediately after it was over.

Over the next several days, I came to understand a few things about hiring out your inn as a movie location.

One: Time is money on a film shoot. The crew wasted as little of it as possible, so filming could proceed with minimal downtime. If they suddenly needed to route an extra cable from the outside generator to inside the room, they chose the quickest, shortest path: a hole cut through my new window screen! (They promised to replace it after.)

Two: Improvised arrangements are the rule, not the exception. If they suddenly needed a rain shower outside the window, then someone scrambled up on my roof with my garden hose and created a downpour using my well water. (They promised to return my hose after.)

Three: The production team will expand to fill all available space. If I hadn't put my foot down, the crew would have taken over my entire parking lot, and blocked access to the inn itself. I would have lost most of my business during the week they were at the Windsong. Yet they had only paid for one room for the actual shoot. As it was, they took a chunk of my parking lot, and made the rooms adjoining Number 11 unrentable due to their noise. (They promised to pay me extra compensation after.)

Four: Special effects are frightening to us civilians. One scene called for the room door to be blown off. I watched, very nervous, as they removed my original heavy door and replaced it with a lightweight special effects door. But the first time they blew it, something went wrong. Half the door came spinning out and smashed into one of their vans, shattering the windshield. Luckily, no one was hurt. They hung another door. This time, it blew up spectactularly, spewing thousands of wood shards over a large area. (They promised to clean up the mess and replace the original door after.)

I did protest all the liberties the production team took with my property. I had never agreed to slashed screens, exploding doors, rain showers, and lost business. But Jerome informed me, with a gracious smile, that unless the contract I'd signed stipulated what they couldn't do, then they were free to do it. It didn't, so they did.

Five: The star is king (or queen, in this case). If she didn't like something, it had to be fixed or replaced to her satisfaction. For example, the pictures in Number 11 weren't to her taste. New pictures were quickly hung. (They promised to replace the original pictures after.)

Actually, I was quite surprised by how mean and surly the star was in real life. She ignored everyone except the director. She kept to herself in her lavish trailer, even eating her catered gourmet meals in there, with just a few of her "yes-people" for company. She caused two people to get fired off the production, because of perceived slights.

And Her Highness couldn't care less about her fans. On the third day of shooting, she happened to walk right past me on the way from her trailer to Number 11. I cheerfully said: "Hi, I'm the owner here and I'm a huge fan of yours!" and stuck out my hand.

She ignored me. Like I wasn't even there. She swept right past me and went into the room.

"Well! How rude!" I sputtered. "Pardon me for breathing the same air!"

A bespectacled little man who had been following her, one of her hangers-on, stopped and said: "Oh, please excuse her. She has a very intense sex scene to do now, and she's totally focussed on that."

"Uh huh. Well, from what I've seen, she's just a –"

"Bitch," finished the little man. We both smiled.

The star's temper got worse as the week wore on. On the fourth day, she had a supporting actress demoted to background extra, blaming her for some dialogue between them that wasn't working. Then she started in on her male co-star, accusing him of hogging the camera and blowing an important scene.

By the fifth day, the director and most of the cast and crew were ready to drown her in the Woebegone River out back. They'd been putting up with her moods and tantrums for weeks now, since the production started in Toronto. (Me, I was counting the days until all of them left and I could have my inn back.)

Things came to a head late on the fifth day. The script called for her to slap her co-star across the face. Of course, it was to be faked; she wasn't supposed to actually hit him. Except that she did. Deliberately and hard. Besides the sting of the blow, her long nails raked his perfectly tanned skin, drawing blood.

The co-star yelped in pain. Harsh words flew: between him

and her, her and the director, her and the stunt co-ordinator. It was pointed out that she had deliberately caused the injury. She lost it then, and railed against the entire cast and crew, calling them useless incompetents.

Not satisfied with that, she then shrieked that she was sick of this little town, sick of this country motel, and especially sick of this stupid dumpy little room.

A few people started shivering; the air had become chilly.

Her tantrum now a violent maelstrom, the star grabbed the vase from the dresser and flung it at a female extra, the same actress who had been demoted. The woman ducked and the vase shattered on the wall behind her. She screamed as the flying glass cut her.

The director went to his star and tried to calm her down. She kneed him in the groin and he fell to the floor, groaning.

The air was very cold now.

The madwoman took hold of the desk phone and pulled, ripping out its cord. She threw it at her co-star, hitting him on the forehead, drawing more blood. He collapsed to the floor without a sound.

The cast and crew fled the room, some of them helping evacuate the wounded. She flung a table lamp to help them on their way; it smashed on the door jamb behind the last person leaving.

If the star hadn't been totally berserk, she would have noticed that the pictures on the wall were shaking. And that her breath was coming out in clouds.

I'd been watching all this from outside, through the window. I suddenly realized what was coming; something like this had happened to Pete in week five. I ran to the door, but it slammed in my face. I pounded on it and pushed against it, but it stood firm.

"No, Brenda, no!" I yelled and ran back to the window, but the drapes jerked shut to block my view just as I got there.

Then something changed in the tone of the spoiled star's shrieking. Now it sounded like raw screams. Of terror. And she wasn't acting.

The medical staff were treating the injured. Jerome and several other crew came up to me, as I stood helpless outside the room. The awful screaming continued inside.

"Man, that is some hellacious tantrum the bitch is throwing today," Jerome said, shaking his head.

"That's no tantrum. Not now, anyway," I replied. "That's Brenda."

"Who?"

I looked at him. "You wouldn't understand. But I'd have those medics ready for when this ... ah ... jammed door opens again."

Several long minutes later, the screams ended abruptly. Silence reigned. I tried the door. It swung open easily.

We found the star in a crumpled heap in a corner of the room. Her clothes were shredded and her alabaster skin bled from many shallow cuts. She was unconscious, her face frozen in a rictus of fear.

When she got out of hospital, two days later, she was a changed woman. She apologized to the people she'd hurt and for delaying the production. She promised to follow the director's instructions and to treat her fellow cast members with respect.

But the production team had to leave the Windsong, because she refused to film any more scenes inside Number 11.

Chapter 19

Formal Requests
And Deadbeat Conniptions

Dear Diary:

The week after that Hollywood mob left, things returned to normal at the Windsong Inn. Or what passes for normal in this business.

(By the way, before they left, the film crew did repair and return the things that they had damaged or borrowed. But only after I nagged them about it. Thank God I'd made a list of everything they'd affected.)

Now that our construction was over, I was again visited by Building Code and Fire Marshal Inspectors, giving our new rooms their final once-over (they had made periodic inspections during the construction process). We'd hired an excellent company in Van Hooydonk, and I hadn't "shaved any corners", so our place received a clean bill of health from both Inspectors.

I fielded many phone calls from local high school kids that week, all trying to book rooms for the Senior Formal (or Prom, as we aging Boomers used to call it). After the first call, I contacted Lodging Ontario for advice.

I again got hold of Brewster, the association manager. He said I should not rent rooms for a Formal. For one thing, most of the kids booking rooms would be under 18. Brewster told me that innkeepers should never rent to minors because, unlike adults, they couldn't be bound by contract. A contract occurred between the renter and the innkeeper when the Guest Registration Card was signed, and the person signing was responsible in case of room damage or theft.

And for another thing, even with those kids who had reached Ontario's Age of Majority – 18 – and were therefore considered adults, the room would be ground zero for Party Central. Which meant noise, rowdiness and drinking. The kids would be below Ontario's legal drinking age of 19.

All of which was a recipe for trouble.

Brewster said we had the right to set our own policies as to parties and noise. And to whom we wished to rent a room – as long as it did not conflict with Ontario's Human Rights Code, which prohibited discrimination on the basis of race, sex, creed, sexual orientation, religion, age –

"Wait!" I interrupted Brewster's drone. "Age! So we can't say no just because of age?"

"Correct, Mrs. Tomlinson. You must not say you're refusing to rent a room because of their age. Just say the same thing you'd say to any adult: You don't rent rooms for parties. Your inn is private property, and under Ontario Common Law, because you don't serve food like a traditional inn as defined under the Innkeepers Act, you have the right to rent to whomever you choose. As long as you don't discriminate, of course."

"Of course."

Whew. That was a lot to take in. And far too much to explain to impatient teens, who were only focussed on the pursuit of party-ness.

So I kept it simple. I just told the kids that we didn't rent to groups for Formals. Period. They were very upset; this place had been known as "easy" under the previous owner – a great place for either a wild Prom party or for sex. Or both.

I replied that the inn was different now; a family place with newly-renovated (and more expensive) rooms. They were still upset as they hung up.

Too bad. I didn't need – or want – that type of business. Besides, this place already had one awful experience with a Prom Night, in 1953. I was living with the consequences of that evening.

One teenage girl got inventive. She had her twentysomething sister call to reserve a room and guarantee it on her credit card. But because of the time of year and the number of calls from teens, I was alert. Certain words the woman let slip tipped me off that she was a front for a teenaged sister and her gang of friends.

"Are you the one who will actually be occupying the room?" I asked, after my suspicions had been aroused.

"Ah, of course, yeah," she replied.

"Fine. Because you should know that we have a policy against wild parties. And you should also know that you, as the person renting and paying for the room, will be the one that is completely responsible for everything that goes on in there – including any damages."

Long silence, then: "Oh."

"Do you still wish to book the room?"

"Ah, lemme think about it and I'll call ya back."

I never heard from her again.

* * * * * *

Those teens notwithstanding, in the wake of the renovations, I was happy to see that its all-new image resulted in the final break with my inn's past. Its former unsavoury reputation had finally been replaced with a more positive one. It had taken almost a year, but the new name, revamped exterior and rebuilt interior, all signalled that it was now a very different property.

Besides all that, I discovered that my higher rates attracted a better class of clientele – the families and commercial travellers that I wanted. People wanting "quickies", or prostitute services, or a cheap place to party, could go elsewhere.

And they did. Case in point:

I noticed that as my occupancy increased, the number of cars each night in the lot of the Big Eagle Inn across the highway did not decrease. That was fine; I didn't want to put anyone out of business. It was good that we were both busy. Still, I wondered why folks wanted to stay at that tired place, with its miserable owner, instead of at my freshly-renovated one.

One day, I got the answer when the foreman of a highway maintenance crew doing work in our area, checked-in.

"Where's your crew?" I asked.

"Staying across the street at the Big Eagle."

"Why? Though our rates are higher, we've got beautifully-renovated rooms with all-new furniture and large screen TVs. They'd be much more comfortable here."

"That's true, but you don't have what he has over there."

"Oh? Such as?"

"The triple-X movie channel, the TSN channel, and ... ah ... how do I say this? The availability of escort services."

"Well! With the possible exception of TSN, we will never have those kinds of ... amenities ... here."

"That's why I'm staying here, ma'am. I'm happily married."

There was a niche for every type of business in this world.

That conversation made me remember a story the Monahans had told me, over coffee last summer. A young couple emigrated from England after World War II, arriving in Canada with only a few dollars in their pockets. Scrimping and saving, they eventually became owners of a motel in Toronto. The neighbourhood was a war zone: crime, drug dealers, prostitutes. They had many harrowing encounters over the years, including being physically attacked – once by a knife-wielding addict desperate for cash. Another time, an angry pimp drove his car right through their front door and into their lobby!

But they boasted at a Lodging Ontario convention that their annual occupancy was over 100%. When asked how that mathematical impossibility could occur, they said with unabashed candour that they rented the same room twice. For one or two hour liaisons during the afternoon then, after the housekeeper had cleaned, for overnight guests. They'd rent to high school students, people having affairs, prostitutes entertaining their "Johns" – anybody with the cash.

Hearing this, many convention delegates shunned the couple, saying they were no better than a "madam" running a bawdy house. Offended, the couple said that if they didn't do it, somebody else would, since there was a demand for that sort of place. So it might as well be them.

And the punch line? When the couple finally sold their motel and retired after decades in the business, they were millionaires, with a huge estate house in the country and a villa in the Caribbean. They had adopted two children who'd been abandoned at shelters, were supporting patrons of the National Symphony, and gave generously to a charity dedicated to getting teenage runaways off the streets.

A niche for every type.

* * * * * *

On a typical day so busy that I wished there were 28 hours in it, I was graced with an unannounced visit from yet another Inspector, this one from the Ministry for Labour and Entrepreneurial Curtailment. He introduced himself as Ted Clennett, and said, with smug righteousness, that he was one of 300 new Inspectors recently hired by the Ministry to visit employers, looking for infractions of the provincial government's countless labour regulations that protected employees.

"But there's only two people working here, and you're looking at one of them and I'm the owner," I said. "Surely you have larger businesses to harass ... I mean, inspect?"

"We look at every size of business, ma'am," Clennett replied, with a loud sniff. "There's so many of us now, that it's a challenge to fill our work week. Now, show me where you have your Employee Health and Safety Policy posted."

I'd never heard of it, so I had nothing posted.

"Humpf," snorted Clennett, making a note on his big clipboard. "Well, what about your Employment Standards Act poster that outlines employees' rights?"

No again.

"Humpf," he repeated. Another note on his clipboard. "How about a copy of the Occupational Health and Safety Act and Regulations for Industrial Establishments? The abridged 450-page handy booklet would be sufficient."

Still no, though I pointed out that the Windsong Inn was not an industrial establishment. That didn't faze Clennett in the least, and he scribbled again on his clipboard.

"Dare I ask if you have a First Aid for Emergencies poster displayed in the employees' area?" he asked haughtily.

"We don't, but that poster sure would have come in handy when my husband used to work here, before he crawled inside a bottle and abandoned me," I replied.

Another loud sniff. More notes on the clipboard. Then he said:

"I understand you're a relatively new owner, and as such and since this is only my first visit here, I'll go easy on you, ma'am. I could hit you with over $1,000 in fines right now for not having all that material posted, you know. Instead, consider this a warning. But I expect to see everything duly completed and posted by my next visit."

I reminded him that technically there was only one employee here: Angie. Wasn't that a lot of paperwork for just one employee? (Did his clipboard have a section marked "overkill"?)

"Irrelevant," he muttered.

He signed the bottom of the long triplicate form on his clipboard with a flourish, tore off a sheet, and handed it to me. He also gave me the address to my local Labour Ministry office, where I could obtain the necessary posters, the 450-page "condensed" Regulations booklet, and a "brief" 230-page Guide to the Act itself that included a sample Employee Health and Safety Policy, which shouldn't take more than five or six evenings "of my spare time" to decipher and complete.

As he left, eager to raise the blood pressure of the next inn's owners, he said:

"When I return, I'll also expect to see your posted policies on Prevention of Violence in the Workplace, Reducing Loud Noises, Prevention of Musculoskeletal Disorders, Working Alone Safely, Prevention of Sexual Harassment, and Training Youthful Employees."

"I don't think I have enough wall space in my small employee area to post all that stuff," I said.

Clennett laughed, adding: "And, on behalf of my colleagues at the Ministry of Health and Perpetual Care, all of your non-smoking rooms must have the official government 'No Smoking' symbol posted in a prominent place, like in the centre of your bathroom mirrors. Now, have yourself an absolutely wonderful day, ma'am."

As he sauntered off, I thought there would be a high risk of violence in the workplace upon his return, accompanied by very loud noises and some musculoskeletal disorders.

If I spent innumerable hours complying with all those Labour regulations, when the hell was I going to run my business? (Maybe I should make Angie a part-owner, so the Windsong would then have no employees at all, just two overworked, barely-paid owners.)

I wondered if a regulation existed to prevent harassment by government Inspectors.

(Actually, complying with the ever-increasing burden of government regulations and forms, soaked up a huge number of hours each month for us small innkeepers. This has *got* to be the most over-regulated industry in Ontario! See the Appendix at the end of this Diary for a list.)

* * * * * *
** ** ** ** ** **

The following week was the end of April, and the pool company showed up to put in my new outdoor pool. It replaced the old one that had exploded in mid-August last year. The men made sure they installed the new pool well away from the underground river that flowed beneath my back yard.

The insurance settlement covering this, had sufficient funds to allow for a large wooden deck to be built around the new pool. It also paid for the filling-in of the exploded pool and re-landscaping over it. I had the men plant a willow tree there; its moisture-hungry roots were guaranteed an ample supply of water.

That week also saw the installation of a computer system for my front desk. Its software was specific for small accommodation properties, allowing me to do reservations, send confirmation letters, do guest bills on check-out, and handle my accounting needs. I was aware that many small innkeepers found computerizing their front desk about as enjoyable as having a root canal done. But I found it easy to master, considering the complicated programs I'd used in my former job as Executive Assistant with a large corporation.

* * * * * *
** ** ** ** **

The week after that, I encountered another deadbeat guest. He was a travelling salesman; quick of talk but slow of cash.

He booked his room for seven days. He told me that his company would pay his bill and gave me an address to send the bill to, after he left. Being a cautious soul, I contacted the company a few days later, to verify his story and to see if I could get a corporate credit card to charge his bill to.

The accounts payable person said the company had no such arrangement with its travelling sales reps. Each one was responsible for his/her own expenses. If I had sent them the bill, they would have simply returned it. Leaving me on the hook, since the guest would have been long gone by then.

When I confronted the salesman about this, he made light of it, claiming it was a new company procedure and he just forgot about it. I asked for a personal credit card as security against the room, as I normally did with every check-in, even for guests paying by cash. He couldn't give me one, saying he "never used such things" (meaning his cards were probably maxed-out). He offered to give me a cheque, but I declined. I was suspicious by then; I figured any cheque from this guy wouldn't be worth the paper it was written on.

So he promised to pay cash when he checked-out in three days.

He would have a big bill, by then. Nervous, I called Madeline Monahan for advice.

"Oh yes, dear, it certainly seems like you have a deadbeat there," she said after I'd finished telling her the details.

"So what can I do?"

"Well, Ellen, you have to be very careful. He'll likely skip out in the middle of the night. Then you'll be left holding the bag."

"So what can I do?" I repeated, flustered.

"You have to seize his property and hold it until he pays what he owes you. The Innkeepers Act gives you that right."

"But I've been inside his room, Maddy. He's got nothing of value in there worth seizing."

"Then take possession of the one thing he has, that is of value."

"What's that?"

"His car."

"What! I can't do that!"

"Sure you can, Ellen. The Innkeepers Act gives you the right to seize any goods of a guest on your property, for non-payment of rent. That includes what's in the guest's room, but it also includes stuff outside the room: cars, boats, motorcycles, horses, trailers – anything, as long as it's on your property."

"I see. But how do I go about seizing a car? I can't very well lock it in a closet."

"Block it with your car. Park your car right across the end of his car, to form a 'T'. Park so close that you're only inches from his bumper. Then don't move your car until he pays up."

I parked my venerable old station wagon as Maddy instructed. Then I returned to my front desk to await the fireworks. They weren't long in coming.

The salesman descended upon me, ranting and raving that I must let him use his car in order to make his living. I replied coolly that he must pay me so I could make my living, too.

He called the police.

A different officer arrived, than the one who came in week 12 about Nora Latimer. He ordered me to move my car immediately, saying I had no right to seize it. Beside him, the salesman smirked and said: "See? I told you that you can't do this, lady."

I smiled and refused to comply. Both cop and deadbeat

bristled. I stayed calm. Just like I did in week 12, I explained my rights under the Innkeepers Act, and produced a copy of the Act for the officer to read. The salesman, not quite so smirky now, read it over the cop's shoulder.

Finally, the officer cleared his throat, tipped back his cap, and said it appeared that I was within my rights to block the car. That caused another explosion from the salesman.

The cop lost patience for this squabble. He said to the bellowing salesman: "Look, buddy, you can resolve this problem very easily by just paying this woman what you owe her. Then she'll move her car. Simple."

Red-faced with anger, the salesman paid cash for his bill. He said, with the icy dignity of a monarch speaking to a peasant, that he was checking-out at once. I replied, with equal iciness, that I would be happy to wave him goodbye.

I moved my car. He climbed into his and roared off.

No loss.

Well, **_Diary_**, that's it for this installment. Oh, look: An entire entry and not once have I mentioned the Pompous Idiot!

Oops.

Never mind.

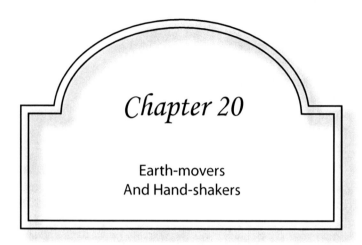

Chapter 20

Earth-movers
And Hand-shakers

Dear Diary:

It was the second week of May, and a glorious spring day full of sunshine and birdsong. I was working in *Pete's Folly,* the Boulder Flower Garden, when I saw the first hole. Then, further away, I came across another. I did a sweep of the area and discovered three more scattered around our front lawn.

Damn! Gopher holes! They weren't there last year. We'd been invaded!

I'd have to get rid of this creature. Besides the damage to my lawn and flowers, its holes would be dangerous to my guests. Children often liked to run and play on our lawn, and I didn't want to have one step in a gopher hole and break an ankle.

Walking to the office, I met Angie. I told her about our uninvited guests and said I was going to call an exterminator.

"Oh, no need to do that, Miz. Ellen," she said. "I'll git my Fred to take care of it fer yous. He's a real good hunter, be easy fer him."

I agreed.

Fred drove up next morning in a battered old pickup truck spewing clouds of blue smoke. How that relic had escaped being impounded under Ontario's Drive Clean program, was beyond me.

It is said that two people married for many years start to look like each other. That sure was true with Angie and Fred.

I'd never met Fred before today, but I'd know he was Angie's husband even if no one told me. He was her male mirror image. Of indeterminate age, he had the same well-worn grungy look. He was slightly stooped, with wayward scraggly hair and weathered skin. I'd swear he had a layer of dust on him, too.

He seemed friendly enough, as he stuck out his leathery hand and said: "How-do, Miz. Pleased ta finally meetcha. Heard lots 'bout yous from Angie. Now, whereabouts is this rodent yous want me ta bag?"

And that's as much conversation as I got out of Fred, in one go. Like his wife, he was religiously laconic.

I pointed to where the holes were. Fred pulled out a long rifle from inside his truck cab. It looked very businesslike, and had a large black scope mounted on top. As he got it ready, I looked at the load in the back of his pickup. There were all sorts of deadly-looking materials in there: iron spikes, sledge hammers, a drum marked "Danger – Acid", and more. Even a box marked "Dynamite".

Fred walked off with his rifle, muttering about "huntin' varmint".

A horrible vision of Bill Murray, as the obsessed grounds-keeper in the movie *Caddyshack*, suddenly came to me. My God! What had I done? I imagined Fred relentlessly tearing up my beautiful lawn and garden, trying to kill that gopher. When bullets failed, he'd work through the entire arsenal in his truck. At the end, after the dynamite explosions settled, there'd be nothing left of my lawn, or of Fred. But the gopher would still be alive, chattering defiantly, doing the boogie to that Kenny Loggins "I'm Alright" song and –

BLAM!

The gunshot shook me back to reality. I turned and saw Fred walking back towards me, carrying something. As he neared, I saw it was one freshly-dead gopher.

"You ... you got it already?" I said.

"A-yep. Varmint obligingly stuck its head up and I obligingly plugged it."

"Now ... now you don't need to use all this ... this stuff in your truck."

He squinted at me like I was insane, then said:

"Naw, Miz. That's gear fer my job. I does blastin'. Fer huntin', alls I need is Ol' Matilda here. She's never let me down." He patted his gun barrel lovingly.

So much for my vision.

* * * * * * *
** ** ** ** ** **

The next day, I was again working in *Pete's Folly*. My official opening was next week, and I wanted the place to look its best. Angie padded out to where I was working and I knew before she spoke that we had trouble again.

"Toilets flushin' sluggish once more, Miz. Ellen," she announced mournfully.

We immediately checked the basement and discovered that just plunging toilets would not solve this problem. Sewage had backed up through the floor drains again.

"Aw, SHIT!" said I.

"A-yep," said Angie.

So once again I called in Stanislas, the sewer line serviceman, who came with his miniature TV camera and auger. Once again, I called in the disaster cleaning company to empty and disinfect my basement. (I wonder if they give Air Miles for frequent users of their services.)

This time, my luck had run out. Stan couldn't find what was blocking my line, by sending his camera through the end of the pipe in my basement. The cable went in as far as it could, but he couldn't see any blockage on the TV.

"We'll have to dig up your clean-out plug under your lawn and go in through it to find what's blocking things further down," said the sewer guru. "Do ya know where the plug is, by chance?"

I did not. So I watched in shock as his men brought in a backhoe and dug a big ugly trench along the length of my buried sewer pipe, looking for the clean-out plug. Ugh! What a mess it made of my beautiful lawn! It least the trench didn't go through

Pete's Folly.

They finally discovered the plug, halfway between the inn and the highway, buried ten feet deep. Uncapping it, Stan sent in the TV camera. He discovered an entire section of pipe that was clogged with roots. A huge wad of underwear and socks (some kid had been having fun!) had caught in the roots, blocking the pipe.

Stan gave me a reproachful look. "When I was here in January, I advised you to cut down them trees along your pipe."

"Ouch. So you did, Stan. I completely forgot, what with all the renovations and personal upheavals that were going on. Sorry."

"Oh, don't say sorry to me, ma'am. It's me that's sorry for you," said Stan in the same tone a doctor would use telling a patient she had terminal cancer. "Sendin' in an auger to chop them roots won't do it this time. Your pipe's been too damaged by the roots. They've been growin' in there for some time. You're gonna need a complete new sewer line put in."

Thank God my property insurance policy covered this. Still, if I thought Stan's men made a mess finding my clean-out plug, it was nothing compared to the havoc they caused by putting in a new sewer line. I was horrified at the damage done to my lawn.

While the sewer platoon turned my front lawn into something resembling World War I trench warfare, I ran around making sure the rest of the Windsong was ready for its coming-out party.

Working fast, so I could rent rooms again, the crew had my new sewer line installed in three days. It went through a part of my lawn that had no trees, so I wouldn't have to worry about root problems again.

But I had other problems.

My official opening was now only days away. And my front lawn looked like hell. Stan's men had filled in the trenches and smoothed over the earth, but the lawn still needed sod – and lots of it. Problem was, at this time of year, all the landscaping companies were booked solid into July. There was no way they could re-sod my lawn on short notice. I finally found a greenhouse that would deliver sod, but had no one available to lay it.

So I had to do it myself.

First thing in the morning, I was out there laying sod as fast as I could. Then I did my regular chores and ran the front desk. In the evenings until it got dark, I went back to sodding. It was back-breaking toil.

I barely made it. I laid the last roll just one hour before my invited guests and the media arrived for the opening. I jumped in the shower, then rushed to get dressed. I decided against a skirt or dress, because then I'd have to wear nylons. I was so tired and so pressed for time, that I couldn't scrub my knees and shins clean enough of the grass and dirt that had stained them through my jeans! Slacks would have to do, though it wasn't my best outfit.

I also needed half a ton of make-up to hide the bags under my eyes, a legacy of the sleep I missed because of my marathon sod effort.

Thank goodness I'd hired a catering company to arrange the food and refreshments, and hang balloons and bunting along the outside of the inn. It gave the place a festive air. The caterers had also brought a huge cake. A podium with microphone had been placed on our parking lot, with rows of chairs facing it.

A horde of local dignitaries arrived, including the mayor, our local MPP, and the CEO of our Regional Health Centre. Cathy, the loans officer from our Wackimac bank, came and she brought along John Oliver, the senior loans manager from their Toronto head office. I was happy he'd made the trip; all this wouldn't have happened if he hadn't believed in me. Angie and Fred were there, along with the Sparrows from the Wackimac Rest Haven. Bert and Madeline Monahan came as well.

I went to the podium and welcomed everyone. I expressed appreciation that the mayor and our MPP could attend. I praised Cathy and John for their faith in me, and their bank for providing financial assistance. At that point, on cue, the caterers let down a large banner that had been rolled and hung along our eavestrough behind the podium. A little surprise of mine, the banner read:

THANK YOU in big letters above the name of the bank. By their expressions, John and Cathy were surprised and pleased.

Before I relinquished the podium to the professional speech-makers, I thanked the Monahans for taking me under their wing and giving me buckets of helpful advice. But I saved my most special thanks for someone else.

"Last, but certainly not least, I want to publicly recognize and thank a very special person." I paused and looked right at Angie. "My housekeeper, Angie Huycke, who does such a wonderful job making our rooms shine, who has put up with many a crisis here, and who is always there when I need her."

I called Angie up to the podium, gave her a big hug in front of everyone, and presented her with a special gift. She blushed crimson at this unexpected attention. But I could see in her eyes that she was very proud.

Then, my invited dignitaries took over the podium. A series of congratulatory speeches were made, each one longer than the last. It seemed that each official tried to outdo his or her predecessor. I was beat from my sod-laying exertions. I was sitting next to Maddy and if it hadn't been for her nudging me awake periodically, I'd have slept through my own official opening.

I was awake to hear the remarks of the Chair of our Chamber of Commerce. He praised my vision and drive in reviving a tired old motel, and stated what an asset the community now had. He waxed eloquent about Wackimac needing more entrepreneurs with my courage and spirit. I almost laughed aloud, but choked it down. In his full-time job, the man was manager of one of the local banks that had repeatedly rejected me for a loan. Now here he was, basking in my glory! Where were you when I needed you?

Hypocrite.

The offices of each of the speakers had called me before today, to confirm their attendance. The callers asked for some background details to work into the speeches (to make it seem like the dignitaries actually knew me). I said that my husband's name should not be mentioned, as he had left the business. (Literally.)

As the podium pomposities were drawing to a close and as Maddy poked me awake for the fourth or fifth time, someone gained the microphone who was not on the schedule: the CEO of our Regional Health Centre.

To my surprise, he called me up to the podium. There, he presented me with a special award, in honour of my "Caring Inn" relationship with the hospital; specifically my Comfort Bears for relatives of patients staying here. The Centre had received hundreds of letters over the past year, praising our establishment.

I was flabbergasted. The audience witnessed a rare sight: Ellen Tomlinson at a complete loss for words.

As I stumbled through some kind of thank-you remarks, a photographer from the *Expositor & Chronicle* snapped my picture. The TV crew from our local station filmed me. All that added to my discomfiture; I wasn't used to the limelight!

Then, mercifully, the spotlight swung from me to the mayor, as she cut the big cake with *Congratulations* written on top. The caterers passed around champagne. I was asked to pose for more pictures: with the mayor, the MPP, the Chair of the Chamber (I had to force a smile for that one and resist the urge to kick him in the shins), my bankers, the Health Centre CEO, and more.

But my favourite photo op was when Fred took one of Angie and I. She squeezed my shoulder hard and murmured: "Thanks, Miz. Ellen. Ya shouldn't of, but I really appreciates it. Fred too."

(My shoulder had a big bruise for days afterward.)

I gave interviews to the newspaper and TV reporters. Later, I watched myself on the six o'clock news. I didn't look too bad; the make-up and the slacks camouflaged the baggy-eyed, dirt-stained lady underneath.

The next morning, I was thrilled to see that coverage of the opening and my hospital award had made the front page of the paper – the actual front page this time. It was the second lead story, with two photos, under the headline: SURPRISE AWARD AT OFFICIAL OPENING OF RENOVATED INN.

The article on my inn was placed alongside the other lead story, whose headline screamed: LOCAL MERCHANTS LIVID

THAT RESIDENTS ALLOWED TO SHOP OUT-OF-TOWN. The article's sub-heading read: "Wackimac Downtown Business Improvement Association Demands More Control".

But on the evening of my official opening, after everyone had left and the caterers had cleaned things up, all I could think about was going to bed. I was not renting any rooms that night; the Windsong Inn was closed.

As my head hit the pillow and blessed sleep overcame me, I felt pleased with how the day had gone. There was just one thing bothering me; a sense of unease that something had been missing.

No, not something. Someone.

Pete.

The jerk.

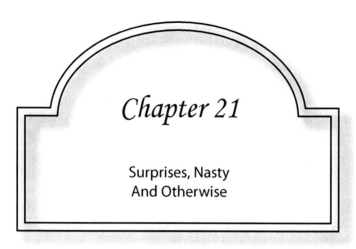

Chapter 21

Surprises, Nasty
And Otherwise

Dear Diary:

Monday of the week following our official opening found me in the lobby, hanging framed copies of the newspaper coverage the inn had received, and the award from the Health Centre.

A tall shadow ghosted over me. Startled, I turned from the wall I'd been facing and stared into a man's chest. I looked up to a dour face high above. He had returned. Ben Rosen, the detective from the OPP Anti-Drug Squad, the tallest – and quietest – man I knew.

"Morning, Mrs. Tomlinson," said highpockets. "Nice to see you again."

"Hello, Detective," I replied. "You're not here to break down another one of my doors, are you?"

For a second, it looked like Rosen would actually smile. Nope. But his eyes twinkled. At least I think they did, from what I could see of them, way up there in the clouds.

"No, not this time. However, I would like to see your guest register, please."

"Sure." (Issues of guest privacy, courtesy of the federal Privacy Act, be damned. Lawyers, who advise innkeepers not to show their register unless the cops had a warrant, be damned. I believe in full cooperation with the police.)

Rosen was only interested in my bookings for this weekend. I accessed the file on the computer, and let him scroll through the names. He went rigid on his seat and whistled softly.

"Here, too," he murmured.

"What is it?" I asked.

"Mrs. Tomlinson, you've got a number of very interesting reservations for this Saturday night."

"Really? Well, there's a big wedding in town and some of the guests are staying with me. They booked half my inn."

"No, not them. It's these other folks booked into the rest of your rooms that interest me." Rosen pointed to about two dozen names. "What can you tell me about these men?"

"Not much. They're all individual reservations, made over the past two or three weeks. As you see, they come from all over Ontario and Quebec. Why do you ask? I don't believe they're connected."

"Oh, they certainly are. But don't blame yourself; you couldn't have realized. These men are known to us. They're all members of motorcycle gangs that deal in drugs."

"WHAT! Well, isn't THAT a nasty surprise! Why did they pick my place? You can see that we're not a seedy motel any more!"

"Yes, Mrs. Tomlinson. Congratulations on your new look, by the way. And on your special award, there. No, you haven't been singled out. All the motels in town have members of biker gangs booked in. These people were very careful; everyone reserved their rooms separately, with no hint of any gang connection."

"So what's going on? Why are they congregating in sleepy little Wackimac?"

"Precisely because it is sleepy. They've booked the arena for a big rally Saturday night, some kind of summit between the gangs. We don't expect there'll be any trouble; they want to keep a low profile. They just want to slip in, have their meeting, and leave. Most will likely not even come on motorcycles. They'll come in pickups or SUVs, so as not to draw any attention. But we've been keeping an eye on them; that's how we knew about this gathering."

"But ... but I certainly don't want vicious bikers staying here!

I've had enough bad experiences with hockey teams; I don't want guests carrying guns and knives! Especially with a wedding party coming here; these are families with children. I'm going to cancel their reservations."

"No, please don't," said Rosen. "We don't want to tip them off that we're on to them. And you don't want these people mad at you, believe me. But don't worry, there'll be no trouble here at your motel."

I must have looked dubious, because the detective went on: "You were very helpful to us with our drug bust last fall, so I owe you one. Tell you what: I'll station two uniformed officers here, for the entire Saturday night. Sound good?"

"Could they also be here in the afternoon, when the gang checks-in?"

"Fine, I'll make it happen."

"Well then, okay."

Rosen swallowed up my hand in his big paw, and shook it. Then he left, as silent as when he arrived.

But I was still very worried. Vicious bikers at the Windsong – at the same time as families with children! What would happen if the thugs returned from their rally drunk or stoned? At the very least, I fretted about damages to my beautiful new rooms. I remembered what gang-related bikers did to poor Graham Sparrow's room last fall, coating the walls in Worcestershire sauce. As a worse-case scenario, I was terrified that someone would get hurt, or raped (there'd be teenaged girls in the wedding party), or killed.

* * * * * * *

It preyed on my mind all week. I told Angie about it, and she suggested that maybe I shouldn't worry so much, since the police would be present. But at night, nightmares plagued me, mostly of gun battles between police and bikers, with whole families being cut to ribbons in the crossfire. Blood and screaming children everywhere.

After two nights of that, I'd had enough. I called private security firms, to hire some men to patrol my inn this Saturday.

Every firm in town was completely booked; the arena and the downtown merchants association had already hired all available personnel.

My stress-meter went higher.

I called the Monahans, thinking maybe Bert could come over to lend moral and physical support. They were away for a week.

I asked Angie if I could borrow her Fred for the night, ideally with his sharp-shooting rifle. Both he and Angie would be out of town, visiting his sick sister, who was battling cancer.

My stress-meter entered the red zone. Well, at least I'd still have the police officers with me.

On Thursday, Ben Rosen telephoned. He was extremely apologetic, but the two officers that he'd promised me were now unavailable. They'd been reassigned to the arena, to help control the rally. It was going to be much bigger than they had originally thought.

"Really sorry, Mrs. Tomlinson. But it can't be helped. Still, please don't worry. I'm sure there'll be no trouble at your motel."

Now I'd be all alone, with deadly thugs on one side and likely-drunken wedding guests on the other!

Stress-meter went into orbit.

When Angie arrived on Friday, I told her about Rosen's call. She was shocked that the promised police protection had been cancelled.

"Aw, I'm real sorry Fred an' I can't be here with yous tomorrow, Miz. Ellen," she said. "But Sarah, Fred's sister, likely ain't long fer this world, an' she's so lookin' forward ta see us fer maybe th' last time."

"That's fine, Angie. Really. Of course, you go see your sister-in-law. I'm not going to impose on a family commitment like that, especially with her condition. Don't you worry about me; I'll survive."

(That sounded pretty good, didn't it? Now if only I believed it.)

That afternoon, I made sure I recharged my cell phone. I'd wear it clipped to my belt all weekend, so I could dial 911 immediately should trouble arise. I went out and purchased two large flashlights; the kind with extra-long barrels. Sure they took a bucket of batteries to power them, but they were heavy and could be used as night sticks in an emergency. Like if I was attacked. I'd keep one behind the front desk, and carry the other with me when I patrolled the grounds.

* * * * * *
** ** ** ** ** **

Saturday morning came. I was on pins and needles. All alone, waiting for known criminals to come sign my Registration Cards. Times like this, I wished I was six feet tall and had muscles like those lady WWE stars. I put on my work boots; the heels gave me an extra inch of height. Every bit helps.

Angie's sister, subbing for Angie while she was away, came in very early to do the rooms. I expected the wedding party before lunch, since it was a 2:00 wedding. I also wanted the other rooms done before the bikers showed up. Too bad Angie's sister couldn't stay with me, but she had family commitments too.

(Wish I did.)

The wedding party checked-in around noon. There was a whole gaggle of teenage girls in the group. My nervousness reached new heights. I hoped the two groups never met; the wedding folks should be gone before the motorcyclists arrived. Then, if I could catch a break, tonight one group would return before the other.

By 1:30, the wedding group had all left, bound for the church and the lavish reception/dinner/dancing afterwards.

No bikers yet.

I took a walk around our property. I tried to admire our lovely flowers, the smell of the grass, the sunshine, the song of the wind through our trees. I usually found those things so restful.

Didn't work. Couldn't get the motorcycle gangs out of my head.

One hour later, a pickup truck drove in. Two beefy guys with well-endowed beer bellies heaved out.

God. Here they come.

"Be brave, little Piglet," I murmured, borrowing a line from

Winnie The Pooh.

The man-mountains clomped into the office, signed-in, took their key, and clomped out. They hardly said five words between them. Both wore kerchiefs on their heads. One man had an eyepatch, the other sported a nasty livid scar running from cheek to ear.

I was so nervous, I was bathed in sweat. And about two dozen more like them were due to arrive! I'd never felt so vulnerable in my life.

There was a sound behind me. I whirled around. *A man was standing in the doorway to my apartment!*

"Hello, El."

It took an eternity to register. When it did, it felt like a freight train hit me.

Pete.

"H-hi," I managed to say. "D-didn't expect to see you around here again."

"Yeah. Well, ah, it was a last-minute decision. I heard you could really use some back-up today."

"Oh, I'll manage. Like I've been managing for months now. No thanks to you."

"Yeah, I've been awful to you. I know that. But I'm ready to make amends and to shoulder my share of the load again."

"Now hold on there, mister. You can't expect to just walk in here and carry on from where you left off. There's been a lot of water under the bridge since you walked out on me."

"I know, El. Look, I didn't come here to fight with you. I came to help. I heard about the biker gangs and I'd like to help – if you'll let me."

I gave Pete a long look. He looked much older than when I'd seen him last. His face had more creases and almost all of his hair was gone now. And he had quite a beer belly.

"Okay, Peter. You can help. I admit it: I'm scared to be here alone with these thugs and I could sure use some support. Even from you."

"Ouch. I deserved that. Well, time enough for recriminations later. Here come more bikers."

So, together, we stood at the front desk as the gang members arrived during the rest of the afternoon. As Detective Rosen had predicted, most drove pickups and SUVs. All shiny late-model vehicles, too. Only a few arrived astride hogs; massive ugly machines with engines that sounded like angry dragons clearing their throats in caves.

Amazingly, the burly, vicious-looking men were very polite. They called me "ma'am" and Pete "sir", and listened attentively as we explained our house rules and gave them their keys. I stayed nervous; they were probably faking us out.

By dinner-time, the leather-jacketed outlaws had left to attend their rally. That made them someone else's problem, for a while. The Windsong Inn was quiet. Time to get some questions answered.

"How did you find out about the biker gangs this weekend?" I asked Pete.

He went over to a chair and sat down heavily. "Angie. She tracked down my dad's phone number and called me. Really tore a strip off me, too. Said I'd been acting like a spoiled brat long enough. Said that you could really use my help today and if I had an ounce of manhood left, I'd get my lazy ass over here and help you. Said if I didn't, she come down there and personally kick my Pompous Idiot backside all the way back to Wackimac."

I chuckled in spite of myself.

Pete chuckled too. "Angie can be quite persuasive, y'know. I never knew she could talk up a streak like that."

"Yeah, it's rare, but she can."

We looked at each other. Long moments of silence dragged on. Finally, Pete said:

"I'm really sorry, El. Angie's right; I've been an absolute ass. You've done a magnificent job here, turned the whole place around, and you had to do it all on your own. I've no right to ask your forgiveness, but I do hope that you will forgive me, someday."

"Someday. Maybe. We'll see."

"Well, I don't deserve it, I recognize that. I'm just asking you to give me a second chance. Oh, and you should know that I've given up drinking. Stopped three weeks ago. Haven't touched a drop since. I looked in the mirror one morning and hated what I saw. I realized that I had fallen into a deep pit and that it was time to crawl out."

"Good for you. Took you long enough."

"Yeah. In fact, even before Angie called me, I was trying to work up the courage to come see you."

"Huh. Well, Peter, I'm glad you're here. I've handled lots of things on my own since you ... lost your motivation. But these vicious criminals under our roof, right next to decent families – well, that really unnerved me."

"It would unnerve me too, El, if I had to face them alone. But together, we always were invincible."

"Yes, we were."

"Maybe we'll be again."

"Maybe."

By 9:30 pm, my bedtime, neither group had returned. I went to bed, fully dressed, after I made Pete promise to wake me as soon as the bikers returned.

About an hour later, he shook me awake.

"Hwazzah? Bikers back?" I mumbled.

Pete's face was grim. "No, worse."

He brought me to our office window and pointed. A big sedan was parked at the far end of our parking lot, engine off, no lights. It was completely black; even its windows were heavily tinted.

"It drove in about five minutes ago, El," Pete said. "It slowly cruised around our lot, then parked over there. It's just sitting there. I think it's Mafia. If the cops got wind of this biker rally, then the Mafia would have too. I've read how the Mob are fighting the bikers over drug turf."

"My God, Pete! I never thought of that! I was more worried about the thugs harming our wedding guests. If you're right, these mobsters are just waiting for the gang to return so they can pick 'em off. We could have a firefight right here!"

I paused and took a deep breath.

"I must find out what they want. I have to go out there, Pete."

"No. WE do."

We each took our flashlight billy clubs and walked up to the jet-black mystery car together. We reached the driver's window and stopped. Nothing happened. Finally, Pete tapped on the glass with his flashlight. Slowly it slid down.

I stifled a gasp. Inside, dimly lit by a red dome light, were four of the biggest, meanest-looking men I'd ever seen. Any one of them looked like he could kill an innocent babe without a twinge of remorse. I gripped my flashlight harder, while my other hand drifted to my cell phone.

"Yeah?" snarled the driver.

"We ... we're the owners here," managed Pete, whose mouth must be as dry as mine. "Who are you and what are you doing here?"

"You two don't need to worry about us, buddy. You just go back into your office there and forget that we're here. Understand me?"

"Look ... Sir. We don't want any trouble. But this is private property. Only registered guests have the right to be here. If you're not a guest, then we must ask you to leave."

"We'll leave when we're done here. Now. Go. Back. To. Your. Office." The tinted window purred closed.

We went back to our office.

There, I called the police. I had memorized the license plate and I gave it to the cop who answered the phone. I said the car refused to move, that four evil-looking goons were inside, that we were positive they were Mafia, and that a gunfight was sure to erupt as soon as the bikers returned, which would be soon.

The cop said he'd run a check on the plate and get back to us.

Five minutes later, the phone rang. It was the police. They couldn't find the plate; were we sure we had memorized it correctly? I was sure; I asked them to check it again.

Ten minutes later, the phone rang again. It was Detective Ben Rosen. The cop at the station had reached him on his cell phone. They had finally found the plate.

It belonged to an unmarked police car. The bruisers inside were all undercover RCMP cops!

Around midnight, the wedding party returned. Most were very well-lubricated. Designated drivers were as rare as promises kept by politicians: They parked their cars all over the place and staggered off to their rooms. We had cars on our front lawn, side lawns, two in back of the inn, and several left hap-hazardly in the parking lot. Not one was parked within the yellow lines in front of a room.

As the last of the revellers were arriving, my worst nightmare occurred. The bikers returned, en masse. I grabbed Pete's arm and braced for violent confrontations.

But the motorcycle outlaws fooled us again. They parked their vehicles neatly between their yellow lines and went to their rooms with no fuss whatsoever. A few of them even said "G'night, folks" to Pete and me as we stood outside our office, watching anxiously.

Go figure. Rosen had been right, after all.

In fact, we had more trouble that evening with the wedding party. The teenagers, many of them girls, spent hours racing up and down the sidewalk, going from room to room, shattering the night quiet with yells, giggles, and hoots of laughter.

You ever try to calm down a pack of giggly teenage girls? You'd have better luck trying to stop the rain.

At first, I was terrified that the noise would rouse the bikers, who'd storm out of their rooms with knives and brass knuckles. And maybe drag some of the girls back in with them. Especially the way some of the teens were dressed, or half-dressed. But the big tattooed outlaws never stirred.

While I was dealing with the teen females, Pete was talking with besotted adult males, trying to get them to park their cars properly. Some cars were even blocking our entrance. Finally, he resorted to asking them for their keys, and parked the cars himself.

One very drunk guy, the Best Man it turned out, thought Pete was a bellhop. He asked Pete to help him carry dozens of boxes of wedding gifts into his room, "for safekeeping". Then he insisted on giving him a tip!

"Look, El," said an exhausted Pete as we returned to the office, "I made ten dollars tonight."

Around 3:00 am, peace descended upon the Windsong, at last. Pete bunked down in the apartment's spare bedroom (we had a lot of things to talk about yet), while I slept in the main bedroom.

I was snoring before my head hit the pillow.

* * * * * *
** ** ** ** ** **

Next morning, a fierce-eyed man, with a huge grey bush of a beard and arms thick and weathered as phone poles, drove up in an all-black Hummer. He went to the rooms of the bikers and rapped on each door until he had roused them. He knew exactly which rooms to go to. Within the hour, all gang members had departed.

While I still wouldn't have taken any of them home to meet Mother (if Mother was still alive, the sight of these men would have given her heart failure!), I must admit that they were still exceedingly polite as they checked-out. I've never been called ma'am so often in my life! And they had treated my rooms well; there were no damages. (Thank God!) Those bikers turned out to be some of the best guests I ... *we*... ever had.

The car with the undercover RCMP squad had left before I got up. When Angie's sister arrived, she was relieved to find both of us unharmed and the place still standing.

The wedding party checked-out very late; some people only in mid-afternoon. The adults were seriously hung-over. The teens looked like death warmed over and several had lost their voice. (Too bad they hadn't lost their voices before they returned last night. We'd all have had a better night's sleep.)

What a weekend! Biker gangs and the return of Pete. Well, I wanted a more exciting life when we bought this place. I should have remembered the old Chinese proverb:

"Be careful what you wish for; you may get it."

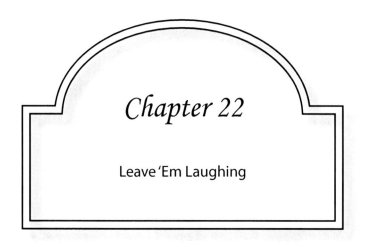

Chapter 22

Leave 'Em Laughing

Dear Diary:

"Erm, pardon me, ma'am, but what are your room rates?"

I looked up and saw a bespectacled little man standing at the front desk, twisting a battered fedora nervously in his hands. I smiled and told him our rates.

"Oh my," said he. "Can't you give me a cheaper rate? All I want is a bed to sleep in, after all."

Still smiling, I replied: "It's more than just sleeping in the bed, Sir. You'll be in the room from now, which is 4:15 pm, to about 9:00 tomorrow morning. You'll consume electricity for lights and air conditioning, maybe you'll use the micro-wave, you'll watch TV, you'll use the bathroom and its soap and shampoo, you'll eat my complimentary fruits and drink my complimentary bottled water. You'll sleep on top-quality fresh sheets, which will have to be laundered after you leave so they'll be fresh again for the next guest."

"Well ... erm, when you put it that way, ma'am, then your rates are quite reasonable. Quite reasonable indeed."

That little encounter occurred two weeks ago, the first of June, the same day I got a letter by courier from the Lodging Ontario association. I had to read it twice, before it sunk in. My first reactions were surprise, then indignation: the both of us? Shouldn't it just be me, by rights? Then I checked myself: let's not be mean-spirited.

I went to our front door and yelled: "Pete! Brace yourself! Big surprise! Lodging Ontario has named us as this year's recipients of their Accommodator of the Year Award, in the Turnaround Category! Get over here and read this!"

Pete gave up trying to start our lawn mower (I could smell the gasoline from here; he'd flooded it again), and came in to read the letter.

"Wow! That's something, Ellen! Really something!"

"Sure is! Huh, I wonder who nominated us?"

"Could be the Monahans, or even the Sparrows. Just to be sure, we better thank 'em both."

The association wanted us at their annual convention to receive the Award and had given us two whole days notice. We scrambled to get ready, including arranging for Angie to mind the Windsong in our absence.

* * * * * *

Around 11:30 pm on the night before we were due to leave, one of the banes of our existence reoccurred: furious pounding on the front door. I heard Pete rise from the bed in the spare room and stumble through the office to answer it. I braced myself for the roar of gunfire, or howling dogs, or even the scream of F-14 Tomcats in a power dive.

Nothing. Pete didn't return to bed either. I heard sounds from the kitchen, then the back door opened and closed. I heard voices in our backyard, and soon the aroma of grilling hamburgers wafted in through my open bedroom window.

What was going on? I hauled on some clothes and shuffled sleepily to our backyard.

Pete was cooking hamburgers on our bar-b-que, and four men were seated at our picnic table. Our rear flood lights lit the area.

"Oh, hi there El," said Pete through thick clouds of smoke that mercifully hid perfectly good beef being charred into oblivion. "Hungry? I could throw one on for you, too."

"What ... what's going on?"

Pete introduced the four men. They were a Ministry of

Transportation emergency road-repair crew that just finished their task, and had come to our inn dog-tired. Our neighbour inns were full and, though we had our lights and sign turned off, they had taken a chance and knocked on our door. Pete booked them into two rooms.

The men were also ravenously hungry. Since nothing in our area was open this late, Pete had offered to grill up some burgers for them. His offer was gladly accepted.

I was amazed. Using the CD player and outdoor speakers he'd hooked up last year, the old Pete would have unleashed the fury of his sound effects CD, punishing the late-night knockers for disturbing his sleep by sending them fleeing into the night. This was new, compassionate behaviour for him.

Maybe he really had changed.

Greedily wolfing down the burgers (they WERE starving, to eat Pete's cooking!), the men thanked Pete profusely for his kindness and vowed to recommend our place to all their Ministry colleagues.

Huh.

* * * * * *
** ** ** ** ** **

Next day found us at the Lodging Ontario convention, standing self-consciously on a stage, flanked by the association Chair on one side and the Executive Director (Brewster, whom I'd talked with several times over the phone during the past year) on the other. The Chair delivered a nice speech about us and all that we'd done to the Windsong, in just one year. Then he presented us with our plaque, while Brewster looked on beaming, as if he was personally responsible for what we had done to win the Award.

We were given the opportunity for some brief thank-you remarks. Ignoring the customary ladies-first rule, Pete startled me by grabbing the microphone.

"Folks, Ellen and I deeply appreciate this unique honour – but there's been a terrible mistake. We do not deserve this Award and we cannot accept it!"

There was a stir among the 230 assembled innkeeper

delegates. I stared at Pete, mouth agape. Brewster made a small whimpering sound, while the Chair glared at him, as if this was his fault. Oblivious, Pete pressed on:

"Yes, a terrible mistake, because the couple before you do not deserve this! This wonderful Award belongs only to Ellen! She's the one who really turned our inn around; single-handed. It was Ellen who fought for and got our financing, who oversaw all the remodelling construction, and who dealt with most of the crises. And she's the one who had the brainstorm of the Comfort Bears too. For many months, I was not even at the property, and even when I was there, I was more hindrance than help – especially when I tried to repair something!

"So Mr. Chairperson and fellow innkeepers, I must insist that the association's records – and this plaque – show that the recipient of this honour is solely Ellen Tomlinson. *She* is your Accommodator of the Year."

He turned and solemnly presented me with the Award. Then he started clapping. After several seconds, the Chair and Brewster joined in. Then the delegates. Soon, the room shook with thunderous applause.

I was overwhelmed. What a nice thing for him to say, and to do! I got so choked up, I couldn't trust myself to speak. Instead, I gave Pete a monster hug, tears blurring my vision.

When we returned to the Windsong, I cancelled Pete's exile in the spare room. I invited him back into our bedroom and into our bed.

We didn't get to sleep for some time that night.

★ ★ ★ ★ ★ ★ ★

Several days later, I was cleaning up yet another overflow mess in one of our bathrooms. With each downward thrust of the plunger into the foulness of the bowl, I chanted: "Damn. *Sploog.* Stupid. *Sploog.* Communist. *Sploog.* Toilets! *Sploog.*"

Afterwards, I expressed my frustration at the need for constant plunging of our new six-litre toilets. Pete readily agreed; clearing toilets had been his least favourite job before the renovations. And now we had to do it much more often.

"This is stupid," said Pete. "What's happening with the Lodging Ontario lobby to amend the Building Code, that you told me about?"

"Going nowhere fast," I replied wearily. "I talked with Brewster at the convention. The association now has dozens of letters from hotels and motels testifying that the new toilets aren't working like they're supposed to, plus letters from independent consulting engineers stating that these water-savers are inefficient for commercial use. But despite all that, the Ministry bureaucrats in charge of the Code refuse to budge an inch until they get more evidence."

"Yeah? Next toilet that overflows, let's bring those bureaucrats over here to personally clean up the stinking evidence!"

"Hah! Wish we could. And that's not all: The environmentalists are lobbying the Ministry to leave the Building Code as is, since the six-litre toilets conserve water. They refuse to see that having to flush twice uses about the same amount of water as the older 13-litre thrones. They don't recognize that toilets are abused more with commercial use and that it's unfair – and unhealthy – for housekeepers or maintenance staff to constantly clean up people's overflows."

"So why don't we have our plumbers rip these out and install new 13-litre toilets?" Pete asked.

"Because, hon, they can't. If they install something in violation of the Building Code, they'll lose their licenses and get slapped with hefty fines. So will we, as the property owners."

"Huh. Okay, then why don't WE do it, ourselves. On the quiet, of course."

Visions of Pete's past experiences in our inn's bathrooms flashed across my mind's eye.

"Ah, I don't believe that we ... ah, have the expertise, honey," I said.

"Oh I agree! That's why I'll take a basic home repair plumbing course at the local college. It's held on a Saturday plus two weekday evenings."

And so he did. Signed up the next day. Course started that Saturday.

Pete got thrown out by noon.

"Broke the college record for screwed-up repairs," he said sheepishly, after he returned.

"Broke a lot more than that, I bet," I said.

So I went to the course in his place. And learned how to change toilets. As well as fixing dripping taps, changing faucets, and more. Hmm. Think I'll sign up for other home handyperson courses. I've known for almost a year that we needed those skills around here. High time I did something about it. Would save big bucks over calling in repairmen, too.

The day after I finished the course, Pete rented a panel truck and drove to Toronto. He returned with ten new 13-litre toilets. He parked the truck out of sight at the side of the motel, and came into our apartment kitchen.

"All set, El," he announced. "Now we've gotta wait until dark, then sneak the toilets into the unoccupied rooms. We must make sure no none sees us. Especially that Patel jerk across the street. All we need is for someone to blow the whistle on us and we're in big trouble. Once the toilets are inside, then you can install 'em during the day, over the next several days. Each night, we'll smuggle out the old toilets you've replaced and bring 'em to that charity place that sells previously-enjoyed building materials."

He threw some bags on the kitchen table. "Because we can't risk being seen, we must dress all in black, just like commandos on a night mission."

"Uh, Pete, isn't this a little over the top, even for you?"

"Not at all, El. We can't take any chances. If we're discovered, there'll be hell to pay."

He had bought two completely-black outfits, including black running shoes.

For me, it was a pair of opaque nylon tights and a spandex bodysuit. He had a black sweatshirt and sweat pants.

"Hey, excuse me, but why do I get a skintight outfit to wear while you get a comfy baggy one?" I asked.

"Because that's how it always works in the movies. Besides, it'll show off your cute butt."

"Uh-huh. Well, perhaps I'd like to see your cute butt, too."

"Later for that," he grinned.

So, with the original TV theme of *Mission Impossible* in my head, we went out at 10:30 that night, to sneak in ten contraband toilets. We extinguished our floodlights over the sidewalk, and dressed in our black outfits. (I drew the line at blackening our faces. That was going way overboard and, besides, I didn't want to terrify any guests we might encounter.)

Luckily, most guests had retired for the night. Except one. He drove up and his headlights swept over two black-clad figures edging into a room carrying a big box between them.

The guest got out of his car and said: "Ah, good evening, folks. This is certainly an odd sight. Usually one sees thieves carrying goods out of a room, not in."

I laughed. "Oh, don't worry. We're ... er, just carrying in some new ... er, furniture."

The man read the side of the box we were carrying. "Yeah, American Standard sure makes excellent ... seats."

He went into his room and we completed our clandestine task without further incident.

Over the next week, I used my newly-acquired expertise to install the smuggled toilets in place of the six-litre ones. As we started renting the rooms with the 13-litre toilets, we noticed the difference almost immediately. The need for constant plunging stopped. We returned to only occasional plunging, such as when some fathead flushed down Pampers or evil brats sent our towels into the netherworld. We resolved to buy more toilets for the remaining rooms.

The phone rang two days later. "Hello, Windsong Inn." I said.

"Yes, hello, we'd like to reserve a room for five days, please, non-smoking, one queen-size bed, you do accept pets, right?" said a breathless female voice.

"Ah –"

The voice rushed on: "We're both dog-lovers, and we have two big dogs travelling with us, they're absolute dears, one's a St. Bernard, the other's a Newfoundland."

"Well, we –"

"You don't have to worry, we have a big crate with us, and of course we do pick up after them, you have a large lovely lawn and lots of trees, I hear."

"CRATE?"

"Yes, because we'll have to leave one dog behind from time to time, while we're staying with you, but they'll be no trouble for you to keep an eye on, even when they snarl at you, they really don't mean it."

"Listen, we –"

"And we're willing to use your vacuum to clean their hairs from your room, they do shed you know, but they don't bark, well not too much, and you'll just love to pet them and hug them, they're such dears."

"We don't accept –"

"And if we like your place, we'll tell all our friends, we're members of a club of big dog owners, well it's the dogs that are big, not necessarily the owners, I mean, and –"

Customer service be damned. I hung up on her.

* * * * * * *

Angie came into work today, highly agitated. Meaning her eyebrows were raised and she was walking fast. She was waving a newspaper.

"Miz. Ellen, has yous seed today's paper?"

I looked at Angie's copy. Two headlines jousted for space on the front page, bellowing: NEW HIGHWAY BYPASS PROPOSAL and COPS CART DRUNKEN MAYOR HOME IN SQUAD CAR AGAIN.

"I assume it's the bypass story that's got you upset? Why?" I asked.

"Look wheres th' bypass is goin' through."

I quickly read the article. My God! Right through our property! If this proposal passed, they were going to expropriate most of our four acres of land! We'd only be left with a small parcel for the inn and parking!

I hollered for Pete as I read the article more carefully. The highway bypass project had been talked about for years here in Wackimac. (Naturally, it was the first we'd heard of it.) Currently, the main highway ran right through the city, twisting and turning like a demented snake through commercial and residential streets alike. Many residents (and travellers!) wanted that volume of traffic diverted around the city. There had been many proposals over the years, all defeated. This was the latest, and now the city would get some provincial funding to make it happen.

Pete came thudding into the office and I quickly filled him in.

"Geez!" he said, passing his hand through hair that he forgot was no longer there.

A big hollow void opened inside me. I felt awful and fought to overcome it.

Pete said: "We ... we can't fight expropriation, honey. No one can. Remember when we lived in Toronto? The city took whatever land it wanted, whether it was motels on the waterfront, factories, even a retirement home. Whatever land the government wants, it gets."

I looked at him and with a steely conviction in my voice that surprised me, considering how I felt inside, said:

"Oh, we'll fight it, Pete. Don't you worry. We'll give them a fight like they've never seen before. There's no way we're going to see this place castrated, our beautiful lawns taken away, our lovely trees cut down! Not after everything we've been through!"

"Ellen, I feel the same way now about this place as you do. You know that. But I think we've finally hit the wall on this one. You cannot fight the government when they want to expropriate. I remember those Toronto cases. At best, you can just delay them for several years through expensive legal challenges. Hell, after

10 years, those two waterfront motels are still fighting for proper compensation in the courts – but their land was taken away years ago.

"Government always wins in the end. Their pockets are bottomless, their lawyers are legion and their patience is infinite. Remember, politicians come and go, but bureaucrats are forever."

I thought for long minutes. "Then we'll use different tactics to make 'em route the highway somewhere else. We'll convince 'em that the lands across the river, which the highway must cross on its way through us, are environmentally-important wetlands. We'll claim that rare ducks and birds nest there. We'll cite pollution and traffic concerns. Perhaps it's an ancient aboriginal site full of religious significance. We'll prove that routing the bypass further east improves traffic flow.

"We'll call the paper and get local public opinion on our side; they can't harm the award-winning inn that's the home of the Comfort Bears. We'll call the national magazine columnist that stayed here and wrote about us: Lorraine Sulieman. Whatever it takes, we'll do it!

"Peter, they are NOT getting our land."

The void inside me had disappeared. I was filled with a righteous energy. I felt like marching down to the Mayor's office right now and giving the hung-over sot a verbal thrashing.

Pete gave me an abrupt hug. "Oh, I agree, El. We won't take this lying down. It's just that, well, I'm not sure we can win this one."

"We'll win it, honey. You'll see. They will not ravage us."

And that, **Diary**, is how our anniversary day started. Some anniversary present, eh?

Yes, I'm writing this on June 15, the first anniversary of our arrival at the inn. We started our new career a year ago today.

Some year!

Several hours later, the couple in Number 19, who looked to

be about our age, came to check out. I had calmed down somewhat by then.

"Wonderful setting you have here," the lady said as her husband did the paperwork. "So relaxing, so peaceful. It's just you and your husband that run it?"

"Yes, with a full-time housekeeper," I replied. "We bought this place a year ago as our semi-retirement project, and we –"

"Yeah, yeah, yeah! Now THAT'S the way to go!" interrupted her husband. "You folks are SO lucky, to be able to live and work here in the country, with fresh air, lots of open space and the slow pace of life. No commuting! No-one to boss you around! Perfect! I bet you have lots of free time to do hobbies and stuff, eh?"

I started laughing.

"Jeez, Susan, we could do this too, y'know?" the man prattled on. "Yeah, yeah, yeah! Sell everything, buy a motel – after all, it's just a matter of making beds and cleaning bathrooms! It would get us out of the rat race and let us enjoy the good life just like these nice folks!"

I was laughing so hard now, that tears streamed down my face. The couple stared at me, then took a step backwards in unison. Apparently convinced I'd taken leave of my senses, they hurriedly quit the office and retreated to their car.

"Boy, what set her off?" Susan asked as they quick-stepped away.

They drove off as I stood in the doorway waving goodbye – still laughing like a maniac.

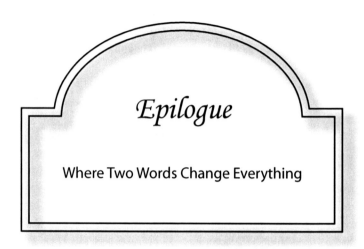

Epilogue

Where Two Words Change Everything

Dear Diary:

Half the trees are green, and half are blazing red and yellow. Fall is here. It's mid-September. We've survived another summer as innkeepers, our second. Things were a little saner than our first summer. Just as hectic, though.

No serious incidents like last summer; no horses in rooms, or squirrel-shooting aunts, or girls' feet stuck in toilet bowls. We did have all sorts of minor incidents, however. Plus that crazy business with the women's soccer team and the male strippers they smuggled into their rooms.

Oh, and those teenagers who decided to hold an impromptu party – on our roof. The guy who smuggled in his pet boa constrictor – then the snake escaped. The cop who stayed overnight with his mistress, and next morning discovered his wife carrying on her own affair – in the adjoining room! The blind gentleman who insisted he had the legal right to stay at our place with his seeing-eye dog despite our strict No Pets policy – and I remembered almost too late that he was correct. The deer that jumped into our new swimming pool – then couldn't get out. The lady who "touched up" her expensive Bombay black cat with liquid shoe polish, before displaying it at a major cat show, and the annoyed beast escaped the bath tub while the shoe polish was still wet and ran all over the bedroom, leaving black paw prints everywhere, even on the new quilt and pillows.

And, to my utter shock, some people *still* showed up with Ellen's Fubar Motel brochures! I thought I had taken care of that last spring, when I dumped all the boxes from Krazy Kathy's at recycling! Forcing smiles, I finally discovered that these brochures came from a gas station over a hundred kilometres away, near Toronto. I called Krazy Kathy; turned out that ever-helpful counter clerk of hers had given a box of the Fubar brochures to Kathy's sister, who owned Looney Laura's Gas Bar and Luxury Spa just outside Toronto. The clerk had completely forgotten about it when I had confronted her last year. FUBAR, indeed.

Okay. I guess we did have quite a summer, after all.

* * * * * * *

Then there was the time our newly-minted provincial Minister of Tourism visited us, as part of his whistle-stop familiarization tour of Eastern Ontario. (There had been a sudden late-June election and we had a change of government in Ontario. The new Premier had decided to give Tourism its own Ministry again, splitting it off from the Ministry of Economic Development, Trade, Technology, Information, Culture, Recreation, Communication and Bagpipe Licensing.) Our new Tourism Minister had barely travelled in his life before being appointed. He had never been on an airplane and had never even visited Toronto before first being elected as MPP (he got lost trying to find the Legislature Building on his first trip there). Naturally, our Premier felt he'd make a terrific Tourism Minister.

After he had toured the Windsong, he congratulated us on running such an outstanding place, considering that it was "just a semi-retirement project". We stared at him, while his handlers – who knew better – fidgeted. Unfortunately, he felt the need to elaborate: He believed that most "Mom-and-Pop motels" were run as a part-time project; either that, or one of the owners had a "regular full-time job elsewhere".

Pete, who had his arm around my shoulder at the time, had to apply pressure to prevent me from lunging forward and attacking the twit. His handlers, seeing our faces redden with anger, swiftly led the novice and naive Minister away.

Our industry's Leader. Boy, does he need a reality check!

* * * * * *
** ** ** ** **

Anyway, we've been enjoying great occupancy since our renovations were completed months ago. Place is doing very well. We get many advance reservations and considerable repeat business, too. Good signs we're doing things right.

Lots of satisfied customers. The letters, notes and postcards keep arriving. Got another gift, too: a lovely original etching of the inn, with our trees blowing in the wind and the river in the background. Guest that did it is quite the artist. I had it framed and hung it in our lobby.

Both Pete and I have volunteered our time with the Lodging Ontario association. We're serving on separate committees, and even though we're still very much the newbies, I think we're making good contributions. Feels good giving something back to our industry. I was also invited to join the Board of our hospital and I accepted. Pete joined our local Rotary Club and works on their committee that's developing the Wackimac portion of the Trans-Canada Trail.

We didn't start volunteering because we now have lots of free time. We don't. It is true that we've got things better organized and we're more familiar with the business, than a year ago. However, the main reason is because we're afraid our brains will atrophy if we don't get some outside interests. Running a lodging business can suck you in 100% if you let it and drain you dry.

* * * * * *
** ** ** ** **

We did get two unwelcome financial shocks. The first was a visit from the federal sales tax people, who audited us to see if we were collecting and remitting the Goods and Services Tax properly. For days, they dug through our files and generally made complete nuisances of themselves – all while we were trying to run our business during its busiest season.

Finally, they announced that everything was in order, except for that time we rented all those rooms to the First Nations people during our third week as owners. The natives had insisted they were exempt from paying any GST, so we didn't charge them. While they may have been sincere, it turned out they were wrong. The federal auditors informed us that natives are only GST-exempt if the good or service is purchased on a reservation or delivered there. The revenue people sympathised with our honest mistake. But that didn't stop them from slapping us with a bill for the GST owing, plus an interest penalty. Ouch.

The second financial shock was when we received our property tax assessment last week. We both almost had heart attacks. The assessed value of our property had doubled! When we contacted our local provincial tax assessor, we discovered it was because of all our renovations and improvements. The property was now worth more, because since our occupancy was much higher, the motel earned more revenue. So our assessment, which was based on our business' income, jumped. We never thought of that when we submitted our financial statements to the assessor upon request, months ago. Now we're bracing ourselves for what our actual property tax bill will be, when the city sends it out in January. Another ouch coming.

* * * * * * *

The whole expropriation issue was on the back burner all summer. City politicians were at their cottages, or on vacation. But it's starting to heat up again, now that fall's here. We're going to be putting in a lot of effort fighting this. We're very worried. Don't know how it's going to turn out. But we'll give The Powers That Be a helluva fight.

The owner of those two Toronto motels – a feisty seventy-something named Ed, who's also a Lodging Ontario member – finally won his decade-long court case for fair compensation for the waterfront he lost. The government promptly appealed the judge's decision. Ed vows to keep fighting, though the appeals process will likely take another two years. "The government hopes I'll die before this thing is finally settled, but I'm too ornery to give them that satisfaction," he said with a grin when we last met him. We may be able to use the precedent established by his case – something called "riparian rights" – in our fight to keep the Windsong's waterfront from being expropriated.

We did meet with a cadre of municipal Wackimac bureaucrats over the proposed highway bypass route. After hours of haggling, they finally offered us a compromise: They would take less land (though we would still lose our waterfront) and in return, we'd get a building permit when we wanted to expand our inn sometime in future. They bluntly stated that if we refused to sign over the required land, then we'd never get a building permit again.

Compromise? More like *extortion.* Bastards.

We said we'd continue to fight and walked out of the room.

..*.*.*.*
** ** ** ** ** **

How about Pete and I? Well, things couldn't be better between us. We went through that rocky patch last winter, but came out stronger for it. We're a team again. Pete's stayed off the booze, just like he promised. And he's much better adjusted to this new life, than he was last year. He cares more about our guests and is calmer – somewhat – when crises erupt.

And me? I just love running this inn. With all its challenges and long hours, it also has its grand moments and rewards. The happy faces on guests who've had a good time here. The tearful appreciation of people when they get a Comfort Bear. The serene beauty of this four-acre property early in the morning, when most everyone's asleep – except me.

I sit here writing this, late on a (rare) lazy Monday afternoon, in my favourite spot: under a big oak tree on a grassy hillock at the edge of our property, overlooking the inn and the river beyond. I'm waiting for Pete to return from his Sanity Day.

I've got two very important words to tell him. Words that he's only heard twice before. However challenging things have been so far, they're going to get a lot more formidable.

I'm pregnant.

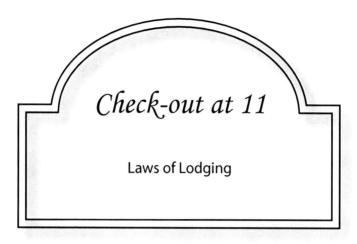

Check-out at 11

Laws of Lodging

Dear Reader:

After reading this book, if you are still determined to own an inn, and if your family and friends haven't talked you out of it, *then they didn't try hard enough.* What kind of family and friends are they? Demand they have another go at you.

Now, after that, if you're *still* going to become an innkeeper, then at least keep these Laws behind your front desk. It may help.

Laws Of Lodging
(In no particular order)

- The number of guests arriving early to check-in increases in direct proportion to the lateness of your housekeeper in starting work that day.
- The amount of government forms needing to be completed expands to fill what little free time you have available.
- When someone comes to your front desk, asks for your room rate, then says they're just going to talk it over with their spouse in the car, put your Guest Registration Card away. They're leaving.
- The eagerness of your child(ren) to help out around the inn usually decreases with age.
- The size of the dog increases in direct proportion to the frequency of the potential guest insisting that "it's just a little

dog." At best, it's really a Great Dane. At worst, it's a Woolly Mammoth. The beast will shed enough hair to knit a coat and will terrify your housekeeper into quitting.

- When you have lots of available rooms, nobody calls. When you're full, your phone rings off the hook.

- Politicians pay attention to tourism businesses in inverse relation to the number of weeks before an election.

- Dinnertime for innkeepers can be anytime, and usually is. And it's always interrupted. Ditto lunch and breakfast.

- Property taxes increase. Always.

- Old innkeepers never retire after they sell their property. They eventually buy another inn.

- The complexity and cost of the repair increases in direct proportion to the ease in which your spouse insists it can be fixed. Especially if the spouse does the fixing.

- Nine out of ten guests are nice people. The tenth is evil. The challenge is to accurately identify that tenth guest, and refuse to rent them a room.

- People who think running a small inn is a "charming part-time job" are mentally challenged. Be kind to them. Better yet, hire them to run your place for a week and treat yourself to a nice vacation.

- The eagerness of a banker to lend you money disappears upon discovering you are an innkeeper.

- You are not alone. Join your industry's trade association. Besides safety in numbers and helpful advice, you'll save money too.

- The stress management guru who advises "don't sweat the small stuff", obviously never owned an inn. It's attention to detail that separates a good place from a great place. And lots of sweat.

- For hours, your phone is quiet. As soon as you make an important call, all your incoming lines light up.

- The quality of the guest checking-in decreases as the time after 10:00 pm increases.

- An annual vacation is a must. Close the place down if you

can't find someone to run it, but go. It's not a treat – it's a medical necessity. Nine out of ten doctors agree.

- The likelihood of one of your valued staff abruptly quitting – without notice – increases as the time you need them the most approaches.
- When guests say all they want is "a clean bed, a good TV, and a nice shower", they really mean they also expect to get continental breakfast, swimming pool, in-room movies, high speed wireless Internet, a daily newspaper, flat screen high definition TV with 80 channels, an extra cot for their kid, and treats for their pet. All at no extra charge, of course. And it would be nice if you washed their car, too.
- The loudness of the party increases with the lateness of the hour. Ditto the slowness of the police to respond to your call to quell the disturbance.
- A tradesman's job quote will perfectly fit your available funds. Especially if you've told him your budget first.
- If you finally sell your inn, don't hold the mortgage. You may have to take back ownership, once the new owner runs it into the ground.
- Old government bureaucrats, like old association executives, never die. They become consultants.
- In Ontario, women taking advantage of their legal right to go topless while sunbathing on your lawn, usually shouldn't. Ditto most men.
- Some religions believe that God decreed Sunday to be a day of rest. He exempted innkeepers.
- The chance of your towels secretly eloping from your rooms increases in direct proportion to their newness and cost.
- *Good Idea:* Deciding to buy sufficient replacement cost insurance for your property.
- *Bad idea:* Making that decision after a devastating fire guts the place.
- Your harmonious relationship with your banker means nothing when it comes time to renew your mortgage. Despite having held your mortgage for many years, with you never missing

a payment, and despite also having all your corporate and personal banking, car loans, your first-born male child, and a pint of your blood every Friday, the bank can still refuse to renew your mortgage. Quotas.

- Being an innkeeper has one thing in common with being a new parent: You are often awakened in the middle of the night.

- Murphy, who wrote that famous Law which states "anything that can go wrong, will go wrong," owned an inn. So he knew what he was talking about.

Appendix

The Regulatory Burden
of Ontario Innkeepers

Dear Reader:

The following is a list of most of the provincial and federal Acts and regulations that must be shouldered by innkeepers in Ontario. *It is all true.* No "artistic license" has been taken to exaggerate it. This list was accurate as of April, 2009.

The Regulatory Burden of Ontario Innkeepers

- *Innkeepers Act.*
- *Hotel Registration of Guests Act.*
- Employment Standards under the *Employment Standards Act.*
- Workplace Health & Safety Regulations under the *Occupational Health and Safety Act.*
- New Fire Code Regulations for all properties meeting the definition of "hotel" (four rooms and up) under the *Ontario Fire Code.*
- Blue and Green Box Regulations from the Ministry of the Environment, including inspections to assess how much a hotel is, or should be, recycling.
- Non-Smoking Regulations under the *Smoke Free Ontario Act.*
- Waste Water Regulations for rural properties with septic systems, from the Ministry of the Environment.

- Regulations governing swimming pools under the *Health Protection & Promotion Act* and hot tubs from the Ministry of Health and Long-Term Care.
- New Disabled Access Regulations under the *Accessibility for Ontarians with Disabilities Act,* specifically the many requirements in *each* of the five Standards for: Customer Service (already law) and (coming soon) Built Environment, Information & Communications, Transportation, and Employment.
- Environmental Impact Studies and Restrictions from the Ministry of the Environment whenever a property, particularly a rural property, wishes to renovate/expand. Also Archeological and Noise Impact Studies. Then, if all the Studies are favourable, you must comply with the Regulations under the *Ontario Building Code.*
- Pay Equity.
- Safe Drinking Water Regulations for rural properties drawing water from a well, lake, or river, overseen by the Ministry of Health and Long-Term Care.
- The *Assessment Act*, governing property assessments for municipal taxes.
- The *Consumer Protection Act,* concerning false or misleading advertising.
- Liquor Law Regulations under the *Liquor Licence Act* for properties licensed to serve liquor.
- Food Handling Regulations from the Ministry of Health and Long-Term Care for properties serving food.
- Privacy Regulations under the federal *Personal Information Protection & Electronic Documents Act.*
- Collecting PST and GST under the relevant provincial and federal Acts, plus remitting Workplace Safety & Insurance Board (WSIB) premiums, payroll deductions, Employer Health Tax, and two Corporate Income Taxes. (For a typical medium-sized inn, it takes the time-starved owner/operator an average of half a day each month to calculate and remit all these taxes, and that is using a computerized system.)

- *Private Security and Investigative Services Act*, governing private security guards.
- *Residential Tenancies Act*, concerning long-term tenants.
- *Trespass to Property Act*.
- Federal Safe Boating Regulations for inns, resorts and lodges that rent boats.

(There's one more Act that perhaps should be added to this mind-numbing list, because it also applies to today's harried innkeepers: the *Mental Health Act*.)